The Reason You Walk

WAB KINEW
The Reason You Walk

VIKING

VIKING

an imprint of Penguin Canada Books Inc., a Penguin Random House Company

Published by the Penguin Group

Penguin Canada Books Inc., 320 Front Street West, Suite 1400, Toronto, Ontario M5V 3B6, Canada

Penguin Group (USA) LLC, 375 Hudson Street, New York, New York 10014, U.S.A.
Penguin Books Ltd, 80 Strand, London WC2R 0RL, England
Penguin Ireland, 25 St Stephen's Green, Dublin 2, Ireland (a division of Penguin Books Ltd)
Penguin Group (Australia), 707 Collins Street, Melbourne, Victoria 3008, Australia
(a division of Pearson Australia Group Pty Ltd)
Penguin Books India Pvt Ltd, 11 Community Centre, Panchsheel Park, New Delhi – 110 017, India
Penguin Group (NZ), 67 Apollo Drive, Rosedale, Auckland 0632, New Zealand
(a division of Pearson New Zealand Ltd)
Penguin Books (South Africa) (Pty) Ltd, 24 Sturdee Avenue, Rosebank, Johannesburg 2196, South Africa

Penguin Books Ltd, Registered Offices: 80 Strand, London WC2R 0RL, England

First published 2015

5 6 7 8 9 10 (RRD)

Author representation: Westwood Creative Artists
94 Harbord Street, Toronto, Ontario M5S 1G6

LIBRARY AND ARCHIVES CANADA CATALOGUING IN PUBLICATION

Kinew, Wab, 1981–, author
The reason you walk / Wab Kinew.

ISBN 978-0-670-06934-7 (bound)

1. Kinew, Wab, 1981–. 2. Kinew, Wab, 1981– —Family.
3. Kinew, Tobasonakwut. 4. Native peoples—Canada—
Residential schools. 5. Native musicians—Manitoba—Winnipeg—
Biography. 6. Broadcasters—Manitoba—Winnipeg—Biography.
7. Ojibwa Indians—Manitoba—Winnipeg—Biography. I. Title.

E99.C6K55 2015   971.27'43004973330092   C2015-905151-7

eBook ISBN 978-0-14-319356-2

Visit the Penguin Canada website at **www.penguin.ca**

Special and corporate bulk purchase rates available; please see
www.penguin.ca/corporatesales or call 1-800-810-3104.

Miigwech Nimaamaa, Miigwech Ndede

Ningosha anishaa wenji-bimoseyan
(I am the reason you walk)
—Anishinaabe travelling song

PROLOGUE

If you were to enter the centre of the sundance circle, then you would understand the beauty of what happens there.

The shake of the cottonwood trees in the breeze ... the swing and sway of prayer flags of every colour tied to the branches ... the chorus of cicadas singing a perfect soundtrack for the sweltering heat ... the feeling of hundreds of supporters standing on the edge of the circle watching you.

THE HOT SAND was starting to burn my feet. The sun's radiance had burrowed deep into my skin, turning it a dark carmine-brown. My dried sweat left a thin layer of salt on my body. I could taste it as I licked my lips.

We had been dancing and fasting in this circle since long before dawn.

Chiefs and headmen formed a procession and walked to the south side of the arbour, where I stood. They took my father's war bonnet from its perch and raised it toward the sky. The dozens of eagle feathers splayed around the headdress like a halo, each representing an act of valour, while the intricate patterns of glass beads caught the light of the sun. The PA system crackled.

When they brought the war bonnet down from the sky and placed it on my head, war whoops and ululations rose from those around the circle. They had made me a chief.

The sundance leader laid down a small box, opened it, and withdrew a treaty medallion. Placing the medallion in my hands, he reminded me of the significance of the treaty relationship: the commitment to share the land with newcomers. On one side of the medallion was a profile of George Washington. The other showed two hands shaking. One hand was European. The other was Indigenous. We are all treaty people.

I nodded and thanked him. I was surprised by how heavy the medal was in my hands.

I turned my gaze to the earth. It had been two years since I was here last. I had strayed off the red road I had been taught to walk as a boy. I had turned my back on Ndede,* my father. I had hurt many people, including those closest to me.

As the son of a hereditary chief, I had always known I would someday rise to this rank, but I assumed that day was far in the future. Perhaps it would arrive after I had achieved something great. Instead, it came when I was at one of the lowest ebbs of my life. My community, my family, and my father responded by giving me a second chance. That which was broken, they tried to make whole again.

All of this took place more than a decade ago. It was not the only time my father would pass something to me that I would commit to carrying into the future.

In the last year of his life, Ndede would go on a remarkable journey of hope, healing, and eventually forgiveness. The journey

---

* *Ndede* means "my father" in Ojibwe, a term my sister Shawon and I used growing up to refer to our dad. The *e* here sounds similar to the *e* in the word *egg*. Written phonetically, *Ndede* sounds something like *in-DEH-deh*.

would take him to the greatest heights of some of the world's most powerful institutions. Yet, in the end, it would resonate on the most basic level of existence that all of us share.

More than any inheritance, more than any sacred item, more than any title, the legacy he left behind is this: as on that day in the sundance circle when he lifted me from the depths, he taught us that during our time on earth we ought to love one another, and that when our hearts are broken, we ought to work hard to make them whole again.

This is at the centre of sacred ceremonies practised by Indigenous people. This is what so many of us seek, no matter where we begin life.

This is the reason you walk.

PART ONE

Oshkaadizid
Youth

1

A CLOUD FLEW LOW across the shimmering waters of Lake of the
Woods. Waabanakwad—Grey Cloud—a tall, lean Anishinaabe
man, studied this bit of mist as it floated by. He broke off a knot
of tobacco in his hand and placed the offering on the water. Then
he craned his neck upward so that when he spoke, his words rose
up into the sky.

"*Ahow nimishoomis, miigwech kimiinshiyin ningoozis
owiinzowin,*" the man said in Ojibwe. "Oh, grandfather, thank you
for giving me my son's name."

Newborn twin boys lay nearby with their mother,
Nenagiizhigok—Healing Sky Woman. They nursed in the lodge
nestled along the line of trees on a point just north of Turtle
Narrows. They had arrived early that morning. Waabanakwad
knew they were a beautiful gift. He thought of what a blessing it
was that his little family was there on his trapline, on land that
had been his father's and his grandfather's before him.

"*Tobasonakwut,*" he said to himself. Low Flying Cloud. He
watched his son's namesake drift past and disappear into the fog

that obscured the far shore. He crouched by the water seeking another vision, a name for his other son.

The leaves of a poplar rustled softly in the wind. The water lapped near Waabanakwad's feet.

That must have been when a small bird landed close to him, cocking its head from side to side, studying Waabanakwad. When Waabanakwad smiled at it, the little apparition jumped into the air. He swooped toward the ground before his wings found their lift and he flew away into the mist.

"*Bineshii,*" Waabanakwad said. Little Bird. He liked the name. His eyes crinkled as a smile spread across his face.

He offered the rest of his tobacco, invoked the spirits of the four directions, grandmother earth, and the grandfather of us all, then walked back to his lodge. He had named his sons, and Nenagiizhigok must have beamed when she saw Waabanakwad return to their home.

The smiles would soon vanish. While still infants, both boys were struck by scarlet fever, but the Anishinaabe medicine helped only Tobasonakwut. Bineshii lived up to his namesake. He touched the ground in this world only briefly before taking flight and leaving us for the spirit world.

Years later, when he became a *gichi-Anishinaabe*—a giant among his people—Tobasonakwut was told by an elder that he had lived such a rich, intense life because he had experienced not just the rewards and challenges that were rightly his own, but also the pain, joy, and heartache that rightly belonged to Bineshii. Tobasonakwut had experienced enough for two lifetimes. This is probably why the Anishinaabemowin word for twin is *niizhote,* or "two heart." Not two hearts, but a duality embodied in one sacred bond. This is what Tobasonakwut would be told by an elder much later in his journey. Even further down that road, those two hearts would become one again. But that would not be for a very, very long time.

First, there was the business of being a kid.

WHEN STILL A YOUNG GIRL, Nenagiizhigok had been playing one day with her siblings and cousins near Sii'amo Ziibing, not far from where her son Tobasonakwut would be born a generation later. It must have been a warm summer day, probably in the morning, when the sun was beginning to bring heat to the forest shade.

The children chased each other, their laughs echoing along the rocky shore. When one of them broke off and ran up a gentle slope into the forest, the others, Nenagiizhigok included, followed. Soon they were in pursuit, slaloming through the pine trees, red-pine needles on the forest floor a soft cushion beneath their moccasins. Though they shouted and giggled, their footsteps were softer on the earth than any of us today could imagine. They broke into a clearing in the woods where tall grasses grew, hiding a swamp beneath them. Beautiful flowers danced among the grasses, swayed by the gentle breeze, and the children were drawn closer and closer, away from the trees.

In a dreamlike state, entranced by the purple and pink blossoms, they kept moving forward. Just then, a soft cascading sound rose up all around them. A thousand tiny rattles shaken at once.

Nenagiizhigok and the others stood frozen as scores of dragonflies ascended from the reeds all around them. The beautiful creatures began to arc and tilt, flying circles around the heads of these little Anishinaabeg.

Slowly, and gently enough to preserve the wonder in the children's minds, the little insects began to sing. It was a calm, soothing melody that traced the contours of the paths they flew through the air. The tones rose to a plateau, hung in mid-air, and then softly landed at a new low. The tiny insect helicopters repeated this pitch before starting their song cycle anew. There was no end, only this beginning—new music.

Many years later, Tobasonakwut heard his mother, Nenagiizhigok, sing this melody to him. She and the other children, now parents, named the lullaby "Kopichigan." He would hear it as he sat in a *tikanaagan*—a cradleboard—while his mother picked blueberries in the August sun, and he would drift off to sleep. He would hear it at night, rocking in a swing suspended above his parents' bed. And he would hear it sung to him when he was put down for a nap.

"*Mehhh, mehhh, mehhh ...*" his mother would softly hum. The gift from the dragonflies worked its way into Tobasonakwut's heart, mind, and spirit. It was a song that came from home. From mother. From earth.

AS A YOUNG BOY, Tobasonakwut lived the happy-go-lucky life that little Anishinaabeg always have in what is now Northwestern Ontario. He had a smile on his face and a slingshot in his back pocket.

Summers were spent at a spot on the Aulneau Peninsula called Neyangaashing, a village built around a Midewin lodge used by the Grand Medicine Society of the Ojibwe. From his parents' home, Tobasonakwut would scale a nearby hill, climb the rounded rock face, and look out over the shimmering waters of Lake of the Woods. He would see fishers passing by in their boats, including his father, heading out to set a net. In August, he and his brothers would sit there and eat blueberries.

One summer day, Tobasonakwut came across a strange sight. He was walking back to the Midewin lodge when he saw an

Anishinaabe man on his hands and knees like a four-legged animal, a leash around his neck. The leash was tied to a post set so deeply into the ground that it did not move when the man pulled on the leather strap. The man was sobbing to himself, unaware of Tobasonakwut watching him. Tobasonakwut was witnessing someone on a vision quest, the man sacrificing his hunger, his thirst, and even his dignity to move closer to the spirit world. It was the first time he had seen such behaviour. It would not be the last.

Things were changing for Tobasonakwut and his people. The Anishinaabeg were being relocated from villages like Neyangaashing to reserves like Big Island and Onigaming, where Tobasonakwut's family was moved. They were told the land where they'd worked their traplines for so many generations did not belong to them. Their traditional way of life gone, they were ordered not to leave the reserve, and they were not permitted to join the new economy being created around them.

Nothing was the same, including the marriage of Waabana-kwad and Nenagiizhigok. Waabanakwad began to spend more time away from the family he loved. Perhaps it was a way for him to reclaim some of the autonomy that had been taken from him. Perhaps he was just chasing women. Perhaps it was a bit of both. Whatever the cause, Nenagiizhigok was left alone with her children and grew distressed and despondent. When Waabana-kwad reappeared after a long absence, the parents would argue in front of their sons, leaving them with unsettled feelings. Colonization is not a good backdrop to family life.

Yet both parents loved their children with all their hearts. Waabanakwad took young Tobasonakwut with him to his broth-er's house, where they would listen to 78s of the Carter Family on the reserve's first record player. Nenagiizhigok, for her part, would tell the children stories by the wood stove all winter long.

One morning, Nenagiizhigok dressed Tobasonakwut a little more deliberately than usual. She made some *pakwezhigan*— bannock—and boiled water for tea. When a respected elder arrived, Tobasonakwut was given the bread and tea and led by the elder to the lakeshore, where a canoe waited for them. The elder paddled the canoe south toward Cyclone Point.

On the way, they came to a rock face that cast an eastward gaze. They paddled to it and pulled the canoe ashore. The old man unwrapped the bannock and poured out two cups of tea. He loaded his ceremonial pipe with tobacco and lit it with a match. He invoked the four directions, mother earth, and the grandfather of us all. The medicine man prayed for the little boy who sat before him. He asked the spirits to be gentle on him. Then he gave the boy bread and one of the cups of tea.

They sat and ate in silence for a time. Then the elder told Tobasonakwut he would become a leader and a spiritual person among the Anishinaabe. For this reason, Tobasonakwut needed to go on his vision quest at a young age. The quest would prepare him for his life's work.

As he chewed the cooked dough, it dawned on Tobasonakwut that this was his last meal before the fast would begin. He must have chewed a little more slowly and listened to the elder a little more closely after that.

The elder instructed him to climb into the open mouth of a nearby cave. He was to remain there for four days.

The boy did as he was told. Cold, hungry, and thirsty, he spent four days alone in the cave. He heard the rain fall, he heard the snakes that shared the cave with him slither past. He cursed his family and the elder who had brought him there. He was lonely and miserable and promised himself he would never force his children to fast as he was fasting. But he did not break his fast.

He honoured his commitment. He completed his quest and he saw his vision.

After four days, the elder retrieved him. They smoked the pipe together and ate some food. As the old man paddled them home toward Onigaming, Tobasonakwut occasionally turned back to study this person who had left him in that cave. He must have noticed that the old man looked as if he had just spent four days in the bush too. When Tobasonakwut arrived home, Waabanakwad encouraged him to leave tobacco under a tree and give thanks for the vision he had received.

2

SO IT WENT. The years that followed were filled with laughter and love, arguing and pain. Life was good, but life was hard. It is the Anishinaabe way.

Yet there was something else, something lurking just out of view that haunted Tobasonakwut's family. It was a deep-seated fear that lay in wait behind the next tree or over the next hill, just as the Windigo, the ice-giant-cannibal with the banshee scream, haunted their ancestors. And, as with the Windigo, the adults dared not speak its name.

The fear became reality one late-summer's day when a man in a black robe arrived to demand that Tobasonakwut come with him.

In that instant, Tobasonakwut's childhood ended. He was placed on a truck with other Anishinaabe children and driven to St. Mary's Indian Residential School outside Kenora, Ontario. He would spend most of the next decade in this institution—run by the Oblate order of Catholic priests—a subject in a large-scale experiment in social engineering, the goal of which was to "kill the Indian in the child."

As soon as he arrived, Tobasonakwut's hair was cut short and he was stripped of the name given to him by his father. The priests and nuns replaced it with a number—54—and an Irish name: Peter Kelly. He was even stripped of the language he had spoken all his life, a language passed down through untold generations of ancestors. Speaking Anishinaabemowin within earshot of his new custodians earned him a beating with a ruler or a belt. In the classroom, he was expected to speak English, but outside that room his keepers spoke French to their charges.

A while later, Tobasonakwut was called by a nun to her room, where the woman raped him. While riding him, she told him, "That's all your people are good for, is just fucking." That was only the first occasion. Other sexual abuses followed, committed by men and women, both while Tobasonakwut was alone and with other children. Throughout his years at the residential school, Tobasonakwut and the other children were referred to by the teachers and staff as *maudit sauvages*.

Tobasonakwut returned to his family at Onigaming for the summer of 1947. As those halcyon days drew to a close, and when the wild rice harvest was completed, Waabanakwad gathered his family for a feast before the children went back to residential school. He showered them with candies and sweets he had bought in nearby Nestor Falls. He led them in traditional songs on his big drum.

The priest arrived to take the three eldest boys—Tootons, Tobasonakwut, and John Pete. Little Tobasonakwut was still singing his father's songs as they drove back to Kenora. He was interrupted when the priest pulled the car over, dragged him from the vehicle, and beat him, telling him, "Never sing those pagan songs again."

That October, Waabanakwad was struck by a car while crossing the highway near Onigaming. Seriously injured, he was taken to

St. Joseph's Hospital. It was there, with his sons standing by his side, that Waabanakwad sang his death song. It was a slow, beautiful, and haunting song without words, only vocables to carry the melody. When he completed his song, he asked his wife, Nenagiizhigok, to make sure his sons remembered it. She kept her promise: it is still with his descendants today.

After he died, Waabanakwad was brought to St. Mary's to be buried in a cemetery in the shadow of the residential school. During the funeral, Tobasonakwut insisted on standing next to his father's coffin, in accordance with Anishinaabe tradition, instead of kneeling as his Catholic keepers had taught him.

Following the service, an assembly was called, and Tobasonakwut was ordered to come to the front of the group. A nun told him to hold his hands out, and he was strapped repeatedly for his transgression. Years later, Tobasonakwut would speak about how he felt at the time.

"I resolved that I'm not gonna cry," he'd say, the edges of his mouth pulled downward. "If that's your best shot, you don't know what I'm going through in seeing my father being buried. And this physical pain that I'm feeling? That's nothing compared to"—his voice cracked as he jabbed his heavy fist toward his chest—"to what I feel."

He would say this some six decades later, when he was a man looking back on his life from the high hill of old age.

But on that day in 1947, the young Tobasonakwut had no one to explain himself to, and no choice but to suffer this injustice in silence. He would take the tears he wanted to shed for his dead father and bury them deep inside, somewhere out of reach of the priests and nuns. He would take the anger at the unfairness of being beaten while the earth on his father's grave was still fresh and use it to push his emotions down even further. There was stress and grief, and the realization that his one true protector was gone. Now there would be no one to save him from this place. All of this was buried. Perhaps his heart hardened. Maybe his spirit petrified. That is what little children did in order to survive residential school.

DURING HIS TIME AT ST. MARY'S, Tobasonakwut became close friends with a boy named Miigoons, who had been renamed Louie by the priests. When Miigoons's father had died, he was abandoned by his mother, who suffered from inconsolable grief after the passing of her husband. Tobasonakwut's and Miigoons's beds were next to each other, and they shared a box at the foot of those beds which housed all of their earthly possessions.

One Sunday afternoon after mass, Tobasonakwut and Miigoons were playing with their toy trucks near a gravel pile on the school grounds. A non-Native man with light-brown hair, dressed in a blue suit, walked over to the boys. As the man approached, Miigoons stood and looked sheepishly at his shoes. The man led Miigoons away toward the cemetery.

Tobasonakwut raced to the top of a nearby hill to get a good vantage point. Arriving at the summit, he saw a group of non-Native men standing in a circle smoking cigarettes and passing around a flask. His eyes were drawn to what appeared to be a pile of clothes in the middle of the circle. Just then, the pile moved. It was Miigoons. One of the men picked the scrawny boy up by his shirt and punched him in the stomach. The boy collapsed to the ground, gasping for air.

Tobasonakwut ran back to the school for help. Finding the principal, he explained what he had seen in a mixture of Anishinaabemowin and English, not knowing much of his second language yet. The father principal stalled and said he would catch up. Tobasonakwut returned to the hill, but Miigoons and the men were gone.

Tobasonakwut would not see Miigoons for a week. One of the other priests, one who spoke Ojibwe well and was kind to the children, came to Tobasonakwut and told him, "*Miigoons ginoonde-waabamig akoziiwigamigong*"—"Miigoons is in the hospital and wants to see you."

Tobasonakwut was driven to a nearby hospital, where he found his little friend in bed. Through Miigoons's hospital gown, Tobasonakwut could see that he was bandaged from his belly button to his sternum. He asked what happened, but Miigoons refused to answer. He did say that his ribs were broken and that he could hardly breathe. Tobasonakwut asked why he had been sent for.

"I want you to have my little toys and my trucks," Miigoons replied. "I want you to take care of my shoes and my boots and my jacket. Everything in that box by our beds I want you to take care of, including my comic books."

Then the priest returned for Tobasonakwut and drove him back to St. Mary's. When he got back to the residential school, Tobasonakwut moved Miigoons's things into his side of the box, just as his friend had asked.

A few days later, a nurse told Tobasonakwut to drag Miigoons's mattress outside into the sun and cover it with a powder.

"What happened to Louie?" Tobasonakwut asked.

"He won't be coming back."

"What happened to him?"

"He's not coming back," the nurse repeated.

"*Giiniboo na?*" Tobasonakwut asked in Ojibwe. Had his friend passed away? At the time, he did not know the word *die*. The nurse had no idea what he was saying.

The priests insisted that Miigoons had died of tuberculosis, but Tobasonakwut knew the truth: his friend had died of his internal injuries, injuries which likely would have made the boy cough up blood.

"They killed Miigoons," Tobasonakwut would later say, the light reflecting off a tear welling in his eye.

HOCKEY WAS AN ESCAPE for Tobasonakwut. Those times were full of fun and laughter. When he had finished his school work and his chores, he could head down to the rink, and he and other boys would spend hours skating circles around each other and working on the fancy stickhandling that characterizes a lot of First Nations hockey. The children were poor. Their skates did not fit. They used frozen horseshit for a puck. But when they were on the ice, those things did not matter. For one shift at a time, they were free.

Tobasonakwut had a soft spot for one of the priests, who was different from the others. He was kind to the children. He never hit Tobasonakwut. He spoke to him about the teachings of Christ and did not contradict them with his actions.

The years spent at St. Mary's had an indelible imprint on Tobasonakwut's spirituality. For better and for worse, endless days of kneeling in church pews, reading the Bible, and saying the rosary worked their way into his spirit. His keepers saw his body as a host for their religion; in Communion, he took the Host into his body.

At their best, these new teachings provided him with refuge. Under instruction from the friendly priest, Tobasonakwut would often pray to Brother André of Montreal, who would later become a saint. He saw something of himself in that man's humble beginnings. At their worst, those religious teachings were used to justify terrible acts committed by supposed emissaries of God.

In addition to his own trauma, Tobasonakwut saw many of his closest relatives abused terribly. He saw his sister Nancy having her head shaved in front of a student assembly after she tried to run away. He saw his siblings led to a cabin where a man he knew to be a pedophile lived. Perhaps most indelible of all was a day not long after his father died.

After Waabanakwad's passing, Tobasonakwut's youngest brother, Kiizhebowse Makwa, was taken from the family early and sent to St. Mary's when he was four years old. On his first day at the school, he was brought into the mess hall while the students ate. A man yelled at him to sit down. Never having spoken any language other than Anishinaabemowin, Kiizhebowse Makwa looked around nervously but did not sit. Tobasonakwut watched helplessly as the grown man walked over to Kiizhebowse Makwa and punched the boy in the jaw, knocking the four-year-old unconscious. At the time, Tobasonakwut was too weak to intervene. All he could do was let the anger build inside. Eventually, he would harness that anger when he fought, but that was years in the future.

The mess hall was rarely the site of joyous occasions. On most days, the children ate gruel for breakfast and often went hungry. And they were being watched.

Tobasonakwut and his brothers and sisters were part of a series of nutritional experiments conducted at several residential schools across Canada. Experimental additives to flour were tested at St. Mary's during the years they were there. As Dr. Ian Mosby, the researcher who uncovered these experiments, points out, a team of government-funded scientists found that children like Tobasonakwut and his siblings were starving. Instead of feeding them, the scientists ran a controlled experiment in which they fed the children prohibited food additives to measure the effects. They also denied dental care to the children to measure levels of gum disease among them. This outrageous racist thinking characterized the residential school era.

TOBASONAKWUT FINISHED GRADE 8, the highest level offered at the
residential school, when he was thirteen, but the Oblates refused
to let him leave. At the time, the high school in Kenora did not
accept Indian students from St. Mary's. So he stayed for three
more years, occupying himself with chores and busy work in class.

One Saturday, the teenage Tobasonakwut stayed behind when
most of the children went to a movie theatre in a nearby town. A
young priest came downstairs and tossed a pair of boxing gloves at
him, promising to teach him how to fight. Tobasonakwut accepted
the offer. The anger he felt over years of beatings and witnessing the
abuse of other children was about to come pouring out.

Two young Anishinaabeg acted as cornermen, lacing up
Tobasonakwut's and the priest's boxing gloves and coaching their
respective fighters. The young man coaching Tobasonakwut told
him not to waste any time and go after the priest straightaway.

When one of the boys rang the bell, Tobasonakwut obliged.
He shot out of his corner across the makeshift ring and planted a
hard punch on the priest's nose. Blood sprayed out over the priest's
face and clothing. For the next three minutes, Tobasonakwut was
the hunter and the black robe was the prey. When the boys rang
the bell at the end of Round 1, the priest said that was enough.
Nobody in the residential school ever hit Tobasonakwut again.

While the priests, nuns, and caretakers exercised control over
the children in their charge, they could not prevent teenagers from
being teenagers. Tobasonakwut was no different. One day, he sat
with his girlfriend in a pew in the chapel, polishing his shoes. One
of the nuns, seeing him from behind, noticed his shoulder moving
furiously.

"What are you doing?" the sister asked.

"Jerking off," he quipped.

"That's nice, don't swear," the French Catholic nun replied from the other side of the language barrier.

Not long after, Tobasonakwut's girlfriend delivered a baby. With both parents in residential school, the infant, whom they named Patricia, was taken from them and adopted by an Anishinaabe family in Saugeen, near Owen Sound. The adoptive parents were very loving, but the irony of having his child taken from him while he lived in an institution that had removed him from his own parents was not lost on Tobasonakwut.

A few months later, Tobasonakwut was set free. He was sixteen years old and could return to his family.

He went back to Onigaming, but things were different. His father was gone, and his younger siblings were still in residential school. His older brother, Tootons, was already an alcoholic. This stoked the angry fire growing deep inside him. Tobasonakwut visited his mother for a short time. Then he went to work.

3

ONE OF THE FEW JOBS open to a young Anishinaabe at the time was cutting wood, so Tobasonakwut went to work in the pulpwood camps around Kenora. Though he was a thin, lanky teenager, he headed into the bush with grown men and worked as hard as any of them.

The days were spent felling trees, cutting them into lengths with a two-man crosscut saw, and loading the logs onto a horse-drawn sled to be hauled to the mill. The work was non-stop, and when the workday was finished, the men welcomed the nights. Tobasonakwut would often lie in his bunk listening to rowdy stories told by older men in the camp. Sometimes, he would even be given a little something to drink before turning in and getting some sleep. There were some comments made about "Indians," but then there were racist comments made about almost everyone, seeing as how most of the camp dwellers were recent immigrants. It was hard work, but sweat was an equalizer. It did not matter where you came from or how you looked; if you could swing an axe and carry a log, there was a spot for you.

The hard work had its effect on Tobasonakwut. The thin teenager who first ventured into the bush that winter emerged a few years later as a muscular young man. And he tolerated no abuse. From anyone. When Tobasonakwut went into town on his days off, he still heard comments like "dirty Indian" or "jack pine nigger," names he had heard when he was a boy. But now he would call the speaker on it, and sometimes challenge him to a fight.

In summer, he would head back to Onigaming, guiding for some of the nearby fishing lodges. It was one of those clients, an African-American boxing coach from Minneapolis, who would offer Tobasonakwut a chance to re-channel the energy he spent brawling in the streets of Kenora into something positive. After watching him punch a heavy bag hanging from a tree, the coach invited Tobasonakwut to the United States, where he could train as a professional boxer. There, in the Twin Cities, he moulded the brute strength of the woodcutter into a skilled practitioner of the sweet science. He also, at one point, revealed a tale that revived some of the fire Tobasonakwut had been trying to bury.

"When I was in Nestor Falls," the coach told Tobasonakwut during a workout session, referring to the town near Onigaming, "I met the woman who ran over your father with her car." He waited for Tobasonakwut to absorb his words. "She said, 'I killed an Indian. Don't I get an eagle feather?'"

Tobasonakwut bit down on his mouth guard and ripped several hard punches off the focus mitts the coach was holding. That which had been buried years earlier was still burning. Now it began to surface.

One day, Tobasonakwut walked into the gym to find a young African-American boxer holding court in the centre of the ring. He would taunt the other boxers, goading them to step into the ring. When they took the bait, the young man would toy with them. He would dance around effortlessly, pivoting out of the way of their mad charges, neatly sidestepping their combinations and raining down punches whenever he saw fit. He did this to boxer after boxer, running through the entire gym. The world would later know this brash young pugilist as Muhammad Ali.

Tobasonakwut was working toward his own ring dreams: the regional Golden Gloves tournament.

But his dreams were cut short. There was indeed a fire burning inside him, or at least it felt like there was. He could feel a persistent burning in his lungs. Stricken with coughing fits, he returned to Canada, where he was diagnosed with tuberculosis and admitted to a sanatorium in Thunder Bay. Tobasonakwut found himself institutionalized for a second time in his life, but this time was different. He had more freedom, and a ton of free time. He passed the days reading and flirting with the younger nurses. After eighteen months, he was transferred to another sanatorium, in Brandon, Manitoba.

As he walked on his healing journey inside this white-walled institution, love re-entered his life. It took the form of a beautiful young Anishinaabekwe, another patient there. They would steal away to unused rooms in the "san" and strip off their white patient uniforms. Their brown skin contrasted as sharply against the discarded clothes as their passion did against the clinical sterility that governed their lives. It was during these rendezvous that they conceived a child. Tobasonakwut would finish his healing journey on his own however; the young woman and her baby died not long after the child was born.

The sanatorium in Brandon offered both convalescence and vocational instruction. By the time Tobasonakwut was cleared to leave, he had been trained in diesel mechanics. Instead of heading into the bush for another winter's work among the trees, he set off with Kiizhebowse Makwa for northern Manitoba, where he had been promised a position as an apprentice on the massive dam being built at Grand Rapids.

After completing his work there, he moved to Winnipeg to work on another large construction project, repairing heavy equipment used to dig the floodway, an enormous ditch designed to divert flood water around Manitoba's capital.

Construction work paid decently, but it could also be dangerous. Tobasonakwut was at work in the garage one day when he heard over the radio that a front-end loader had stopped working. When he arrived, he saw the machine perched on a slope, its bucket facing uphill. A few workers had gathered around it to assess the situation.

Tobasonakwut began approaching the loader and was about a dozen feet away when he realized the parking brake was not engaged. Suddenly, the loader began rolling backward down the slope. He watched helplessly as a man was pinned underneath, the pressure shattering his skull and sending brain matter and blood spewing out into the mud beneath.

Tobasonakwut moved on again.

He had a lot to live for. He and his new wife, Margaret, originally from Fort Frances, Ontario, started a family together. They welcomed three children into the world: Darryl in 1961, Diane a year after that, and Danny in 1965.

After bringing Darryl home from the hospital, Tobasonakwut would carry him in his arms late into the night. He would hold the sleeping baby boy for so long it left an impression of sorts, a lingering feeling in the crook of Tobasonakwut's arm. That impression would stay there long after Darryl had grown. Diane grew up exhibiting the boldness that would later see her become a politician and lawyer, the first female First Nations lawyer called to the bar in Manitoba and Ontario, and the first female grand chief in modern times of Treaty #3.* Sometimes her confidence put her boyfriends at the mercy of her dad. She would flaunt their relationships in front of him, and Tobasonakwut would respond by attempting to burn a hole through the suitors with his gaze.

Where Darryl and Diane had the smarts and the leadership qualities, Danny was the life of the party. Good looking, with an easy charisma and a natural sense of humour, Danny could make fun of you but have you feel good about it. He also inherited the family's stubbornness. At one Anishinaabe celebration, Tobasonakwut dressed Danny in his powwow regalia, complete with feathered bustle, feather fans, and a roach on top of his head. The boy, looking like a miniature Anishinaabe warrior, refused to go out into the dancing arena.

"I'm not going out there dressed like a bird."

That was the end of Danny's powwow dancing career.

THOSE IDYLLIC SCENES played out under brewing storm clouds. Back in Kenora, Tobasonakwut found a town whose racism toward Indigenous people was growing more vile and hateful by the day. First Nations people were still not allowed to eat in most restaurants in the city. One bar downtown had a line taped on the floor. This barrier divided the room, with one side for non-Native people and the other reserved for the "Indians." There were two exceptions to the segregation, Ho-Ho's and Ted's Cafe, both owned by

---

* Treaty #3 is the agreement between the Queen and the Anishinaabeg from North-western Ontario and southeastern Manitoba signed in 1873. It is preserved in the Paypom Treaty, the Queen's version of the treaty and the oral history of the area. Since the Anishinaabeg of this region share spiritual and linguistic characteristics, the term "Treaty #3" is also used to refer to a distinct cultural group in this geographical area. It is also shorthand for Grand Council Treaty #3, the political organization that represents the First Nations in this area, an organization that Tobasonakwut, Kiizhebowse Makwa, John, and Diane would lead as grand chiefs at different times.

immigrants, both rewarded with loyalty from Indigenous customers for generations to come.

First Nations people who drank in the streets were beaten randomly. Anishinaabe women were plied with booze until incapacitated. Other times, they were abducted and raped by non-Native men. Kenora's oral history says some victims were dumped into Lake of the Woods along the city's harbourfront. Those who swam to shore lived to tell their stories. Others were not so lucky.

Tobasonakwut and his brothers John and Kiizhebowse Makwa, now known as Fred Kelly, the name he'd been given in St. Mary's, rejected any idea of becoming victims of the prejudice that coloured life in Kenora. Whenever one of them found himself targeted by non-Native men on the street, he fought back and won.

One day, the three brothers were walking along 2nd Street South when they saw a large crowd gathered on the sidewalk. In the middle of the crowd, a friend from St. Mary's was getting a licking from a non-Indigenous man. Tobasonakwut—his fists clenched, anger raising his hackles—watched his friend take a beating while the rest of the crowd cheered on the non-Native.

"Fucking hit him!" he shouted to the Anishinaabe. His friend paused, absorbed the moment, and decked his foe, sending him backward. The crowd caught him. A brawl broke out. The flame inside Tobasonakwut was rekindled.

The problem with rekindling a fire is that once it catches, you can't always contain it. The beatings at residential school, the years cutting wood and fixing heavy equipment, the boxing training—they combined to make Tobasonakwut a fearsome street fighter. To John and Fred, their older brother was both a mentor and a model where self-defence was concerned. They shared his anger and much of his ability, bonded by the attachment that exists

between brothers. They were the "Kelly Boys," and they built a
name for themselves on the streets of Kenora.

It may have started on the streets, but their rage in response to
racist attitudes and aggression eventually grew into an important
part of the Indigenous rights movement in that part of the country.
In fact, it helped usher in civil rights activism in Canada in general.

Non-Native allies, both in Kenora and from across the country,
helped the Kelly Boys funnel their energy and righteous indigna-
tion into more political arenas. In 1965, with the aid of an Indian
Affairs employee in Winnipeg, Tobasonakwut headed to St. Francis
Xavier University, in Antigonish, Nova Scotia, to study community
development. Completing this program and earning one of the
university's iconic X graduation rings was very important to him. It
was proof that he could make the most of educational opportunities
denied to him in his residential school days. That same year, Fred
organized a silent march through Kenora by Anishinaabe people
and their allies to demand change. Some of their demands, such as
the creation of a safety patrol and help for addicts, were met. The
brothers succeeded individually as well; John was among the first
Anishinaabe men to earn a master's degree.

Thus began the political careers of the Kelly Boys. Politics may
seem an unlikely career choice for a group of "Indian kids" who did
not have the right to vote until they were in their twenties (the
franchise was denied to First Nations until 1960), yet they excelled
in this arena. John, Fred, and Tobasonakwut would all go on to
become grand chiefs.

Their activities, within the crucible of racial tension in and
around Kenora, drew media attention as violence between
non-Natives and First Nations people continued. Some people
began to predict that "race riots" similar to the violence that was
tearing apart many urban centres in the United States would erupt

in the small city nestled among the jack pines in Northwestern Ontario. TV, radio, and print journalists descended on Kenora, many of them turning to Fred, John, or Tobasonakwut for interviews.

One of these profiles about the Kelly Boys appeared in *The Toronto Telegram*'s weekend magazine and was seen by a young woman in that city who was just starting to learn about and work with First Nations people.

4

ANNE KATHERINE AVERY—"Kathi" to her family and friends—grew up in the Beaches neighbourhood in Toronto. Her mother was a homemaker and her father an advertising executive in the era immortalized in popular culture by the *Mad Men* television series. Sister Lynne was a few years older and popular at school.

Kathi was a rowdy but kind child. She inherited her mother's smile and relished the time they spent together working on arts and crafts. Her father's charm and work ethic rubbed off on her as well. She did not mind some of the perks that came with his career either, like the time he took her and a friend to see the Beatles when they first touched down in Toronto.

Kathi spent her teen years watching movies at the Fox Theatre and hanging out with her friends at the Garden Gate Restaurant, nicknamed the "Goof" for its neon sign promising "Good Food," which never seemed to have a functioning *d* in "Good" or *ood* in "Food." There, they would chat and order "pine floats"—water with a toothpick in it. The price was right, but it may not have won them any fans among the restaurant's management.

Summers were spent in the lake-filled Muskoka area north of the city, where Kathi and her family and friends swam, water-skied, and fished for bass. Winter was the season for school and family. Kathi's diligence at school paid off; after earning a BA in social work at the University of Toronto she went to work on a master's degree.

A folkie at heart, Kathi developed a passion for social justice that was in line with the protest music of the 1960s. Looking to her own backyard, she saw that First Nations people in Canada faced unprecedented discrimination and inequality. She set out to get involved. One of her first jobs was working on the Rama reserve in Southern Ontario for a summer, where she first met Anishinaabe people and was introduced to their culture.

A few months later, she was back at U of T. There, she would meet a man, and together they would change each other's lives in ways neither could have imagined.

THE YEAR WAS 1968, and Tobasonakwut was in Toronto searching for an escape from the unrest back home. The problem had grown beyond the violence in Kenora, which continued without let-up. Now it was personal. Tobasonakwut had dug himself into a deep hole with the people he loved most.

What started with a few sips of booze in the pulpwood camps had progressed into full-blown alcoholism. He had quit when Darryl was born, but now, some seven years later, he had picked up the bottle again.

That raging fire, the anger burning inside him since boyhood, was now manifesting itself with ugly symptoms: more drinking, more fights, and more women. During this period, Danny, Darryl, Diane, and Margaret saw Tobasonakwut at his worst.

Soon, Tobasonakwut was gone not just for a weekend or a few days but weeks at a time, without a word to his wife or children. When he did return, he was not always welcomed by them.

One day, Darryl was with his school friends when he saw his father, drunk and dishevelled, walking down the street toward them.

"Isn't that your dad?" one of the boys asked.

"No," Darryl said, and looked away.

Tobasonakwut hung his head and faded away into the background. His relationship with Margaret was soon over and the children remained with her.

TOBASONAKWUT DECIDED the way to put his life back on track was to focus on education. Having earned a diploma from St. Francis Xavier University, he wanted to continue, but nothing was available around Kenora. So he headed to the University of Toronto to begin work on a bachelor's degree.

It was in and around the First Nations education scene of Southern Ontario that Tobasonakwut and Kathi first met. The Anishinaabe man with the confident air, the Indian Affairs glasses, and the pompadour haircut caught Kathi's eye. She studied him, curious, maybe even enamoured. He returned Kathi's gaze.

Soon, Tobasonakwut and Kathi were seeing each other—and learning about each other. Listening to Tobasonakwut describe life as an Anishinaabe in Canada, she began to see his charisma, appreciate his sense of humour, and grasp the source of his anger.

Tobasonakwut learned about Kathi as well. He met her friends from high school and university. He visited the Toronto spots she grew up around. He was polite, and patient, at least by his standards. They would talk for hours on end. In her, he found a match for his smarts, but also a foil for his sharp edges—where he was rough and tumble, she was gentle and nurturing.

Eventually, Kathi told Tobasonakwut she wanted to introduce him to her family. This might have presented a major challenge to some. In the climate of the 1960s, bringing a First Nations man to her upper-middle-class Toronto home would have provoked anxiety and concern for most young women. But Kathi wasn't like most young women of the time; she was kind and idealistic, someone who believed in equality and expected the same of her family.

Tobasonakwut viewed things a little differently. He had no qualms about visiting Kathi's parents; he cared about her deeply, after all. But he recognized the scene for what it was—the Canadian equivalent of *Guess Who's Coming to Dinner*. And he was playing the part of Sidney Poitier.

Tobasonakwut arrived at the family home before Kathi was ready. He walked through the foyer, registered the comfortable surroundings, and sat down with her parents and her aunt Betty. Together they made small talk as they waited for their mutual interest to join them.

Finally, Kathi came down the stairs in full view of everyone in the room. She made quite an impression, wearing a buckskin jacket and skirt, with long fringes hanging from her arms and a smile on her face. No one made any comment until Kathi dragged Tobasonakwut to another relative's house close by.

"My, aren't we looking Indian tonight," their new host quipped.

Kathi and Tobasonakwut managed to contain their giggles until they left, but then promptly broke out in laughter. They would smile about the scene for many years. Sometimes, they would laugh at the family member's comment. Other times, they would be laughing at Kathi's wardrobe choice.

Kathi's parents had no problem with their daughter dating an Anishinaabe man. They did, however, object strongly that he was still married. They also worried that the amount of time Kathi was spending with Tobasonakwut might put the completion of her master's degree in jeopardy. (It did not, she graduated that year.)

Kathi's parents were among only a few who did not make much of the two young lovebirds coming from different walks of life. Their interracial relationship was uncommon at the time, even in Canada's biggest and most multicultural city. Occasionally, the intolerance threatened to drift toward violence. On more than one occasion, a male friend of Kathi's pulled Tobasonakwut aside and hinted at the kind of misfortunes that might befall a young Indian dating a "white girl." Tobasonakwut would typically brush him off.

But the tension ran both ways. Tobasonakwut returned to Onigaming after elders called him home to help the Treaty #3 organization. It meant putting his studies on hiatus, but the relationship he had found at university continued. He missed Kathi.

Privately, he wondered how he would be perceived if he brought her back to the reserve. He had heard people back home make negative comments about his first non-Native wife, Margaret. He pondered whether Kathi would be able to contend with such disapproval. He wondered how his mother, Nenagiizhigok, would greet a second partner from a different culture.

Tobasonakwut shared his doubts with an elder he often turned to for advice. Perhaps he was looking for an easy way out, half-wanting this guardian of Anishinaabe tradition to tell him not to bring the "white girl" home. But when Tobasonakwut finished explaining his dilemma, the old man thought for a few minutes. Then he said, "Well, if you love her, then you should bring her home."

Soon after, Kathi made the long trek north to join Tobasonakwut.

It was a promising beginning. Tobasonakwut's political activities continued, and Kathi worked with him to build up the Treaty #3 organization. The happy times seemed to belie the concern Tobasonakwut had felt about asking her to join him. Kathi loved his kids, and she began adapting to his culture and learning his language, Anishinaabemowin. But there were challenging times as well, times when Kathi would wait for hours in a car parked outside a bar as Tobasonakwut got drunk inside.

Tobasonakwut had known for years that he had to change. He'd seen the truth of it in his children's faces. Heard the quiet protest of his new partner, who refused to join him inside the beer parlours. Felt the revulsion inside as he robbed himself of his spirit's vision.

The pressure built up within him until one night, sitting with friends in a bar in Thunder Bay, Tobasonakwut watched a waitress make her way toward his table. He pointed at a bottle of Labatt's beer on the tray she was carrying and said, "See that beer? That is going to be the last beer I ever drink."

His friends scoffed. Their laughter rang out through the air of the dingy bar. Their cackles cut through the smoke and sliced him open. He had not meant it as a joke. He choked back a mouthful of the swill and set the bottle back down two-thirds full. He stood up, staggered slightly, and walked out of the bar. He went back to his hotel room, where Kathi was reading. The next morning, they drove the six hours back to Onigaming. Tobasonakwut would never touch another drop of alcohol again.

It wasn't easy. For several days, he stayed in a dark room alone, in deep withdrawal from alcohol. He sweated. He shivered. He felt his skin crawl. The room shook, alternating between menacing, expansive darkness and claustrophobic, smothering black.

At one point, he lay on his back, studying the ceiling. Hundreds of small black spiders appeared, their eyes glowing red in the dark. They lowered themselves from crystalline webs and threatened to land on him like countless tiny paratroopers. He squirmed and squeezed his eyes shut.

Once the hallucinations passed, he slept for a long time.

THINGS CHANGED for the now-dry Tobasonakwut. In 1972, he was elected grand chief of Treaty #3, representing some twenty-seven communities in the Kenora, Dryden, and Thunder Bay areas. He pushed for improvements in these communities, negotiating with provincial and federal governments to reclaim land that had been unlawfully seized, all the while encouraging other First Nations leaders to pursue the same sobriety that had changed him. He cleaned up the operations of Treaty #3 and transformed chiefs meetings into a forum where things actually got done.

Soon, things began to change for Darryl, Diane, and Danny as they approached their teenage years. While Tobasonakwut and Margaret never reconciled, the kids spent more and more time with their father, eventually coming to live with him. Together they built a house on a beautiful point overlooking Lake of the Woods, the first on the reserve with a basement and one of the first with running water.

Tobasonakwut had long ago nicknamed Darryl "Dad," an allusion to the young man's precociousness. Tobasonakwut still liked to joke around with his son in this way. "Let's go for a ride, Dad!" he'd call, walking down the front steps of their wooden porch. Darryl would smile and reply, "Okay, Dad!" They would climb into the cab of Tobasonakwut's truck and set out to visit friends and relatives all around Lake of the Woods.

Around the same time, Tobasonakwut's nephew Pee-wee began staying with them as well. Living just a few doors away, Pee-wee's father, Tootons, drank almost every day. It was a scourge that began when he was thirteen years old and still in residential school. One of Tootons's boys had been getting in trouble with the law. Social workers apprehended the other children, but Pee-wee managed to escape from a Children's Aid foster home. Tobasonakwut's home offered refuge.

Tobasonakwut appealed to his brother to quit drinking. Tobasonakwut told him how he was working with all his might to stay clean and was finally doing it, thanks to the help of Alcoholics Anonymous.

"I want to take my own life," Tootons said. "But I don't have the heart to shoot myself in the head. So I use this bottle instead." Tobasonakwut never gave up on his brother, despite the fact that he drank until the end of his life.

DARRYL, AT NINETEEN, showed promise of following in his father's footsteps as a leader. He had returned to Onigaming after working as a page in the Ontario Legislature. Tobasonakwut encouraged him to pursue a career in law. But it was not meant to be.

The love of Darryl's young life left him after learning that another woman was carrying his child. Darryl was heartbroken. He turned to his father for solace. He told Tobasonakwut that he, too, was contemplating suicide.

Instead of comforting his son, Tobasonakwut laid into him. "It's never been an option for me," he snapped. "I've never thought about giving up!"

The little boy he had held in his arms on so many late nights was hurting and crying out for his father again. He needed his father to tell him it was okay. He needed his father to tell him he knew he was suffering. He needed his father to hold him tight and never let him go.

But the anger his father had felt for so many years, the emotional sickness that had been growing inside him like a cancer, had crowded out his nurturing impulses—the love. It seemed as though all his father knew how to do was fight.

When Tobasonakwut finished tearing a strip off the boy, he stormed off.

That would become one of his greatest regrets.

Not long after that, as Tobasonakwut and Kathi unloaded wood they had just cut, a single gunshot punctured the early afternoon calm.

The shot had been way too loud. Way too close. It had been fired inside the house. Tobasonakwut knew in an instant what had happened. Darryl was gone.

SAGE SMOKE ROSE THICK in the air, filling the living room. Two elders stood over a large blanket. They picked up opposite ends and brought them toward each other, like two soldiers folding a flag at a military funeral. They tied two corners together, then gathered the other two corners, wrapping all of the young man's worldly possessions in the blanket.

The two elders, Kwekwekipiness and Kizhe-Manito (a nickname which means "kind spirit," but contains connotations of the Creator, conveying a deep respect), had been called to help put Darryl's belongings away. These things would stay tied up for a year, then they would be given away. The two old men prayed for the family. They shared teachings with them. They consoled the inconsolable.

Tobasonakwut had known heartbreak before, but never like this. He had lost his "Dad" all over again. All of the promise, the smarts, the wit were gone. Nineteen years earlier, he had cradled and carried his first-born child. Now the boy was gone. When the grief did not haunt him, the guilt did.

He was truly at a loss. He did not want to talk about how he felt. Throughout it all, the two old Anishinaabe men kept watch, witnesses to the parent left behind by his child.

In the wake of that loss, a second tragedy washed over the family that year. It came one July night in 1980. There was chaos. Confusion. Young people shouted for adults. They said that Pee-wee was lying in the middle of the highway, not far from where his grandfather Waabanakwad had been fatally injured. Pee-wee was lying there and waiting. The bright high beams of a postal truck dawned over the crest of the hill. A horn blasted. But it was too late for the truck to stop. The wheels pounded the young Anishinaabe man into the pavement. Kathi heard the screams and ran out into the middle of the highway. She gathered Pee-wee into her arms and held him. Her tears washed his face. Pee-wee was already gone.

THERE HE WAS. *On the far side of the arbour, with the other dancers. As clear as day. Darryl. Tobasonakwut had seen him only for an instant, but he would never mistake that face. Pushing through the crowd, he could not bear to spend another second away from the one he missed so much, the one he loved so much.*

Tobasonakwut woke up. He was back in Onigaming. In the same rez house. The same wallpaper and linoleum floors. The same ugly reality: Darryl was gone.

The visions visited Tobasonakwut regularly. The language of the spirit was speaking to him, calling him to action. The spirit was telling him that he could be with his son again. If only he could find that arbour.

Tobasonakwut brought tobacco to Kwekwekipiness, the elder who had stood with him during his darkest hours. He told the old man about his dreams, described the arbour to him and spoke of the dance. The old man listened and nodded, staring out the kitchen window from his seat next to the little Formica-topped table. From time to time, the old man would retrieve a pack of Player's Lights, pop out a cigarette, place the tailor-made between his lips, and strike his BIC lighter.

When Tobasonakwut finished speaking, Kwekwekipiness contemplated all that was and had ever been within the span of a few drags of his cigarette. Then he spoke.

He told Tobasonakwut that the vision he had seen was of a sundance, but it was not an Anishinaabe sundance. It was a Lakota ceremony. In traditional times, the two peoples had been at war. Now Tobasonakwut needed his former adversaries.

Kwekwekipiness told Tobasonakwut to seek his vision, to go and find this sundance, to walk the path his spirit was calling him toward.

And he left Tobasonakwut with a final piece of advice. "Don't let the enemy cut you," he said in Ojibwe.

Then Kwekwekipiness butted out his cigarette and looked back out the window.

DARRYL'S DAUGHTER was born not long after his death in 1980. She was named Melissa. Her birth was a new beginning for the family, the first of many grandchildren.

Diane gave birth to her daughter Jennifer not long after. The baby had brown skin and blond hair. Her little sister Wendy arrived about a year later.

Danny also welcomed a baby into the world. Dan Junior was born premature, but he would grow into a strong young man as charming and good-natured as his father. Then Danny begat Jay. And then he begat Matthew. And then he begat Lisa. And then he begat Danielle. And so on. You get the picture. There were a lot of new babies in the family over the next few years.

Some rays of light began to shine through the cloud of grief. Tobasonakwut had lost his first-born son, but he had been blessed with several grandchildren.

5

AN EARLY MORNING GREY CLOUD shimmered above the frozen waters of Lake of the Woods. The tall, lean Anishinaabe man studied the cloud as it diffused the powerful light of the faraway sun. It had been a long time since another Anishinaabe man had stood on a different shore of this same lake and named him Tobasonakwut. He thought of his father. He pulled a pinch of tobacco from its pouch and placed the offering on the snow. He dipped his head and faced the earth. *"Ahow nimishoomis, miigwech kimiinshiyin ningoozis owiinzowin,"* he said softly. In English, it means, "Oh, grandfather, thank you for giving me my son's name." Tobasonakwut would give his father's name to this new baby boy: Wabanakwut.

Tobasonakwut looked east toward Kenora's harbourfront, then west to the Lake of the Woods Hospital, where his wife, Kathi, lay resting with their new baby son.

My life began in that hospital on that morning, the last morning of 1981.

My mother had been wheeled into the operating room. The doctor made an incision. Inside her womb, I was upside down. The doctor reached in. He pulled me out—all ten pounds eleven ounces of dark-brown me—from my blond-haired, blue-eyed mom. A nurse gasped in surprise. My mom laughed at the nurse as I was passed to my aunt Nancy, who held me and welcomed me to this earth.

Our first stop on our way home from the hospital was at the Washagamis Bay First Nation to visit the home of Allan Paypom. Elder Paypom was extraordinarily well respected as a former grand chief and as the keeper of the treaty. He carried the Anishinaabe version of Treaty #3, ours being one of the few where the Indigenous people recorded the promises that were made to them—a document that lists more promises than the Queen's version of the treaty but makes no mention of land surrender. It was the carrier of this "Manito Masina'igan," as our elders refer to it, who held me and blessed me. Then my parents took me home to Onigaming.

Each day, from the time I was a few weeks old, my mom would bring me up the hill to the house of her friend Baatiins, who also had a newborn. In this way, Baatiins became like a second mother to me. Her husband, Ronny, became like a second father to me. And their youngest son, Waabishki-Makwa—White Bear— became my friend and brother.

When I got to be a little older, Ndede—my father, Tobasonakwut—would bundle me up in layers of blankets, set me on a small wooden sled, and pull me for hours over the frozen surface of Lake of the Woods. He would check on me now and then, as we spent time outdoors in the freezing cold, on the same land our ancestors had inhabited and passed to us.

Around this time, my mother began seeing the visions. Visions of fire. Visions about her son. Visions that scared her. If it were one dream, she might have chalked it up to her nerves as a new parent. Another dream she could have dismissed as a second aberration. But the dreams persisted. She slept. She saw flames. She worried.

Ndede took her and me to see Kwekwekipiness. They gave him tobacco and he brought his wife, Auggie, to sit with him and listen to my parents describe the visions my mother was having.

When they were finished, Kwekwekipiness spoke. "This boy needs to be given another name," he explained in Ojibwe. "Come back in one moon and I will conduct the ceremony."

In the Anishinaabe way, when a person enters a new phase of life they are instructed to receive a new name. The name conveys to their spirit and to the spirits around them that the person has undergone a change. I was only a few months old, but the elders Kwekwekipiness and Auggie believed it was time for me to enter a new level of existence.

Before twenty-eight days had passed, Kwekwekipiness and Auggie came to Onigaming. Kwekwekipiness smoked the pipe and said his invocation. Then he and Auggie sang some traditional songs before asking my parents to bring me to them. Placing his hands on my head, Kwekwekipiness announced my new name.

"*Kwekwekipiness kidizhinikaaz*," he began.

Tobasonakwut's face brightened at the sound of the words. Kwekwekipiness continued. "*Kwekwekipiness kidizhinikaaz, Kwekwekipiness kidizhinikaaz, Kwekwekipiness kidizhinikaaz.*" He lifted his hands from my head and smiled.

Kwekwekipiness had not only given me a new name, he had given me *his* name, taking me as his young charge, someone to help carry on his legacy. "I'm giving this boy my name," he said in Ojibwe, "because he will live to be an old man, even older than me."

My mom must have smiled as she looked down at me.

LIVING IN THE HOUSE at Onigaming, I was bathed in the same sink my nephews Dan and Jay were bathed in, and I played with my nieces Wendy and Jen every day. We were raised in that same house together through those early years. They were my brother's and sister's kids, but my nieces and nephews were like siblings to me. When I wasn't home, I was at Waabishki-Makwa's house, up the hill and across the highway.

Early one morning, when we were about two years old, Makwa's mother, Baatiins, called our house in a panic. Her baby was gone and she could not find him.

As Ndede listened to the panicked mother, he glanced out the window and saw a buck-naked Anishinaabe toddler in our front yard, picking chokecherries from a tree and stuffing them into his mouth. The little boy did not have a care in the world. He didn't worry about the highway traffic or getting dressed or telling his mom that he was leaving. He wanted chokecherries, and it was as simple as that.

My clearest memories of my older brother Danny were formed then. He always seemed to be in a good mood. Even if he was teasing me, he would still make me smile. He had that magnetic sort of personality.

Danny, his partner, Corinne, and their two sons moved to Winnipeg to live with his mother, Margaret. On a night not long after that, his two sons Dan and Jay woke up suddenly.

"Dad!" they both yelled, their little voices ringing through the apartment. Corrine told them their dad was still on the highway, driving back from a road trip.

"No," little Danny told his mom, "Dad was just here."

Jay nodded in agreement.

At about that time, in Morris, Manitoba, their father's car was sideswiped by another vehicle. Danny took his first steps toward the spirit world. He stopped to say goodbye to his two young sons before moving on.

Danny, Darryl, Pee-wee, and two other cousins died in close succession. Our family buried five of its children in five years in the early 1980s.

I RAN AWAY FROM NDEDE, who was screaming at me. I forget what I had done, either left the phone off the hook when he was expecting a call or hung the phone back up when he wanted the line left busy to get some silence. All I remember is being chased across our living room. I scurried under the table for cover as he berated me, spittle shooting from his mouth.

Scenes like that were pretty normal. When I did something wrong, I was yelled at for being stupid. When I got hurt and cried, I was yelled at for being weak. When I sat inside for too long, I was yelled at for being lazy. When my mom did something to aggravate my father, she would get yelled at too.

Ndede had stopped brawling. He had wrestled the illness of alcoholism into submission. But one sickness remained—anger— and it didn't live far from the surface anymore.

In fact, it only seemed to grow, a malevolent presence in our family life. Every time he yelled at me, it only served to make me angry, and I learned to bury that anger inside me, just as he had once done. While he never hit me, I learned to fear Ndede. And I learned to hate him.

THE TRAIN MOVED WEIGHTLESSLY along an airborne track as the scenery flew by beside me. I scanned the terrain and saw that I was passing through many different territories. First it was the plains, carpeted with green and brown grass, then the yellow sand of the desert.

Soon, whitecapped mountains and wintry glaciers flew by. Finally,
I was back in the rocks and lakes of Anishinaabe country.

As I travelled these four territories, I saw the pipe. It was beautiful.
The light-brown cedar stem. The dark-red pipestone bowl. Four little
eagle feathers hung from it, fastened by brass furniture tacks. The pipe
held my rapt attention. It dominated my field of view, even as the
scenery rolled by.

An eagle flew down and gripped the pipe in its talons. The scenery
faded and became the darkness of my bedroom in Onigaming. I lay
there. I could still see the eagle.

The eagle flapped his wings three or four times, as though trying to
lift off from a tree branch. He clutched the pipe. He was a golden eagle
but had the speckled light marks of youth. Then he vanished, and so did
the pipe.

"NDEDE!" I shouted into the darkness. Both parents knew
something was amiss when I called for my father rather than my
mother. I heard muttering, then Ndede shuffled into the room and
asked what was the matter.

"The eagle visited me."

I tried to explain the vision to him, struggling to find the
words. I was three, maybe four, years old. Ndede listened patiently,
then urged me to go back to sleep.

Not too long after that, we were back in Wauzhushk Onigum-
Rat Portage speaking to Kwekwekipiness, who nodded and smiled
while listening to my father describe my vision. He accepted our
tobacco and discussed the matter with Auggie. As the daughter of
a very powerful medicine man, her opinion on spiritual matters
carried a lot of weight. She said that even though I was very young,
it was clear I should receive a pipe, a very high spiritual calling for
an Anishinaabe to receive. Kwekwekipiness would make the pipe

with his own hands. It would be beautiful, exactly like the one in my dream. Auggie would make a buckskin pipe bag, with intricate beadwork and sequins on each side.

I was presented this gift in front of the elders of Treaty #3 at the old roundhouse on Powwow Island, in Wauzhushk Onigum. Some of them still recall the occasion and tell me about it to this day. I was just a little boy, but I was made a pipe carrier and took my first steps on the path to becoming a spiritual man.

WHEN I WAS OLD ENOUGH to attend school, we moved to Winnipeg, which offered better schools than the reserve. At the same time, Mom and Ndede returned to university, where my mother went to work on her PhD.

My little sister Shawonipinesiik—Southern Thunderbird Woman—was born in January 1986. When I went to visit her in the hospital, I brought her a little stuffed lynx, our clan animal. I sat nervously on the bed as they handed her to me, bundled tightly in hospital blankets. Just as she was about to settle in my arms, I lost my balance and began falling off the bed and onto the floor.

In mid-air I made a split-second decision to protect her. I tossed her back onto the bed, where she landed safely. I hit the floor, probably bruising my ego more than anything. It is a good thing I didn't hurt her, though; that little baby would wind up becoming the brains of the family.

Things were different in the city. For one thing, I was the only Anishinaabe kid around. School was an adjustment, and I struggled through my first few years. I was the last person in my Grade 3 class to learn how to read. Finally, one Saturday, my mom sat me down in the bedroom of our apartment and started to teach me how. I went through many of the stages of childhood rebellion in one sitting. First, I got punchy and started giggling. Next, I threw a fit and got angry. From there, I tried to cry and throw myself around, exaggerating my agony. Through it all, my mom was patient and firm. Finally, I gave in, sat down, and began to read the damned book. Within a few months, I was in the gifted program at my French immersion school.

While we were in Winnipeg, my father began to follow his visions of Darryl. He travelled to South Dakota, where he visited many sundance ceremonies, and spoke to many spiritual people among the Lakota.

One day at a Lakota powwow, he looked across the arbour and caught a glimpse of a young man who looked just like Darryl. He harkened back to his dream. The young man. The arbour. His son. Ndede pushed through the crowd and caught the young man just as he turned to walk away. Ndede introduced himself. The young man said his name was Tommy Charging Eagle.

Soon, Ndede's truck was kicking up dust on the back roads of the Cheyenne River Reservation. He stopped at a tribal office and announced that he was looking for Tommy's father, Steve Charging Eagle, a well-respected elder and powwow dancer. One of the clerks called to the back.

"Harold, this guy's looking for your father-in-law!"

Harold Condin emerged and introduced himself. The two men spoke for a time. Ndede told Harold his story and said he needed to meet Steve (Harold was married to Steve's daughter Geraldine). Harold obliged, and soon the two of them were pulling up to Steve's ranch on the reservation.

Ndede told the old man about his vision. He asked Steve's advice. The elder Charging Eagle said they should do a *hunka* ceremony—a traditional adoption ceremony. They parted ways, agreeing to make their preparations and meet again a few months later.

The *hunka* adoption was held in the centre of a powwow arbour during one of the annual celebrations of the Lakota people. Dancers adorned with eagle feathers and regalia lined the arbour, singers sat around their big drums and spectators kept up their conversations, doing their best to ignore the uncomfortable bleachers they sat on.

When the ceremony began, Ndede and Tommy stood side by side. An elder offered a prayer. As the elder finished his invocation, a man rode in on a painted horse, carrying a spear. The horse turned and charged toward Ndede and Tommy. The two men held still even as the ground beneath them shook with the pounding of the horse's hooves. At the last second, the horse stopped and reared up on its hind legs, and its rider tossed the spear into the ground directly in front of them. The tip of the spear buried itself deep into the earth.

In this way, the Charging Eagles became a part of our family and we became a part of theirs. They would travel north to see us and dance at Anishinaabe powwows, and we would travel south to participate in Lakota ceremonies. Tommy was my dad's son and my brother, and his sisters were my sisters.

Our families would share many laughs and even some tears in the decades that followed. We were bound as solidly by the ceremony as we might have been by blood, and neither side made much of the fact that our two nations had once been bitter enemies.

The adoption was part of the healing path that Ndede walked in grieving Darryl and Danny. Tommy was not a replacement; he provided a new outlet for the love trapped inside my father since the loss of his eldest sons.

And there was more: the Charging Eagles took him to many sundances, ceremonies that would help him put himself back together.

NDEDE BENT AT THE WAIST, exhausted. His torso was bare and sunburned. He wore a sage crown on his head and a blue-and-red skirt wrapped around his waist. Blood streamed down his back.

I could tell you many things about the sundance. That it is a ceremony of thanksgiving, and that after fasting for four days we pierce our flesh. I could explain that we do this because we believe the only meaningful thing we can offer to the Creator of all that exists is a little piece of ourselves.

I could tell you those things, but nobody really tells it like that to us when we are growing up. Instead, we watch. We learn. We participate. It was August, and the sun radiated intense heat. Cedar smoke blew across the arbour as the beat of the drum picked up again, signalling another piercing song. Hundreds of dancers stretched across the arbour. In the centre stood the tree of life, adorned with tobacco ties and flags in every colour, all of them dancing in the breeze.

My father stood in front of a dozen buffalo skulls, maybe fourteen. They were tied together, forming a long train along the ground. Tatanka, the bison. This was the life-giving force that sustained the Lakota for millennia. Two wooden pegs pierced the skin on Ndede's back, one above each shoulder blade. A sisal rope attached the skulls to the pegs. My father had dragged the skulls around the arbour four times, his pierced skin stretched taut. It was discoloured, grey, and ashy. The skin was dead, but still attached to him. It was still a part of him.

Ndede was ready to break the skin, but the cuts were too deep. Whenever he leaned forward, the skin would not give and the skulls moved with him.

This was how he wanted it. He had asked the cut man to pierce him deep. He wanted to feel pain. He wanted to sacrifice something for those two boys, for his nephew, for his own father.

It was time.

A large sundancer called out to me and the other children, raising his voice to be heard above the sound of the drums and the singers.

"Okay, kids," he said. "Come sit down on these skulls!"

A few boys took seats on some of the skulls. I sat on one too. The dancer held an eagle fan in front of our faces. It was to protect our eyes from shards of buffalo bone fragment.

"*Hoka!*" someone yelled.

My dad ran forward.

The wooden pegs sprang out of his back. Blood sprayed from his wounds, and for a moment the rope harness danced in the air. Ululations rose from the women. A few men let out war whoops.

I looked down the beaten path. My father was running ahead of me.

MY PARENTS ENCOURAGED ME to share my culture with my classmates in Winnipeg. So I put on powwow demonstrations at my elementary school. I would get into my traditional dancer's regalia, break out the boom box, and get down to some Whitefish Bay Singers. My parents helped me explain the significance of the different songs and the dances. This was years before First Nations culture started to be brought into most schools.

Having progressive parents didn't protect me from racism. I saw its ugly face at school, and at the hockey rink.

"Indians are stupid," "dirty Indian," and "stupid fuckin' boggin" are some of the phrases that stand out. Part of the reason I hate the word *Indian* so much is because when I was growing up I never heard it used without an ugly adjective before it. *Dumb. Drunk. Dirty.*

The Anishinaabe people I grew up with in Onigaming were none of these things. We were proud, funny, hard-working people. Somehow, when we came to the city, that language was translated:

proud became *dirty, funny* became *dumb*, and *hard-working* became *lazy*.

With Ndede gone most of the time, I navigated this myself. And as great a parent as she was, my mom could not teach me much about having the blunt end of racism shoved into my face.

These are the sorts of things I heard from friends, coaches, and teachers—people I considered to be on my side. The things I heard and endured from people who were not my friends were worse.

In Grade 5, a substitute teacher choked me in class after I talked back to her. I can still feel her fat fingers constricting around my neck. I struggled for a second. She tightened her grip. I stopped struggling.

"Are you done?" she asked. Then she whispered a quiet slur into my ear.

"My dad is going to kick your ass," I told her.

When I got home, my mom and dad were waiting for me at the kitchen table. They told me there had been a call from school and that I was in trouble. I tried to explain what happened, but my dad interrupted me and scolded me. Only contempt held back the anger from overtaking his voice. He asked if I had told the teacher he would beat her up on my behalf. I said yes. He sneered and looked away in disgust.

"I'm not going to fight anyone for you," he shouted. He said he would let her beat me up, as if we were talking about another kid on the playground and not a teacher who had physically abused me.

The tears stayed deep down inside. The only change I betrayed on my face was a flaring of my nostrils and a grimace.

I felt sick. I didn't have words to explain how I felt about being choked by a teacher. I was bewildered by my dad's reaction. The teacher did not substitute at our school again. I stayed home from school for a few days, but I am not sure if there was any follow-up

other than that. If a teacher choked a student today, there would
be a lot more outrage.

A few years later, I was leaving the Southdale Community
Centre, near my parents' house, with my mom and a few friends after
a lacrosse game. I yelled, "Under the B—52!" as we walked by the
open doors of a bingo hall in the centre and made our way outside.

Almost at once, I felt a big pair of hands gripping my neck
and strangling me. I froze. Was this one of my older friends
playing a trick on me? Was this someone I knew taking things a
little too far?

I turned around with the stranglehold still on my neck and
saw that it was a fat, middle-aged man—the bingo caller.

He was a fully grown man, at least a hundred pounds
overweight. I was a skinny little kid who had yet to hit a growth
spurt. He kept throttling me.

My friends froze. My mom started screaming at him. My eyes
welled. He swore at me and used a racial slur. I broke free of his
grip, pushed myself away, and walked to the car, tears streaming
down my face. I threw my lacrosse stick and gear inside and
covered my face with my arms.

In the aftermath, there were no charges. The man wrote a
half-assed apology addressed to my parents in which he attempted
to justify himself. My parents left it at that.

Ndede made a much bigger deal a short while later when I got
hit in the face by a puck while tying my skates at the same community club. As I held an ice pack to my face, he shouted about what
a pussy I was. I had an eye swollen shut, but all Ndede cared about
was that I had not rushed to fight the kid who accidentally fired
the puck over the boards. After the yelling stopped and the tension
dissipated enough for me to feel like moving again, I jumped into
the car with my mom and we drove my friend Makwa to Kenora.

He'd been visiting our family in Winnipeg for a few days. On the long drive back home, I wondered why Ndede refused to stick up for me when a grown man had attacked me but had been so harsh when I didn't attack another child who had hurt me by accident. At the time, I did not know that he had grown up in a dog-eat-dog environment with no one to stick up for him. All I knew was that he was an angry, angry man.

I FELL IN LOVE WITH HIP-HOP MUSIC one night in 1993. A friend of mine was at my house for a sleepover, and we were up late, hanging out and watching music videos on TV. At one point, a black-and-white image popped onto the screen and things began moving in slow motion while the sampled sounds of a keyboard wailed in the background. Four emcees took turns rapping about the object of their affection.

"This," I thought to myself, "is the greatest song ever made."

I had heard a lot of different styles of music growing up. Country, rock, and folk music from my parents, and 1980s sounds from Prince, Madonna, and Cher whenever I visited my sister Diane's house. But from the night I first heard Pharcyde's "Passin' Me By," I was devoted to hip-hop. I went to rap shows, I wrote rhymes, I even started making beats on the computer.

It was a painstaking process. I would copy and paste one sound over and over—a hi-hat, say—for the length of time I wanted it to play during a song. Then I'd repeat the process for each track on the song and synchronize them later. (I have always been a huge computer nerd.)

Through rap shows and mutual friends, I met others who loved the music as much as I did. We called ourselves Dead Indians, and our logo was the cartoon mascot of a famous baseball team with his eyes crossed out. Soon we were doing shows at dances and performing as the opening act for local hip-hop crews. Over the next few years, we travelled south to the furthest tip of the continental US and into the far north of Canada performing our music. It was a heck of a ride.

AT SIXTEEN, I entered the circle I had grown up near and became a sundancer. A family friend made my skirt, a relative gave me a medallion to wear, and I bought the tobacco I would need for offerings. I was ready.

Soon enough, Ndede and I drove down the winding South Dakota road that led to the sundance grounds. I stared out the window at the buckshot marks obliterating the paint on the signs that once read Bureau of Indian Affairs Highway 7.

"Do you think you'll pierce?" Ndede asked.

I sat silently in the shotgun seat, letting the song on the radio breathe. "I don't know. Maybe."

My father waited a few beats before saying, "I think you will." He smiled and looked out at the cottonwood trees flying by, their leaves basking in the long golden rays of the magic hour.

A few days later, I was standing in the middle of the circle. I could feel the warmth of the buffalo robe I was standing on. I noticed the fur because I was wiggling my toes while the cut man used a surgical scalpel to pierce my virgin chest, free until now of the scars that marked the chests of many of the men I grew up around. The blade felt cool at first, but it started to burn as he sliced through layers of my skin. When the scalpel found the other side, he pulled the skin away from my pectoral muscles as another man slid an ebony peg through the hole.

I stared into the distance. The cut man and his helper repeated the process on the other side. When they finished, I was led around the arbour before a horse pulled the pegs out of my chest.

That night, Ndede smiled as we sat beside a campfire. "One of the other chiefs was looking at you while you were piercing," he said. "You didn't make a face when they cut you." Then a pause. "No brain, no pain," he teased.

The words echoed in my head as the dark South Dakota night enveloped us.

In years to come, many family members would join us in that place, sitting around campfires like that one. But that night, it was just Ndede and me. Me and my dad. And I knew that he was proud.

THROUGH MY TEENAGE YEARS, I struggled to make sense of my Indigenous identity. I was never ashamed of it, but I was not sure how I fit in with the rest of the country. The racism I experienced left a bitter taste in my mouth. I turned to hip-hop for a reference point, a medium that offered space to voice an outsider's perspective. I oscillated between the influences of Indigenous culture, hip-hop culture, and the mainstream.

I worked steadily from my early teenage years. First at the Onigaming band office, writing up cheque requisitions, then at community development organizations in Winnipeg. The money I earned covered meals and gas for trips to ceremonies in Northwestern Ontario and northern Minnesota.

My father attended some of the ceremonies, but not all of them. He had begun spending more time in the United States, first working with some of the Great Lakes tribes in Wisconsin, then moving on to a teaching gig at the University of Minnesota. There, his deep knowledge of our peoples' ways and language made him a hot commodity in the burgeoning Anishinaabe culture revitalization scene.

He attracted a following of sorts. They were a mix of older professionals keen to rediscover their culture after a lifetime of living in the American mainstream, and young urban Anishinaabeg who wanted culture to be a part of their university experience. I was jealous of those people. I would wonder what the hell Ndede was doing down south teaching these things to people he had known only a short time while I drove hundreds of kilometres on my own to learn more about our ways

Maybe because of my father's absences, I grew closer to Kwekwekipiness, the elder who had named me and made me a pipe carrier. Each Wednesday night, I made the two-hour drive from Winnipeg to Wauzhushk Onigum, where I would sweat with him. I would usually stop at his grandson Vernon's house and visit for a while. Then the old man would join us and sit with a gentle smile, listening to our conversation. From time to time, he would interrupt with a long soliloquy in Ojibwe. When my face betrayed confusion, Vernon would translate for me. Otherwise, I did my best to soak up the knowledge in Anishinaabemowin.

Vernon built Kwekwekipiness a small roundhouse, the traditional building of the Anishinaabe, about twelve feet in diameter. It was there that I learned many traditional Anishinaabe songs. And it was there that they explained the meaning of the travelling song to me, the song I had heard sung to close community gatherings since I was a child. Kwekwekipiness said that in this song, the Creator speaks to us and says, "I am the reason you walk."

Kwekwekipiness was a generous teacher, but he was also very stern—firmly a member of the old school. Over the years we spent together, he chastised my father, his grandson, and myself at different times. Once, he even stopped a sweat lodge when a woman in attendance began crying, telling her, "Stop. We came here to pray."

His approach may have been harsh, but he taught me the fundamental humility, independence, and dignity that are hallmarks of the Anishinaabe. When he prayed, he never asked for anything for himself or complained about the ailments that descended upon him in old age. He prayed only for others to be well.

One day in the sweat lodge, the steam flowing all around us, he said, "When you say your prayers, always thank the Creator last." Such is the Anishinaabe world view that even the most powerful put themselves last.

When he could barely lift an axe, he still tried to cut his firewood by himself. Even when he could barely use the washroom on his own, we knew not to wait for him to ask for help. Whenever I see a young man asking for charity today, I think of Kwekwekipiness, shuffling outside in the cold, carrying wood through freshly fallen snow. He lived the true Anishinaabe way.

AFTER GRADUATING from a private high school at age seventeen, I faced a crossroads. Based on my SAT scores, I had been offered a full scholarship at a school in the States. I gave the idea a lot of thought, but at the last moment I declined the offer and enrolled at the University of Manitoba to study economics. I thought I could save the world through economic development. I also wanted to spend more time with Kwekwekipiness and learn as much as I could about the Anishinaabe road. I knew Kwekwekipiness would not be around for much longer, and I decided to make the most of the time we had.

My immediate family did not object to my turning down the scholarship. But my cousin Sonny couldn't believe I could decline such an opportunity. "Why didn't you go?" he demanded the next time I saw him in Onigaming.

He nodded through my rambling reply before he interrupted me. "You know what?" he said. "An elder once told me that no matter where you go, you are always the centre of your own culture."

He stared into my eyes to underline his point.

It was the kind of wisdom I believe Kwekwekipiness would endorse.

6

"DID YOU KNOW NDEDE has another baby in the States?"

Shawon's question came out of the blue. All I could offer in reply was, "What?"

"No, he does," she continued. "He has another baby with a woman down there."

My younger sister, Shawonipinesiik, had found a box full of papers and letters in Ndede's room. They did not detail the entire affair, she said, but it was enough to be sure of what had happened.

I went and found this box for myself. She was right. There was no reasonable doubt.

I found a card from this woman in America—a well-known author—telling Tobasonakwut she did not want to hold him back. And there was a baby picture. I had another little sister, now probably several months old.

I studied my new baby sister's name. I had seen it before. It was my paternal grandmother's name—Nenaa'ikiizhikok.

The discovery left me a little conflicted. I was happy to learn of this new little sister, but I worried for my mom. And to be honest,

I felt a little guilty for not being more upset with Ndede. At the time, I did not have a framework in my head to deal with adultery. I assumed that everyone was faithful, that if one partner wanted to see other people the two would break up. I was pretty naïve.

Not long after that, I let Ndede know that I knew. "I would like to meet her someday," I said, when I brought it up.

Ndede smiled. He explained how he had met this woman and they had started seeing each other. He understated the depth of their relationship. I know now that they spent a lot of time together and had their own unique bond.

Yet in spite of this, and in spite of his betrayal, Ndede kept coming back to my mother. He told my mom about the new baby shortly after she was born.

"Just get out of here!" was all she said at first.

So he did. He moved out of their bedroom into a room across the hall. That is, of course, when he was not gone to America. They settled into a new normal. She told him that if he wanted a divorce, he would have to initiate it, that he would always have a home with us.

"She didn't kick me out," he said to me later. "She said, what really matters is you guys, the kids. She wants you guys to get along."

I nodded. "You know, the one you really have to worry about is Shawon."

"She knows," he said. She had already confronted him and yelled at him.

To Ndede, the end of the deception meant that the matter was settled. But that was only the beginning. He had damaged his relationship with my now-second-youngest sister, Shawon.

GROWING UP, drugs and alcohol never held much appeal for me. I abstained for most of the first eighteen years of my life. There were a couple of exceptions, like the time I shared a joint outside a suburban dance in Winnipeg when I was eleven, or when I sipped a beer on the reserve when I was thirteen. Mostly, I was content to follow the spiritual path laid out for me. But at eighteen, at university, I discovered partying and young women. Things changed.

The first time I had a real drink, it was a shot of whisky at the apartment of a young half-Filipino woman I was seeing. I can't explain the decision to stop being a straight edge other than my attitude was "fuck it." I asked the girl to pour me a shot. She raised her eyebrow. I insisted. I tossed back the whisky. It felt like the amount of blood in my head increased.

My friends started laughing and got excited when they saw this going on. I cracked a few jokes and started to loosen up. I asked for another shot. Cameras flashed. Soon, I was the life of the party ... for about half an hour. The next thing I knew, I was in bed with the young woman. She was smiling at me. It was morning; I had blacked out.

It was like that most of the times I partied—just a young dude having fun, cutting loose on the weekends. I would not always drink, but I started to get drawn more into the party lifestyle. With it came other things, like the occasional fight or another blackout, and more time sleeping in and less time at school. That pretty much sums up the party lifestyle in Winnipeg—sex, drugs, fights, and blackouts.

One of those early mornings that came hot on the heels of a late, late night, I woke up, left without waking the young woman I was lying next to, and drove myself to the university. It was 7 A.M. I stumbled into the library, pulled up to a computer, and pounded out a ten-page essay. I handed it in at 10:30 or 11:00 that same morning and got an A. That became a curse in disguise. I thought

I could go out and party and still do well in school, and I managed to do it for a time.

Neither my mom nor Ndede drank, so I hid my drinking from them. If I was hungover, I would head for the basement when I came home. If I had alcohol on my breath, I would stay at a friend's house. Eventually, I moved out, in part so I wouldn't have to keep up the appearance of being a clean-living individual. They would find out the truth soon enough.

BIG WET SNOWFLAKES fell slowly through the air, like a scene from a Christmas movie. It was only six or seven o'clock in the evening when I pulled up to my friend's house, but it was already pitch-black outside. I walked in and headed downstairs, where two buddies were making beats on a drum machine. A TV played in the background, filling the silence between loops of the drum machine and lulls in the conversation. Old cigarette smoke and the smell of stale beer filled the air.

One of my friends laughed as he pulled out a forty-ounce bottle of Bombay Sapphire gin. We may have said we were going to make music, but basically we just wanted to drink. Several glasses of gin and juice later, we decided to go to a club.

I was drunk at this point, and it crossed my mind to call a cab, but due to either laziness or cheapness I made a stupid decision and said I would drive. We hopped into my truck and headed for downtown Winnipeg.

I saw the lights flashing, red and blue, in my rear-view mirror. The roads were covered in a thick layer of slush. I put my foot down on the gas and felt the wheels spin beneath me.

I made a right turn here, a left turn there, and rolled through every stop sign. I checked my rear-view mirror and saw no more flashing lights. I had lost the cops.

I was too drunk to notice how fast I was going. Once we hit a bridge, I caught the wheels on a patch of ice, which sent the truck spinning. The ass end of the truck turned toward the front and the front end slid toward the guardrail. I twisted the steering wheel as quickly as I could and steered into the spin until we came full circle. When the truck was about to complete the 360, I floored the gas pedal. The spinning wheels cut through the slush and gripped the pavement. The truck found traction and roared forward. We were going to make it. Or so I thought.

Later, I would read in a police report that more than one person on the road that night saw me spin out on the bridge and called police. With an update on my location, the police tracked me down quickly. The flashing lights were in my rear-view mirror again.

The cops caught up with me as I turned into a downtown parking lot. Glass exploded everywhere as a nightstick smashed through the driver's side window. The next thing I knew, I was face down on the pavement, handcuffs on my wrists.

I spent that night in jail. The next day, I was released on a promise to appear in court to face charges of refusing a breathalyzer test and impaired driving. Outside the courthouse, I met my mom and the woman I was seeing at the time.

"I never thought I would see you wearing those blue khakis," the young woman said, referring to the jail uniform. *Neither did I,* I thought.

"Were you drinking?" my mother asked in her quiet manner. She still held out hope that this was all a misunderstanding.

"Yes," I replied, "I was drinking." I made a long, uncomfortable confession of what I had been up to the past few years.

"SO YOU'RE THE JAILBIRD, huh?" Ndede said as we drove to a restaurant for lunch.

I scanned his expression to get a read on what he meant. He had a big smile stretched from ear to ear. He was teasing me. I was an adult now, but I had half-expected him to tear into me the way he had when I was a kid.

"That's okay," he said, still grinning. "I went to jail a few times when I was young. The police in Kenora used to come and round us up at two in the morning, if you were standing on the street corner, and take you to the drunk tank. Didn't matter if you were drunk or not. Just if you were Indian."

I appreciated his attempt at humour, but our experiences were very different. His run-ins with the law had been the result of injustice. Mine was caused by my own bad judgment.

"I used to hate sitting in that drunk tank, stone-cold sober," he said, "counting down the hours until they would let me go. Let all of us go."

Some things repeat themselves across the generations, though they vary with the changing times like a mutation in the genetic code. As a child, Ndede was thrown into extremely stressful situations when he was powerless to change them. That suppressed feeling of weakness had made him angry, and that in turn had caused some of his dysfunction. But he was also the target of some very racist attitudes and policies. In my life, I did experience a lot of racism, but some of the stress came from my own family, particularly Ndede. Like him, I felt powerless to change the situation, and, like him, my suppressed feeling of weakness had made me angry, which was now manifesting itself in other aspects of my life.

Though Ndede faced much more inequity and oppression than I did, he made things better for himself when he accepted responsibility for changing his self-destructive behaviour. I was still a long way from accepting responsibility for my own life.

IN MAY 2003, I walked across a stage at the University of Manitoba wearing a cap and gown. A beaded medallion hung from my neck, the Ojibwe floral design contrasting with the black robe. I shook hands with the university president, walked off the stage clutching my parchment, and set off on the next phase of my life.

I was also honoured, along with the dozens of other Indigenous grads that spring, at the U of M's convocation powwow. When they read my name out, Ndede walked down from the stands to shake my hand. We stutter-stepped as we approached each other, readying for a handshake, then hesitated in one of those awkward half-hug manoeuvres before settling for a combination handshake-and-pat-on-the-shoulder-with-the-opposite-hand type deals. Singers beat the drums in celebration and the audience applauded, as they had for each graduate. My dad and I let go of our half-embrace and returned to our respective seats.

As I rejoined the drum group my friend Ed, seated at his drum, leaned toward me and said, "It looks like you're embarrassed to hug your dad."

"Nah," I replied. What I did not say was that we had never hugged.

I had assumed a bachelor's degree in my hand meant jobs would start coming my way. That was not the case.

I managed to get contract work doing research on First Nations economic development, which paid decently, but those gigs were few, and I didn't make enough from them to support myself.

So I started working casual labour and picking up work at temp agencies. I would wake up early every morning, and call the agency to see if they had a job for me, taking the bus to wherever they sent me. Some days I filled soda bottles at a bottling plant. Other days I was in a warehouse lifting heavy boxes onto endless matrices of shelves. And so it went. Construction projects, warehouse gigs, manufacturing jobs. Whatever came along, I accepted.

I would work for eight or nine hours a day, and a week later a cheque would arrive for fifty dollars. It was not the most rewarding work, but it kept me busy.

I applied for other jobs but rarely got a callback or a second interview. This had nothing to do with my legal troubles but everything to do with me being a young Native man who wore baggy clothes in a city where that look is equated with being a gangster.

In the evenings and on weekends, music began taking up more and more of my time. I worked with a group called Slangblossom, doing PR and touring with them. I also made guest appearances on recordings by Rezofficial, and stockpiled songs I wrote with my own crew, Dead Indians. All of the small local success went to my head, and I decided I deserved to party it up with other rappers whenever I felt like it. Which, of course, led to more problems.

Growing up, I had been raised to see myself as a warrior and to prove myself as one. Yet I was also an angry young man, imitating the male role model I had grown up with. Now I was caught up in the party lifestyle that goes hand in hand with the music scene.

These influences collided with my ego in an ugly way. I managed to take the worst from each world: I had the need for the validation of a young warrior, but the only avenues I considered proving myself in were drinking contests and street fights. I had inherited the grammar of the proud, noble Indigenous person but adopted the vocabulary of the angry, self-centred city dweller.

I developed a mean streak. After a few beers, I would shift from cracking jokes and having a good time to trying to mess with people. I would get in someone's face and insult them until they either backed down or fought me. Either way, the goal was the same—feed my ego.

Most times, the fights were settled fair and square. A few times, things turned into brawls that spread beyond me. In one particularly bad incident, my friend was beaten badly and I had to take him to the hospital. After another, I was arrested and charged with assault. I spent a few days in jail waiting to make bail.

With each fight, each time I threw an opponent to the ground, each bump that formed on my knuckles, my head grew. I thought I was the shit. I was about to learn that when you suffer from overconfidence, life often finds ways to humble you.

One night, my friends and I were already a few beers in and looking for more. We walked across downtown Winnipeg and stopped for some drinks at a friend's house. Then the mean streak kicked in. I insulted our host until he asked us to leave. Another case of me being the man, I thought. My friends and I spilled out of the apartment and headed back downtown. We hopped in a cab, then hopped out without paying. The driver caught up with us and pushed me. I turned and shoved him back. A passing cabbie saw what was happening, stopped his taxi, and jumped out to help his fellow driver. He swung and hit me in the face. I grabbed him and swung back. We stood in the middle of the street, arms flailing in full-on hockey fight mode. Then the police showed up and tackled me.

The next morning, I woke up in a holding cell. What the hell had happened? I had one hell of a headache. I couldn't remember why I had been fighting, but apparently it had cost me my freedom. I began to cry.

When I spoke with my lawyer, he told me I was facing an assault charge, as well as numerous breaches for violating court conditions imposed after my other arrests. He explained that I could probably make bail this time but that if I had another run-in with the law I would likely do real time.

Over the next couple of days, I spoke Ojibwe to my cellmate. I told him how sad it was that I could speak Ojibwe to someone my age in jail but had never done so in university.

I read a copy of Alcoholics Anonymous's "The Twelve Traditions." I lifted weights. I ate shitty food—a boiled egg for breakfast and a hot dog for lunch. I talked to the other guys on the tier with me. Most faced charges of armed robbery and drug dealing. They were poor kids and addicts who saw a quick way to small-time money. But what the hell was I there for?

If it was from a desire to prove myself, what exactly had I proved myself to be? A criminal? A thug? A dumbass? It certainly was not the warrior I had been taught to be in the sundance circle.

My girlfriend April visited me. She had been through the doors of the justice system before, after her brother Joseph "Beeper" Spence was murdered when he was thirteen. His shooting helped galvanize attention around the issue of street gangs in Winnipeg. April's family had been the subject of intimidation during the trial but had seen the process through to the conviction of Beeper's killers. Now she was engaged in the system again on my account.

So were my parents.

"I can't be myself in here," I said to Ndede.

The way I phrased it must have struck a chord with him. He thought I was suicidal. I was certainly down on myself, but not that far. I just meant I couldn't be my computer-nerd, artsy-musician self; I was stuck with the partying tough-guy facade I had created in my own head.

I made my bail application by video link. When I put my foot in my mouth, saying I was not likely to listen to her conditions, only to my family's, the judge told me to shut up.

Ndede spoke on my behalf. He said he would take me back to the sundance and see I joined AA, the same program that had helped him stay sober for more than three decades at the time. The Crown objected, saying I had already been to the sundance. Ndede assured the court it would work.

The judge asked what would happen if I kept drinking or ran away.

"Then I would turn him in," Ndede replied.

She asked why she should believe him.

"Because of my honesty and integrity," he said.

A pause ensued in the courtroom while I watched via the grainy video link. My father's confidence seemed to echo in that space.

The judge believed him. I was set free under the condition that I abstain from alcohol and live with my parents under house arrest, leaving only to attend AA meetings and ceremonies. Few things are more humbling at age twenty-two than having to move back in with your mom and dad. Where I thought I was a warrior, it turned out I was still just a dumb kid.

I began the process of putting my life back on track by going to AA meetings daily, sometimes two or three times a day. The rest of the time I would make music, lift weights, and read.

One evening, my mom and I took the dog for a walk in the humid summer air.

"I used to worry about you," she told me. The old animal pulled on his leash and began to lead us home. "I didn't know where you were or what was happening to you."

I pursed my lips, silently urging her on.

"You've changed. You're not the same little boy I raised. What happened to you?"

She was right. I had been raised better than this.

7

NDEDE AND I WERE TOGETHER AGAIN on the same winding road, headed for the sundance grounds. But this time we were late. The ceremony had already started. As we pulled in, I could see the cottonwood tree standing tall in the centre of the ceremony, prayer ties hung from its branches. The beat of the drum rang across the valley. The voices of the singers reached to the heavens.

It had been two summers since I was here. Something inside had told me to stay away while I was partying. I was late, and I was in rough shape, but I was back.

That night, we went to Chief Leonard Crow Dog's camp and spoke with him as the sun set over the trees that stood in the west. Ndede told him about the things that had gone on in our family. He explained why we were late. I told him what I had been up to.

Leonard nodded his head as he listened, then said, "*Aho*, son. It's good that you're back." He smiled. His dark eyes sparkled.

It was the next day that they made me a chief. Leonard and his sundance leaders vested their confidence in me, but they also handed me a great responsibility.

Leonard began by introducing me to the crowd. He explained my heredity and why I was to become a leader.

As I walked around the circle that day, I understood that Ndede was giving me his bonnet for a very powerful reason. Leonard conducted the ceremony with the very same motivation. They wanted to remind me to lead a good life, not because I deserved it in any particular way, but because it was the bare minimum I owed to my family and to my community.

I had been afforded so many opportunities—from being born into a good family, to being given a pipe and a name, to getting the chance to attend university. I owed it to my family and community to pay back some of that good fortune by being a positive influence on those around me. And so they placed this responsibility on my shoulders.

It was a risky move. I could have dishonoured them by receiving the bonnet and going right back to partying. But they took that chance. I like to think I have made them proud.

That year, I pierced three times. I had a lot on my mind. A lot to be thankful for, too—after all, April and I had decided to have a baby together.

NINE MONTHS LATER, just after two in the morning, I stood in a delivery room at the Women's Hospital in Winnipeg. April was in labour. The resident physician, in near shock, tripped over his words. It must have been his first birth, because inexperience seemed to be sweating from his pores.

An older doctor came into the room and took over. For half a second, he looked at the resident as if he were an idiot. Then he stepped forward and pulled the baby out. Boom. Done. Next.

"Do you want to cut the cord?" a nurse asked.

I agreed. The nurse handed me the bundle of blankets, and there he was. My son.

I studied the little face, his furrowed brow. Then I counted his fingers and toes.

His eyes blinked open for the first time ever. The dark pupils were huge. My son's eyes locked with mine. He squinted slightly, studying my gaze. I began to sing. I chose a song from Lake of the Woods. I wanted the first sounds my son heard in this world to be ones that appealed to his ancestors—the same happy, melodic tones the old-time Anishinaabeg used to love. When I finished the song, I spoke to him and told him his name.

"Boozhoo ningoozis. Oshkii'anang kidizhinikaaz, Oshkii'anang kidizhinikaaz, Oshkii'anang kidizhinikaaz, Oshkii'anang kidizhinikaaz."

Four times, I told him his name in Anishinaabemowin. He remained silent the entire time, listening to me. I kissed him softly on his head and handed him to his mother.

A vision had given me his name about a month earlier. In the dream, I was visited by the elders from our sundance. They explained the night sky to me in great detail, and they related that each pole in a tipi pointed to a star above us. When they arrived at the final star that they had yet to explain, I knew it was my son's.

"Which star is this?" I asked.

"That's the new star," the leader replied.

So my little boy had an Anishinaabe name, meaning New Star, before he even joined us in this world. We also chose to name him Dominik and Joseph, after April's deceased brother.

I was very nervous leaving the hospital. I checked the baby seat over and over again. I examined the clothes Dom was wearing. *It cannot be this easy*, I thought. Ndede drove slowly. My neck was on a swivel. Danger seemed to lurk around every corner.

Despite all my imagined threats, we made it home to our apartment safely and began settling into life as a little family.

FROM THE TIME he was two months old, Dominik slept through the night and woke each morning like clockwork at 6 A.M.

These are some of my favourite memories, my son and I starting our day together in the quiet of early morning. I would change him, feed him, and sit with him as I drank coffee and read the news on the internet. We would play with his toys and I'd walk around the apartment with him in my arms, singing powwow music to him until he fell asleep again. When April got up, I would start my workday.

This was our routine, and it was happy for a time, but things began to change. April and I had met on the powwow trail. She was a beautiful, good-natured, and funny young woman, but after the baby arrived things soured between us. It might have been undiagnosed postpartum depression. Whatever it was, we muddled through for more than a year.

Every relationship needs two sides to fail, and I contributed my share. After one of our arguments, April took Dominik and her things and drove to her mom's house in anger, saying we were through.

She was gone only a few days, but during that time I met a stunning young woman through mutual friends. She caught my eye with her beauty, mocha-coloured skin, and a brilliant white smile.

It was a hot summer day. I made her laugh. She made me smile. I walked her back to her apartment and she invited me inside.

When April returned, we began to reconcile. But I did not stop seeing the other woman.

MONTHS PASSED. I worked for temp agencies and casual labour joints. Here and there, I picked up contracts to do research reports on economic development. I was earning enough to get by, but not enough to get ahead. My life was simple—I spent time with my son in the morning, worked during the day, and spent more time with him in the evening. Yet when I looked at the little guy, I knew I had to do more for him.

When I first thought of bringing him into this world, I was in the haze and confusion of a young man battling himself and addiction. Now, a couple of years later, I was trying hard to live a productive life, a good life. My son had been my motivation to change for the better. In return, I owed him every comfort and opportunity I could provide.

Around that time, I wrote a letter to the editor of the *Winnipeg Free Press* about Canada's Olympic hockey team, of all things, and it was published. A few weeks later, my phone rang. It was a producer from the CBC's local morning radio show. She had seen my letter in the newspaper and wanted me to come in and turn it into something for the radio. The CBC, even a local radio show, was a big deal to me. As a kid on the reserve in the summertime, the public broadcaster was our window to the world. That was how I had watched the First Gulf War and the Oka Crisis. I agreed.

At the CBC story meeting a few weeks later, I pitched some ideas and contributed to others. The producers liked the life experiences and perspective I could provide and offered me work as an associate producer. Soon, I pitched my own music show, *Live by the Drum*, about how cultures around the world are united by rhythm and percussion. After building my skills on the radio side, I moved to TV reporting and began to work my way up the ranks of the local newsroom.

I was still creating music. My group, Dead Indians, began touring the southwestern United States in 2006 after the internet opened up new audiences for us. I realized the power of social media when, as soon as I stepped out of our rented minivan and onto the red dirt of Kayenta, Arizona, a young Diné man greeted me.

"Wab!" he barked. "'I miss my son every time I gotta leave him, but he can't wear hugs and the love won't feed him.'"

There I was, thousands of miles from home, in a place I had never been before, and a stranger was quoting my own lyrics back to me. I was fascinated. These trips introduced us to new people and new friends, and we spent a lot of late nights partying with them. I began to have a social drink now and then, maybe even the occasional joint. We also spent a lot of other late nights travelling to remote parts of the desert landscape. It opened up a cultural exchange between the scene we had built in the north and the one they had in the south. Tours followed, along with concerts at marquee events like the Gathering of Nations, in Albuquerque, New Mexico. We travelled across the Yukon. Some nights, we performed for hundreds of people, a few times for thousands. There were also many days when shady promoters would skip town on us or deliver us to audiences of ten people. None of the tours lasted longer than a couple of weeks, but every time I left I missed my son.

APRIL WAS ALREADY seven months pregnant with our second child when we went to the sundance that year. Leonard Crow Dog's wife, Joann, and others looked after her and gave her advice on what to expect with her second child. They would sit in the shade and talk as they cooked, while the rest of us made preparations for the ceremony that was about to begin. Everyone in our extended family was happy to have another little relative joining us.

A few days later, we were in the middle of the sundance circle. I had just finished piercing. The blood was starting to dry on my skin in the hot sun. I walked toward the tree to have my wounds cleaned. Ndede stopped me. He had something to share with me. A vision.

"I had a dream," he began. "There was an old man from Buffalo Point. He experienced the worst of the worst that Anishinaabeg suffered."

The man's community of Buffalo Point, on the western side of Lake of the Woods, was on the American border. He lived there during the time our people were being forced onto reserves. As an accident of history and bureaucracy, he ended up being dispossessed in two countries rather than one. The Americans told him to live in Canada. The Canadians told him he did not belong on their side of the border. The old man became homeless in his own homeland.

"After his land was taken away, he was poor," Ndede continued. "He lost his children to residential schools. He lost his wife to an accident." My father listed off the injustices both big and small that this man encountered.

"Finally, one night in the wintertime," Ndede said, "he froze to death. He was outside, walking alone in the blizzard. They found him wrapped up in a package of insulation, trying to keep warm." My father shot me an emphatic look. Then he went on.

"This old man appeared to me in my dream the other night. He came to me and said, 'Ni-noonde-pimaadiz!'"

Ndede delivered this last line very sternly, with conviction. The old man from Buffalo Point had told Ndede, "I want to live!"

"His name was Bezhigomiigwaan—Lone Feather," Ndede said. "This is the name you should give your new son. I want him to have an Anishinaabe name first."

I nodded, and we turned and walked to the tree together. Bezhigomiigwaan was born six weeks later.

APRIL AND I BROKE UP on Christmas Day that year. Ndede had a blastomycosis infection, likely picked up from the soil in Northwestern Ontario or northern Minnesota. Being the stoic Anishinaabe, he told us not to worry, he would simply sleep it off. Instead, over the next few days, he nearly died in hospital.

In the middle of all his reassurances and our awareness that we needed to take Ndede to the emergency room immediately, April and I began arguing. The war of words escalated until things were said between us that could not be taken back.

I told her that we were finished and would never get back together. She demanded I drive her to her parents' house. After taking her there, I did not see my sons for several weeks. I spent a lot of that time with Ndede in the hospital. It was the first time I really thought about his mortality.

Ndede recovered. My relationship with the mother of my children did not. This was the most difficult period of my life. The guilt I felt at not seeing my sons, the sadness at losing a relationship with someone I loved, the shame at having it play out in front of the people I held closest—it all rocked my world. Yet I knew I could not turn back. I knew there would be more arguing and fighting in front of my sons if we tried to reconcile again. At least this way, things would be a little better for them. They may not have the benefit of a two-parent home, but I could still be an active father, provide for them, and remove one source of dysfunction, the broken relationship, from our lives. The stress of this sort of moral calculus, a kind of domestic utilitarianism, pushed me to my wits' end. I actually contemplated suicide, but my better judgment kept me in this world, motivated to do a little bit better by my young sons.

I survived by putting my head down, working long hours at
my job, putting in more hours at the gym, and listening to a lot of
slow, sad, emo rock.

I made it through the rough patch, and a few months later
things got easier.

8

IT IS NOT OFTEN that you know before it happens that history will be made. Canada experienced such a moment in early 2008, when it became clear that the federal government was about to apologize to survivors of Indian residential schools, which included people like Ndede.

As a young journalist with the CBC, I covered this historic event. Almost immediately, I encountered pushback from the Indigenous community. Some looked forward to the apology, but others wanted no part of it. "Too little too late," one said. Blues musician and residential school survivor Billy Joe Green asked, "Where are the criminal charges?"

I assured them that they were welcome to share their views with us. "We're going to get things right," I would say. While I was trying to explain the CBC's position to one of these people who was skeptical of the apology, an all-staff notice came across my computer screen and changed my optimism.

The memo said that those who went to residential schools liked to call themselves "survivors" but that this term was technically incorrect, and it offered a dictionary definition of the term as supposed proof. "Survivors," the definition went, were persons, plants, or animals that outlasted disasters that killed others of their kind. In our coverage, we were to avoid saying "survivors" and use the government's chosen term: "former students."

I hit the roof.

Marshalling my anger into a letter, I argued a few key points. First, I pointed out that the dictionary definition of "survivor" applied, because these were people who had survived a disaster that claimed thousands of their peers. In some areas, nearly half of the kids who were sent to residential schools died there. Next, "survivor" is the term those people use to identify themselves when telling their own story, and to override this would be an act of paternalism oddly parallel to the type of thinking pervasive in the residential school era. Finally, we would be doing all Canadians a disservice by failing to capture the horror of this era in our language. If we used the term "former student," my reasoning went, then in fifty years students visiting the CBC archives would assume these Indigenous children were in schools similar to the ones they themselves attended. *But they were not.* The residential schools were institutions of cultural genocide. The term "survivor" conveyed the experience correctly, and would help the CBC fulfill its mandate of telling Canadians our own history.

The CBC's response came in the form of a phone call from members of the journalistic policy committee that sets its standards. The answer was basically, "Thanks, but no thanks." The edict would stand.

I slammed the phone down and sat fuming for a few moments. Then I called my bosses and told them that if this policy was not changed, I would resign in protest. After that, I walked out the door into the warm early-summer sun.

I drove to my sons' daycare, picked them up, and took them to a playground close to our house, where we spent the afternoon. Dom ran up and down the structure while I carried little Bezh around in my arms.

My challenge kicked off a flurry of meetings, phone calls, and negotiations behind the scenes at the CBC. My boss, the broadcaster's regional director for Manitoba, and others became involved and supported my position. There was pushback from high-ranking journalists and editors on the committee. Finally, a conference call was scheduled to settle the matter. The call would include members of the journalistic policy committee, some allies, and almost every Indigenous journalist working for the CBC at the time.

The night before the call, I drove to my parents' house to sit with Ndede and explain the situation. I told him that I fully intended to follow through on my threat and quit the CBC. Two years into my broadcast career, it would all be coming to a voluntary end.

When my sister Diane, then the grand chief of Treaty #3, arrived, Ndede said to her, "Isn't it a good thing that he's doing?" It was one of the few times I can remember him expressing pride in me while I was present to hear it.

Diane nodded and said to me, "Yeah, but it's too bad you have to lose your job over this."

She was right. Good jobs for young people were hard to come by, to say nothing of jobs in broadcast journalism.

When I was about to leave, my father offered me some advice based on his years as a politician. "You know," he said, "when you're in a situation like this, you can't aim to humiliate your opponent. You have to give them a way out, you have to give them a way to save face and feel like they are doing the right thing."

I thought about all the things he had faced in his life. Being taken from his parents as a child. Being jailed as an adult. Being denied basic rights like freedom of mobility, suffrage, access to food, and more, all in his own homeland. Yet in the face of these transgressions, he still offered those on the other side a chance to maintain their dignity, even as he fought to assert his own rights. I could see this wisdom as he sat in the soft yellow light of the kitchen that night.

"They must use the term 'survivor,'" he said. Then, after pausing briefly, he added, "But I think it would be all right if we let them use 'former student' too."

The next day, I was in Portage la Prairie, Manitoba, at the Long Plain First Nation's residential school museum, itself a former residential school. We were there to prepare for a concert to honour the survivors, which would be held that night. It would air as part of the coverage of the apology a week later. My plan was to fulfill my commitments to the survivors who would be a part of the event by making sure it was a success, and then tender my resignation the next day.

In the shadow of that old building, I dialed in to the conference call.

Introductions were made. The editorial committee outlined their rationale and their willingness to listen. I restated the arguments I had made in the letter. They said they admired my passion. Then came the moment of truth. We went around the horn and asked each journalist what they thought. I tensed up, fully expecting to have my fate sealed over the next few minutes.

But I had too little faith.

Voice after voice, person after person, in their own words and in their own way, said that it had to be "survivor," that using the term would be the right thing to do, both for Indigenous people and for all Canadians. I was floored.

After we hung up, I stared down the dirty rez road at the old building where hundreds of little children had been housed for a large chunk of the previous century.

A few hours later, an all-staff notice went out. The previous memo was rescinded. In all of our coverage across CBC's myriad platforms and outlets, reporters and presenters were to use the word "survivor" when referring to those taken from their families and placed in residential school. The term "former student" would also be acceptable. I remembered my dad's words and knew this outcome was the right compromise.

To this day, whenever I hear Peter Mansbridge say "residential school survivor" on television, I do a little fist pump in my mind. Not because I won anything but because we did right by my country, my people, and my family. Full credit to the senior journalists who were a part of that process. They may have put up a fight at first, but in the end they did the right thing.

That night, we held a concert in which three generations who had felt the impact of residential schools in our community sang away their pent-up feelings. The stolen children, now elders, stood and danced in the aisles. I watched Ndede and my mom laughing and visiting old friends. Singer and fellow survivor Percy Tuesday joined Billy Joe during his set for a cover song. He neatly summarized so much of the pain and confusion that had followed children like him through residential school and into their adult lives when he sang "Wasted Days and Wasted Nights."

I could relate. Now, we had a night with a purpose.

ON JUNE 11, 2008, in a room on Parliament Hill near the House
of Commons, Tobasonakwut lit a smudge, the sacrament of sage
we use to purify ourselves and our spiritual items. The burning
sage sent a rich plume of smoke into the air, its scent filling the
room. He held the feathered war bonnet of the national chief over
the smoke and moved it in a slow, deliberate circular path. He
offered it to the earth. He offered it to the sky. He said a prayer.
Then the bonnet was blessed.

Tobasonakwut carried the bonnet to Phil Fontaine and raised
it before placing it on Phil's head. He straightened the ribbons and
ermine skins, then smiled at Phil and shook his hand. Traditional
protocol had been followed.

Moments later, Phil and a handful of other Indigenous leaders
walked into the chamber of the House of Commons to a standing
ovation. The eagle feathers stood out with quiet elegance against
this backdrop of pomp and ceremony adopted from England.

When the guests were seated, Prime Minister Stephen Harper
took centre stage and apologized to Phil, to Ndede, and to the
eighty thousand residential school survivors alive at that time for
what was done to them as children. For taking them from their
families, for trying to destroy their identities, and for often putting
them in harm's way. Harper acknowledged that the intent had
been to "kill the Indian in the child."

"The burden of this experience has been on your shoulders for
far too long," the prime minister said, in perhaps the most eloquent
passage of the apology. "The burden is properly ours as a government, and as a country. There is no place in Canada for the attitudes
that inspired the Indian residential schools system to ever prevail
again. You have been working on recovering from this experience for
a long time and in a very real sense, we are now joining you on this
journey. The government of Canada sincerely apologizes and asks

the forgiveness of the Aboriginal peoples of this country for failing them so profoundly." He then apologized in both official languages and in three of the other founding languages of this country—Cree, Ojibwe, and Inuktitut : *"Nimitataynan," "Niminchinowesamin,"* and *"Mamiattugut."*

It was a remarkable moment.

Part of the pain Tobasonakwut had felt all these years was now recognized by the descendants of some of those who had caused it. This brought one part of the journey—the fight for recognition— to a close. The quest for justice that Ndede and thousands like him had been pursuing was reaching some manner of resolution. It may not have been perfect, but at least it was something. Sadly, many, like my uncle Tootons, my uncle John, and my grandparents, never lived to hear the apology.

Watching the moment on a TV screen back in Winnipeg, I was moved. It had taken some very painful stories told in public for many years, and billions of dollars' worth of class action lawsuits, but the survivors had demanded justice of this country. For its part, the government may have resisted until almost the last minute, but eventually it did the right thing.

Back in the CBC Winnipeg newsroom, I could see the stress of the day wearing on my colleagues. They were reporting and sharing one brutal story after another told by residential school survivors, and it was taking its toll.

"I can't fucking take this!" a non-Native colleague yelled as he threw his headphones at his desk. He brought his hands to his face. Tears welled in his eyes.

I put my hand on his shoulder.

I told him it was going to be all right.

IN 2009, TOBASONAKWUT accompanied Phil Fontaine as part of another important delegation. This time, they travelled to Rome. Vatican City, to be exact.

There, they heard Pope Benedict XVI give an "expression of sorrow" over the suffering of children in residential schools. Many people criticized this language, saying it fell short of the forthright apologies delivered by the government of Canada and the four other churches involved in running the schools. My father had a different take.

On the way to the meeting in the Holy See, Ndede was unsure of what to expect from the occasion he and his friends had travelled across the ocean to attend. "I didn't know what to think," he told me later, "but I figured I would offer the Pope the eagle feather. Then I'd know if he's for real."

In our Anishinaabe way, the eagle feather reminds us of the time the Creator came to visit us on the back of an eagle. As such, it is a spiritual intercessor that connects us to God. Most recognize the eagle feather as an emblem of Native American spirituality.

Tobasonakwut was forcing the Pope's hand both literally and figuratively in offering him the feather. "If he took it, then I would know he is genuine and that he really wants reconciliation," Ndede told me. "But if he didn't accept the feather, then I'd know that nothing has changed."

In the Vatican, my father met the man who was the head of the church he had been thrust into as a boy. As he approached the frail Catholic elder, Ndede offered him the feather. He was pleasantly surprised when the Pope took it in his hand and said a prayer. The men smiled at each other.

This moment does not excuse the sins or abuses of the past. Nor does it fix policies and views held by the church, which are still harmful. It is a sign, however, that the institution can change. If reconciliation is to be possible, both sides need to move, and Indigenous people have already come a very long way.

While in Rome, Tobasonakwut struck up a friendship with James Weisgerber, the archbishop of Winnipeg. The friendship blossomed when they returned to Canada. They met for lunch and discussed how to move reconciliation forward. My father began to attend mass on occasion, and would ask the archbishop to bless him.

His Grace would soon take some significant steps toward the Indigenous community as well. That summer, he became a sundancer.

He rose with us before daybreak and crawled into the sweat lodge. He danced with us from before sunrise through to the evening, fasting all the while. He even joined us during the piercing ceremony, supporting me and other members of our family when we were cut. Through it all, he was there, soaking it all in. Perhaps it aligns somewhat with the place of Christ's passion, his torture and flagellation, in Catholic tradition. Or perhaps the archbishop had meant what he said a few days earlier when he offered a prayer beside our campfire in which he asked us to understand and enjoy each other in all of our unique expressions of humanity.

The archbishop also got an earful at the sundance. Several people gave long speeches decrying the pain caused by the residential school era in particular and the Catholic Church's role in colonization more generally. His Grace listened and nodded.

At one point, Chief Leonard Crow Dog called him over and offered him a cigarette. The two men sat in folding chairs below the pine boughs that offered shade around the edges of the sundance arbour. They took turns pulling drags from their off-brand American smokes. They watched the circle, now empty as the dancers took a break, and shared some quiet words. They had both been praying for their people and caring for their flocks for a long time.

My sister Diane and I studied the two men from across the arbour, their legs wrapped in traditional sundance skirts. Their bare chests were red from the sun, though the chief's was several shades darker, a ruddy brown next to the reddish pink of the archbishop's. Both men wore beaded medallions depicting the sun around their necks.

"Now, that is a Kodak moment," Diane remarked. "Who would have ever thought that you'd see a priest dressed like a sundance chief?"

I was asked what the archbishop's intentions were at the sundance. Was he playing a long game, eventually hoping to convert us? Or was he genuinely trying to understand the Indigenous way? I was not 100 percent sure, perhaps because these were not the right questions to be asking. In hindsight, the more important thing was that he was there to pray with us, and pray with my dad.

I WALKED carrying five-year-old Dominik in my arms. We followed Ndede as he pushed up the gravel path and through the lush green trees. We came to a small clearing interrupted on one side by a rock face. A small grotto was carved into the stone. "This is where we used to pray," Ndede said.

We were back in Wauzhushk Onigum at the site of Ndede's old residential school, St. Mary's. He was about to tell us his story, not just to Dominik and me but to a national TV audience. A camera crew was with us. I had been asked to prepare news stories for the launch of the Truth and Reconciliation Commission of Canada (TRC), taking place in Winnipeg in the summer of 2010.

As part of that coverage, I had put together accounts from many survivors, but there was one that I was most intimately familiar with—my father's. Normally, a journalist would not insert himself so personally into a story, but I had an idea for a powerful ending. When I pitched it to senior editors, they agreed.

So here we were, at the site that had caused so much of the pain my family suffered for at least seven decades.

I remarked at how small the stone grotto was. I studied my old man and the way he dwarfed this little thing now. But it still meant a lot to him. It was here that he told us about how he was raped by a nun in a building not far away. He recalled the feeling of depression that followed. This was also where he spoke about his father's death, and how he was beaten for standing, not kneeling, beside his grave.

His voice cracked as he described the beating and how he had told himself he would not cry, though his world had just been torn apart and he was being punished for trying to honour that passing like a good Anishinaabe son.

"That's nothing compared to"—he said, choking up—"to what I feel."

I put my arm around him. "It's okay, Ndede."

This was the first time my father had explained to me the depth of his sadness. It was also the first time we had embraced as a way of consoling one another. In one way, that moment was the two of us experiencing something very small. On another level, we were overcoming something massive—the emotional, physical, and familial gulf confronting survivors who never learned how to parent their children, one of the worst legacies of the residential school system.

The strange part was that we did all of this in front of a national television audience.

We walked the grounds of the old school and heard more of the old man's life story. We made our way to the south side of the big green hill where the school had once stood. It had been demolished decades earlier. In the cemetery, Ndede picked up an old wooden cross. "This is my dad's cross," he said, as he dusted it off.

He spoke again of his father's funeral, and of the lost sons he had once cradled in his arms. He spoke of their pain, the pain he had caused and the pain he felt when they died. He spoke of feeling this pain at the sundance.

Just then, a fawn bounded out of the woods nearby. I watched it, still holding young Dominik.

"What Anishinaabeg say when you're going through a lot of pain," Ndede said: "The Creator puts something in front of you to forget your pain."

I carried Dom in my arms to get a closer look at the deer. When we got within a dozen feet of it, the little animal turned and ran back into the forest.

Back on the hill, my father and my son sat together looking at black-and-white photos from the old man's school days. "And there were little guys there just like you," Ndede said to his grandson.

Positioned with the crew a few feet away, I delivered to camera the ending I had composed.

"My son is five years old now," I told the TV audience. "He's the age kids were when they were taken away from their families. When I look at him and see how frail he is, I wonder if he could take a beating from an adult like my dad did. I hear him cry for his mom sometimes, and I wonder if he could survive for ten months without his parents. Seeing my son at this age makes my father's residential school experience hit home. I understand why he screwed up so much later on in life, and I forgive him. Now it's up to me to make things a little bit better for my son."

A bald eagle soared overhead.

We wrapped for the day and ate at a Boston Pizza before driving back to Winnipeg.

The response to that piece was a powerful lesson for me in bridging gaps between communities. Indigenous people said they felt the story did justice to their experiences. Non-Indigenous people felt it helped them relate to the residential school experience better than black-and-white photos alone did. Seeing my son with his grandpa, they were delivered to a place where they asked themselves what they would do if their children disappeared, or what would happen if all the children in their neighbourhood vanished. To me, getting viewers to ask these questions is the beginning of building empathy, and empathy is the beginning of reconciliation.

The day before that story aired, Ndede gave his testimony to the Truth and Reconciliation Commission of Canada. He stepped into the private hearing with a plan. Instead of only focusing on the abuse and mistreatment he suffered, he gave an impassioned and eloquent account of the richness of Anishinaabe tradition, culture, and spirituality. He also pointed out that he had been robbed of educational opportunities that he had the intellectual capacity for, as evidenced by his diploma and degree. What is more, he delivered this statement entirely in Anishinaabemowin and directed it toward his descendants. Knowing that the TRC would preserve his statement for posterity, Tobasonakwut used the forum to help preserve the language, culture, and family that the residential schools had been designed to erase. He appropriated the setting in which he was expected to play the victim and instead demonstrated how he was the victor.

On the home front, things were stable. I had given up alcohol completely. I shared custody of our sons with April, and made every effort to provide a rewarding life for them. This meant choosing good schools for our kids, buying them nice things, and coaching their hockey teams. Simple things. Things we may take for granted. Things that I recognize not every generation in my family has been able to do for their children.

WE WERE IN HAWAII on a family vacation when he first felt the pain. My boys and I were swimming in the ocean surf while Shawon and her boyfriend, Jesse, watched from some nearby lava rocks.

Ndede stood on shore, clutching his gut. He said something was bothering him. Shawon and I looked at each other and assumed he was laying the groundwork for an excuse to leave the beach and not spend time with the family. But this magical time and this magical place marked the early stirrings of another journey for the old man.

The pain he felt would later be identified as the first signs of cancer in his abdomen. It was also, however, the start of something much more. It was a call that would lead him to embark on the journey to confront all that remained of the pain in his past. In the process, he would show us how things that had been broken apart long ago could be brought back together and made whole again.

At the time, however, we were all just playing like children in the sun.

I SPENT MUCH OF 2011 maintaining the hectic pace of a daily-news journalist. A once-in-three-hundred-years flood and the return of professional hockey to Winnipeg were some of the more memorable stories I covered. This meant working many days that stretched through fourteen or sixteen hours, or even longer.

Finally, by summer, I had banked enough time to take off for three weeks. For the first two weeks, I took Dom and Bezh to Onigaming. Here, we lived, just the three of us, in a way very similar to how I had lived as a boy. Playing in the sun. Swimming in the lakes. Camping on the islands. Studying the rock paintings. Offering tobacco to the thunderbirds when it rained. It was perfect.

Yet there was something missing. After a full day of playing outside, after we had said our prayers in Ojibwe and the boys had gone to sleep, I would be left alone. Outside, the night must have stretched on for infinity. I was lonely. I did not have a partner.

I had met Lisa a few years earlier at a bar in Winnipeg, but nothing really came of it. She was a catch, to be sure. Beautiful, funny, and—oh, by the way—a medical doctor.

Inviting me to breakfast, she told me she had watched the documentary about Ndede's residential school experience. She said she had participated in a self-help program called "Returning to Spirit" and thought I would be perfect for it because it dealt with the legacy of residential schools. I told her it sounded like Scientology.

She insisted that I consider it. "I'm serious," she said. "You would be the perfect person for this program to help."

She was stubborn, but she had such a nice way about her you almost didn't realize it.

"If I do this program," I said, "then you have to come to the sundance with me."

Lisa agreed. It was a win-win. Worst-case scenario was that I participated in a lame self-help workshop yet got to spend time with this beautiful woman. Best-case scenario was that the workshop changed my life for the better and I still got to spend time with this beautiful woman. As it turned out, it was more of the latter.

I persuaded Ndede to take the plunge into the self-help program with me, though he was skeptical. In fact, several times on the first day he tried to leave, saying the program was superficial. There may have been some truth to that, but he did experience a breakthrough of sorts.

On the second or third day, we were all tasked with carrying out an imaginary conversation with somebody who in the past had hurt us. We were to speak to them honestly yet also without blame. Ndede chose to speak to Darryl—his eldest son, my brother—who had committed suicide thirty years before. But he refused, at first, to engage in the exercise. Then he spoke directly to the facilitator without attempting the suspension of disbelief necessary to speak to the one he had missed for so long. He kept this up for a long time. Another facilitator stepped in and tried to explain the exercise in Ojibwe. Ndede snapped that he couldn't understand the man's dialect. And on it went, until I said, "*Gego zegiziiken Ndede, ganoonzh Asineobitangiban.*" "Don't be afraid, Dad, to speak to your late son."

Ndede stopped to ponder the direction. Finally, he spoke.

"Why the *fuck* did you do it?"

The room stayed silent for a moment. Ndede had touched a nerve, his own. But from then on, he would engage with his emotions rather than casting them aside or burying them. Some of the best times in those five days came when we were driving home. We found ourselves speaking to each other directly and openly, putting the things on the table that had built barriers between us earlier in life. I told him how I had resented the anger with which he had dealt with me as a boy. He told me how disappointed he was in me when I got in trouble with the law. We were becoming friends.

I called Lisa to tell her I had finished "Returning to Spirit" and that she should prepare for the sundance. Later, she would tell me she had never in a million years expected me to follow through on my end of the bargain, and so she hadn't given much thought to attending the sundance. That probably explains the surprise I heard in her voice that day. But she kept her word. The sundance is a holy place, but that is also where we started dating.

Lisa lived in Dauphin, about three hours from Winnipeg, and we saw each other on weekends. She travelled with me to Toronto, where I was spending more and more time that fall on a new television series called *8th Fire*. When we finished shooting, we would go out for dinner or check out the nightlife. It was fun and amazing. It was also too good to be true.

It came to an end. Perhaps I was too quick to anger. Perhaps she was too quick to leave. Either way, we went our separate ways in November.

I put my head down for the rest of the year and focused on the one thing that had always gotten me through rough waters—work.

The new series, *8th Fire*, examined the relationship between Indigenous people and the rest of Canada. It covered both the negative and the positive stories, which was something rarely reported in the media. It was an ambitious undertaking, involving producers across the country.

By Christmas, the show was basically complete, and it would launch me on a new journey of my own. I would experience new heights in my career, new opportunities for my family, and eventually new freedom to deal with the thing so many of us wish to change but never get around to confronting—the past.

PART TWO

Kiizhewaadizid
Living a Life of Love, Kindness, Sharing, and Respect

9

SOMETHING had spooked the horse.

It was shortly after we passed a police checkpoint a few miles up the mountain from Real de Catorce, Mexico. A dozen officers had stood shooting the breeze on the road carved out of a mountainside, assault rifles hanging lazily over their shoulders. Thanks to the drug war in Mexico during early 2012, it was difficult to avoid the presence of the narcos. But on this mountain, you were likely to run into something other than marijuana or cocaine. It was home to one of the oldest peyote gardens on earth.

This was where the Wixárika people, called Huichol by outsiders, carry on their ceremonies in much the same way they have been practised for several millennia. Each year, the Wixárika journey for hundreds of kilometres on a sacred pilgrimage to this mountain they call Wirikuta.

At one point, I noticed that someone had spray-painted, in Spanish, a message that alluded to a showdown I had seen play out countless times before in Canada. "We support both jobs and Indigenous culture," it said. The supposed dichotomy between economic development and Indigenous spirituality was being used as a wedge issue here in the heart of Mexico.

As we passed the circle of cops, I had grunted "*Buenos dias*" to them, doing my best imitation of a local accent. Hearing me, one of the officers tilted his aviator shades toward me, smiled, and nodded. Nothing to see here, he probably thought. Just a six-foot-one Native dude from Canada riding an old broken horse down the side of a mountain. The knot in my stomach began to unwind, and I was relieved that they didn't stop and question me and the sundance brothers with me. The horse, however, did not share my comfort. With the police behind us, he took off at a gallop.

The horse picked up speed. Maybe, I thought, the police were not my biggest concern. Maybe it was this old horse. I looked to one side and saw a rough rock face stretching to the sky. On the other side a sheer cliff dropped a hundred feet or so to a riverbed. Suddenly, I felt very mortal.

The horse's hooves kicked up dust as we charged down the dirt path.

"Stop!" I shouted, attempting a commanding voice. "Whoa!" I tried, mimicking old Western movies I'd seen. "*Alto!*" I said, assuming he understood Spanish better than English. Judging by the way he picked up speed, he did not.

Barely hanging on to the horse, now rushing down the mountainside, I realized words alone wouldn't work. I tried stroking the side of his neck to calm him while I focused on soothing thoughts, attempting some sort of mind meld. Given the exotic landscape and the local confrontation between Indigenous people and resource extraction, I was thinking *Avatar*. Maybe I had some sort of psychic connection with the beast I was riding. Apparently I didn't. He continued at full tilt. If you picture one of the windy mountain paths from *The Road Runner Show*, you'll have a sense of the situation, with me playing the role of Wile E. Coyote.

Then I noticed the black leather reins flopping on the horse's back in front of me. *Right,* I thought. *That is how you slow a horse. Not with mind melds or psychic energy, but by pulling on the damn reins.* Sometimes, we need spiritual answers. At other times, we need practical solutions. I began to haul back the reins, slowly but firmly. The horse slowed, pranced once or twice, and finally stopped and snorted into the air as though saying, "Dude, you finally figured it out."

My sundance brothers showed up a few moments later. "That horse took off on you!" my friend John said, and all I could do was nod humbly.

THE LESSON I LEARNED that morning was very pragmatic. The day before, I learned something that resonated on a much more spiritual level.

I had gone to a Catholic church in nearby Real de Catorce, an old town that looks like a village from Renaissance Spain or Italy. Cobblestones were everywhere, and the church marked the highest point in the town. As I entered the stone structure, I was surprised to see a statue of Saint Francis of Assisi dressed not in the traditional brown robes of the mystic but in the multicoloured psychedelic embroidery of the Wixárika. The priests here, I thought, knew who they were preaching to. After praying to the Creator for my children, I visited the gift store and chose a long rosary with light-brown wooden beads for Ndede.

Later that afternoon, we rented horses, including the one that would give me the scare. Riding up the mountain, we passed generations of Wixárika climbing on foot to their destination. An old man wearing traditional white linen pants and shirt, marking a sharp contrast against his dark-brown skin, carried a bundle of mesquite wood on his back, leaning forward as he walked to keep it balanced. When he smiled in my direction, his happiness washed over me. I would see someone else on another such journey soon enough.

I saw a young mother climbing the rocks with a baby in her arms. She was tired but waved off our offer of help, determined to carry her child herself and reach her destination under her own power.

Much had changed since the ancient Wixárika were first instructed how to use the medicine placed here by the Creator. Empires had risen and fallen around them—first the Aztecs, later the Spanish, and now modern Mexico—and still the Wixárika came back.

What was it like, I wondered, to see the world through the Creator's eyes? To see civilizations grow and collapse? To watch rivers turn hills into canyons? Throughout all these changes, a small group of Indigenous people continued to practise their spirituality as they always had. Many things in their lives had changed—Spanish became the lingua franca, and many pilgrims now arrived at the foot of the mountain in tour buses. Yet the stories that explained who they are and what they did here, and the ceremonies used to commune with the universe, had not changed. The people kept following the Indigenous way of this part of the world.

That night, outside the ceremony location, I wore both the rosary and the treaty medallion I had been presented when I was made a chief.

We spent the night a hundred metres below the summit of the hill, without sleep, supporting those who were conducting their annual ceremony. We heard about the traditional ways. We listened to the beautiful music played on traditional violins, accompanied by feet stomping on the earth.

I brought my pipe out, loaded it with tobacco, and said an invocation in support of the people participating in the main ceremony up the hill. I passed the pipe to those around our fire.

A Wixárika shaman came to explain how to use the medicine. When he finished, he paused for a few moments, chewing on some medicine and studying us. He looked back and forth at each of us before speaking as he would to a group of children. "Go ahead and eat it," he said in Spanish. "It's not going to hurt you."

The effects of the medicine made me think of mothers, grand-mothers, and all women. I stared up at the full moon, luminous above the darkened landscape. I could see the contours of the hills and plants around me and watched as the moonlight radiated toward the earth. The moon seemed to breathe in and out against the night sky. I felt the love of my mother. I knew that back home she had probably smoked her pipe tonight, as she does on every full moon, in accordance with Anishinaabe tradition. You often hear of Indigenous people becoming assimilated into the mainstream, but our family experience was different. We participate in the broader society along with others, but we also bring many previous outsiders into our culture and into our world view, my own mother included.

The mountaintop and landscape, the blanket of stars, and the shining moon all combined to remind me how infinitesimally small we are in the grand scheme of things. Awestruck by the night sky, I watched the moon breathe in and out. Standing in witness of the heavens, I heard a woman's voice in my head say, "She's probably wondering why you haven't called."

The voice was referring to Lisa. Had it been three months since we'd broken up? Had we really not said a word to each other since then?

Some people go on a vision quest and meet their spirit animal or see grand prophecies of things to come. Others, apparently, have visions that tell them to pick up the phone and call their ex.

The sun began to rise, and I looked out over the stunning vista surrounding us. Rays of light cascaded across the horizon, and the sea of clouds, hundreds of feet beneath us, looked like an ocean of frothy whitewater. The peaks of mountains miles away pierced the clouds like islands in a sea, a reflection of the earth in the sky.

Only a certain kind of non-clinical insanity would drive people to put an open-pit mine in such a place. My sundance brothers and I, along with countless others, had been invited to this place because a silver-mining company from Canada had secured the mineral rights to the area around Wirikuta, threatening to place the sacred mountain under siege. The Wixárika had called for allies to join them in prayer and witness their 2012 pilgrimage. We had responded to the call.

The town of Real de Catorce, at the base of the holy mountain, is home to one of the oldest mines in the Americas. The Spanish founded it and used Indigenous labour to extract silver to be shipped to Europe. This colonial history made the showdown between a modern multinational corporation and the local Indigenous people all the more poignant.

The Wixárika had launched a public relations campaign. Some protested at the annual general meeting of the silver-mining company, while their allies held concerts for huge audiences to raise awareness of the company's plans. Then there was the spiritual component. Peyote is a sacrament to many Indigenous peoples and is used in the Native American Church, the biggest organized religion among Indigenous people in the United States. The prospect of seeing the peyote gardens damaged rang alarm bells.

Wherever Indigenous people stand up to safeguard their homelands or sacred sites, it seems the prospect of job losses is used to whip up opposition to them. It's as if people cannot have both jobs and spirituality. I would like to think we can make a living and still respect the earth.

On the sacred mountain, I understood how much the land meant to the Wixárika. It meant as much to them as Lake of the Woods means to me, to Ndede, to my grandpa. The land is inextricably bound up with us and connects us to our grandparents and our grandparents' grandparents. That is why some Indigenous people are not prepared to negotiate or allow development on their lands. For some, it would be like selling a family member. If the land loses its integrity, so do we. If we do not fight for our mother the earth, then we have failed our families.

After that night on the mountain, and wrestling with the spirit of Crazy Horse the next morning, we drove to the city of San Luis Potosí and found a hotel room. I called Lisa from there. I don't remember much of what we said to each other, except for the last thing she said: "I'm glad you called."

I headed home considerably more humble, contemplating the spiritual guidance I had received and mindful of Lisa's words.

A few months later, the Wixárika saw their sacred mountain Wirikuta protected from mining when the Mexican government bowed to pressure from the Indigenous people and their allies and put the development plans on hold.

The world is always changing.

10

THE YEAR 2012 began with a spark for me when CBC Television's *8th Fire* began generating buzz on social media.

The show was a chance to tell a more complete truth about Indigenous peoples in Canada. We sought to balance the usual dismal news coverage with positive stories, sharing examples of people across the land working hard to build bridges between communities. We tackled the challenging issues, but we also highlighted the growing number of success stories.

The title *8th Fire* alludes to a prophecy of the Anishinaabe people that suggests now is the time to fix the relationship between Indigenous people and others. Embracing a way of life built on spirituality, respect for one another, and respect for the earth will create a fire that can burn forever, which is the way for us to build a sustainable society that can last long into the future.

The late William Commanda, who carried a wampum belt depicting the prophecy, shared his teaching with the team that created *8th Fire*. An elder and spiritual leader, Commanda deserves much of the credit for the series' name. His granddaughter Claudette carries on this legacy, and is the one to whom tobacco should be given if one wants to learn more. Edward Benton-Banai has written his own account of this teaching in *The Mishomis Book: The Voice of the Ojibway*.

The rollout of *8th Fire* began with a short video I wrote and performed for the CBC show *George Stroumboulopoulos Tonight* in which I debunked five stereotypes about Native people in two minutes. Logging on to Facebook the next morning, I saw that every notification on my screen was maxed out. Apparently, we had struck a chord. People were starving for a more accurate representation of First Nations, Métis, and Inuit people

Each episode of *8th Fire* generated a huge response. Facebook and Twitter were flooded with coverage, and the DVD set became a bestseller. Educators continue to give the series life by using it as a teaching tool in classrooms.

The true impact of the series really hit home for me one night in a hotel room on the way back from a Baja vacation with my boys. We were in Vancouver, spending the night on a layover, and I turned on the television to watch the latest episode of *8th Fire*. When my face appeared on the screen, I was a little embarrassed to look at myself, so I studied my sons' reaction.

My two little Anishinaabe boys were sprawled on the king-size bed, eating room service pizza and chicken. They watched an Innu surgeon who ran across Quebec inspiring young people. They witnessed a Mi'kmaq chief who brought his community from poverty to multinational business success in one generation. They met a young Kanienkehaka woman who stands strong for LGBTQ rights and teaches healthy attitudes about sexuality to young people. My sons did not think twice as they absorbed these images of proud Indigenous people on national television. To them it was normal.

That was huge to me. All my life, I had seen Indigenous people portrayed poorly in the media. As a child on the reserve during the summer of 1990, I remembered images of the Oka Crisis beamed into our homes. I wondered why the army was deployed in a community where the people looked like my cousins, aunts, and uncles. I bristled whenever I watched old Western movies on TV. And as an adult, I cringed every time a story reminded me of the bigotry that still existed in my country.

Sometimes the prejudice and insensitivity is overwhelming. Remember the 2009 H1N1 influenza scare? Manitoba First Nations were hit hard by the disease. Rather than sending enough Tamiflu to treat the residents of Indigenous communities, Health Canada sent body bags. Whoever made that decision did not see the people on those reserves the same way they see other human beings. These daily injustices may seem tiny in the grand scheme of things, but they add up. They misinform the public and feed into stereotypes about Indigenous peoples.

They also affect the way we First Nations people see ourselves. Over a lifetime of internalizing the message that you are "less than," you start to believe some of the lies you hear about yourself. It lowers your sense of self-worth and influences your behaviour. You begin to censor your own thoughts and actions or make choices because of the way you expect to be perceived as an Indigenous person.

That is why it meant so much to watch my kids seeing people like them depicted as achievers. I hope they live in a world where they are less likely to be made to feel ashamed of who they are or who their grandparents were.

Thanks to its success, *8th Fire* unleashed a torrent of speaking invitations for me. They came from all directions. One of the largest multinational corporations in the world requested me to speak to their people, as did a Toronto college. Another asked me to visit a small reserve in Southern Ontario. There were many more, most falling into those three categories—First Nations, corporate, and educational. I turned them down in the beginning, even though they were lucrative offers. My first commitment was to my career as a broadcast journalist.

ON THE FIRST WEEKEND I spent in Winnipeg after returning from Mexico, Lisa and I met at Little Mountain Park, a dog park on the edge of the city where the industrial lots meet the prairie. Everything was blanketed in white. We went for a walk in the snow, both of us speaking tentatively at first. Sitting together on a park bench, we watched the sun set over the tundra, the scene framed by groves of oak trees on either side. We talked about what had happened months before. I told her about the ways I had changed. She spoke about her insecurities. We both agreed that we missed each another.

Lisa looked beautiful in that cold blue-and-gold setting. Her soft café-au-lait skin caught the shimmering light of magic hour. When I told her I wanted to start over, she agreed. We moved closer to hold one another in our parkas and ski pants, and kissed each other gently for a long time.

Then we walked back through the frozen twilight to our vehicles and drove in opposite directions down the highway, secure in the knowledge that neither of us would be alone anymore. We had each other.

THE NEXT DAY was a typical Monday at work, coloured by the gnawing thought in my soul that I should be out on the plains hunting buffalo instead of sitting in a field of fluorescent-lit blue cubicles. After I finished my hit on the six o'clock news, I crossed

the street to the University of Winnipeg. I was about to start
something new.

Down the warm hallway, the glazed doors were coated in
condensation from the cold. When I turned the corner to enter
the classroom, my breath was taken away by the sight. The room
was filled with people, all of them patiently waiting for me to
arrive and teach the class.

This would be the first session of a free Anishinaabe language
class for families, to be called "Anishinaabemonotawaataanig
Abinoojiiyag," or "Let's Speak Ojibwe to Our Kids." When I had
approached officials at the university about starting a language
program for the community on a volunteer basis, they'd agreed.

Indigenous languages contain the world views of our ancestors.
They give us a common identity across a variety of communities,
where some are traditionalists, others Christians, and others atheists.

My mom and Ndede had told me that the first word I
spoke was *saabkeshii*—"spider" in Anishinaabemowin. Even though
Anishinaabemowin was my first language, I did not have the same
easy conversational facility with it that the older generation had. I
considered those old-timers to be the real Anishinaabeg, sparring
with each other in long strings of Anishinaabemowin interrupted
by fits of laughter. In turn, I looked at myself as something less than
them. I'd had a vision, I had become a pipe carrier at a very young
age, I had started sundancing as a teenager, and I had learned
hundreds of songs. Still, I felt I was not as Anishinaabe as they were.

As an adult, I worked hard to understand the language better.
I launched an Anishinaabemowin "Word of the Day" series on
YouTube. Yet I wanted to increase my impact, and that's what led
me to the classroom on this evening.

The room was crowded with young mothers and fathers
accompanied by their children. Their grandparents and elders were

there as well. In all, about sixty people had gathered in a classroom built for no more than thirty. My two sons were waiting for me with their grandparents. I hugged them and took off my coat, sweating a little.

Ndede saw that I was nervous. "*Gego zegiziiken*," he said. "Don't be scared. Just go for it."

I nodded and took a deep breath before addressing the group. "*Ahow ndinawemaaganiidog. Miigwech kipiizhaayeg*," I began, greeting the group as my relatives and thanking them for coming.

We returned two nights a week for the rest of the winter to learn the language together, and things soon settled into a routine for me: work, Ojibwe, gym, boys' hockey; work, Ojibwe, gym, boys' hockey; and so on.

It all changed in February, when Ndede received bad news. The cancer he first felt on that trip to Hawaii had been treated with surgery and two rounds of chemo. He felt well and assumed things were under control. That assumption was mistaken. Now he was told it was far from being under control. He would need an aggressive round of chemotherapy. The doctors said he only had a few months to live.

Ndede did not tell me the prognosis at first, only that he had to have another round of chemo. Phrased that way, the news did not seem so grim at first. Ndede had had health scares before and bounced back. *He's a fighter*, I thought. *He will fight this too.* So I carried on with my routine.

One night, I drove through thick snow to visit my parents in their bungalow on the other side of town. When we were sitting at the dinner table, I asked my dad about his health, and he tried to reassure me by saying, "Everything is fine." Which set my alarm bells ringing.

That was the line he used whenever everything was definitely not fine. Ndede is one of those tough, don't-worry-about-me, that's-not-a-tear-I-just-have-something-in-my-eye old-timers. Had he reacted with anger, it would have been all right, even reassuring. Had he sworn at the cancer, that would have been fine as well. Those reactions would have made sense; I could have understood them. But it did not make sense for him to be calm. Maybe he was afraid. Maybe something had changed. Driving home that night, I thought about what it meant.

I considered how our relationship had changed. As a boy, I had been afraid of Ndede. He had always been angry, even if I did not know why. Now that I was an adult, he was the one biting his tongue whenever he saw me getting upset with my boys for not listening to me. Other things had changed. When I was young, people would often say to me, "You're Peter's boy!" Now Ndede heard, "Oh, you're Wab's dad!"

So many things had started to change for the better between us. Yet there were still things left unsaid and left undone.

NDEDE WAS AN INSTRUCTOR in the University of Winnipeg's master's program in Indigenous governance, where he taught a course titled "Pathways to Indigenous Wisdom." We joked that his office was actually at a nearby restaurant, Dessert Sinsations, where you could find him most days, holding court with his students.

That's where I joined him one snowy day. I showed him a lesson plan that had been developed by another university volunteer. The class would teach kids in our Ojibwe class how to build rockets, and we spent a few hours translating every detail. It began with an introduction to the night sky, the destination we aimed to send our rockets toward.

I knew the simple terms in Anishinaabemowin that were relevant, like "sun," "moon," and "stars" (*giizis*, *dibeka-giizis*, and *anongook*). Ndede was able to provide the richer vocabulary for words that identified constellations and the universe itself. He also had the deep grasp of the cosmology that lay beneath that lexicon.

Years earlier, Ndede had taken me with him to "Science Dialogues" in places like Santa Fe, New Mexico, and Kalamazoo, Michigan, where physicists engaged in long philosophical discussions with Indigenous knowledge keepers. These dialogues were premised on the awareness that many Indigenous languages describe the natural world in terms of process, action, and flux. In some ways, this reflects the reality posited by contemporary physics more closely than static, noun-based English. The dialogues were an attempt to broker insight and innovation on both sides through collaboration.

It was my good fortune to attend these events and hear people like Dr. Leroy Little Bear, Sakej Henderson, and my father give rich accounts of Indigenous linguistics, science, and philosophies. As a result, I have never had much time for those who think Indigenous peoples do not have an intellectual tradition.

This came back to me at the restaurant table. The possibilities were exciting. Not only would we be able to teach the kids Anishinaabe; we would teach them science. We could also normalize the academic environment and let students know that their people had a rich intellectual life reaching back through the centuries.

A few days later, our lesson plan became reality in an old chemistry lab. First, we reviewed the astronomical terms in Anishinaabe, then we set out to build cardboard rockets propelled by Diet Coke and Mentos Mints.

The children loved it. I watched my son Bezh combine the elements in a small film canister, and we started counting down in Anishinaabemowin together.

"Midaaswe … shangaaswe … nishwaaswe …"

When we got to "eight," the pressurized fizz popped the container's lid off, sending the attached rocket into the air for a few centimetres. Bezh laughed and said, "I'm a mad scientist!"

Looking around at other families, I saw Dominik sitting with his grandparents. My older son had been frustrated by the chemicals reacting too quickly for him to get the lid back on the canister until Ndede stepped in and snapped the lid neatly in place as soon as Dom added the soda and candy. When Dom's rocket flew into the air, a sweet smile lit up his face and Ndede grinned from ear to ear. Ndede's eyes squinted behind his glasses when he looked over to my mom. He may not always have been like this when I was growing up, but now he made a perfect grandpa.

We wrapped up the class after everyone had a chance to launch their rocket successfully and describe the process in Ojibwe. I was overjoyed.

Bezh and I left the chemistry lab holding hands. On our way to Ndede's Buick, Dom walked on the sidewalk ahead of us between his grandparents.

Ndede's Buick was more than just a car. He had put a down payment on it a few years earlier when he received his initial disbursement as part of the Indian Residential Schools Settlement Agreement. Later, he received more money based on the abuse he suffered. "Ever since I was a little boy, I've always wanted a Buick," he told me, when he first drove the car home. It was fitting that he bought it with money paid in compensation for the pain he suffered in his childhood.

We stood on Spence Street in downtown Winnipeg beside the Buick, which was in an accessible parking space. A blue parking permit hung from the rear-view window, identifying the driver as handicapped. The simple white lines on the permit formed the recognizable hieroglyph of a person in a wheelchair. This, I realized, was new.

I hugged my mom and then awkwardly shook hands with my dad, reprising the half-hug, half-handshake from my convocation years earlier. "*Gigawaabamin minawaa*," I said, telling him I would see him again.

"*Weweni sago*," he replied, telling me to take care. Then he shuffled to the driver's side of the car, his back hunched slightly. Those glory days of Golden Gloves boxing were long behind him. Watching the world-beater become frail would be an adjustment, for me and for everyone.

Later, my friend Leonard and I saw a movie called *50/50*, about a young man battling cancer. On the way home, I was recalling a scene in which the man's best friend was reading a book about how to support someone with cancer. "If Seth Rogen can buy a book about cancer," I told Leonard, "it's the least I can do."

A few nights later, I pulled just such a book from the shelf of a local bookstore. It promised to reveal twenty things that people with cancer want you to know. After scanning the book, I took it to the counter, paid for it, and went home to read for the rest of the evening. This book helped me immensely over the coming months. It helped me understand that though my father needed help and support, he also needed us to respect his dignity, pride, and independence. Most important, perhaps, it helped me realize that I had to learn how to have his back without needing to rationalize the situation. Suffering from cancer is a situation without rationale, and any response, whether anger, sadness, or denial, is understandable.

THAT WEEKEND, my sister Shawon called me from Italy. She had travelled back and forth overseas for the past few years, researching

Renaissance art for her doctoral dissertation. Shawon is the true achiever of our family. By the time she finished her undergraduate degree, she had already been published in academic journals, and Ivy League schools were competing for her to attend their PhD programs.

"How's it going, Bruddy?" she asked. Bruddy was the nickname she invented for me when she was a kindergartner.

"Not bad," I said. I walked outside to sit on my front steps. The weather had warmed, so being outside in Winnipeg no longer hurt. The smell of spring had returned.

Shawon cut to the chase. "What's going on with Ndede?" she said. "Mom told me that his cancer is back but that I shouldn't worry."

"Yeah, it is," I said. "I don't know much." Thanks to our parents' humility, neither of us knew exactly what my father's prognosis was or what was in store for him. "I do know that he is going for chemo," I added.

We parsed each word we had exchanged with our parents on the subject, especially with our mother. We rearranged fragments of information over and over, hoping a clear picture would emerge from the puzzle. We also shared the unhelpful bits of internet research we had conducted. All we knew was that it was serious.

"I'm thinking of coming back to spend time with Mom and Ndede," Shawon said.

"Well, I know Ndede wants you to stay in Italy and finish your PhD," I responded. "But yeah, you've got to do what's right for you."

"Mom already said Ndede doesn't want me to come back for him," Shawon answered, and she told me about a young woman in her cohort who had taken a year off to spend time with a sick family member. The interruption in that woman's studies had caused problems, but she had worked it out. "I could put my studies on hold and return to the program next year," Shawon said. "I just wonder if this is the last chance I'll get to spend time with Ndede."

I thought about their relationship. Shawon loved him so much. She had chosen Harvard over another school she preferred primarily because of Ndede's long-time desire to see one of his kids attend the famous institution. At the same time, my father's unfaithfulness had wounded her.

"Well, I'll be honest with you," I said. "I've been thinking of leaving the CBC so I can spend time with him."

We discussed the pros and cons of changing our lives to make the most of the time our father had left—learning from his wealth of traditional knowledge, fixing the shortcomings in our relationships with him.

In that light, the downsides to the idea seemed to lose their importance. What would we miss out on? Steady paycheques, stability, timelines we had set for ourselves? We agreed that family came first. Our careers could wait. "Ten years from now, will I regret missing a few months of working at the CBC? Or will I regret not spending the time with our dad before he died?" I asked rhetorically, summing up the way I felt.

"I think we'll both regret it if we don't spend the time with Ndede," my sister concluded.

Before hanging up, we said we loved each other in Anishinaabemowin.

I looked down my street. I could still see ugly patches of sand and snow here and there. But some of the trees had bright-green shoots emerging from the branches.

The next day, I walked into the CBC and asked for a leave of absence without pay, explaining that I wanted to help my father fight his illness. I was granted the request immediately. Within a week, Shawon was back in Winnipeg.

On March 29, we were free. Free from work. Free from studies. Free from a regular paycheque. Most important, we were free to follow Ndede on his journey.

Ndede and I with Treaty #3 elders at Neyangaashing, the spot where he grew up.

Ndede with his grandfather Kakagewanakweb at St. Mary's Indian Residential School. Kakagewanakweb surprised my father with an impromptu visit to check on his wellbeing.

Ndede with schoolmates at St. Mary's as he approached his teenage years.

My older brothers and sister—Danny, Diane, and Darryl—in the 1970s.

My mom and I at my convocation from the University of Manitoba. At twenty-one, I was going through a rough period in my life and partying too much, but I still managed to get my B.A. in economics. Mom supported me throughout.

Shawon and I circa 1988. We were all dressed up outside our apartment in Winnipeg for some event, but ended up playing a spy game outside a nearby park.

My son, Bezh, and I back when he was a baby. We were getting ready to head to his first sundance. Well, if you don't count the sundance he attended while he was in his mother's belly.

Dominik as a baby with his mother, April. That cute little face motivated me to get my act together and build a career so I could support Dom and his brother.

Performing at a CD-release party back in my rap days, circa 2009. A CD used to be these reflective discs we put music on back in my day ...

Ndede, Phil Fontaine, and Pope Benedict XVI in 2009. My dad offered the feather as a symbol of reconciliation. That the pontiff accepted it in his hand signalled his willingness to embrace Indigenous culture in a way his predecessors had not.

Shawon, Archbishop James Weisgerber, Ndede, and I at the 2012 adoption ceremony. It was a powerful day where we witnessed residential school survivors taking a priest as their kin.

Ndede and Sundance Chief Leonard Crow Dog—two spiritual leaders who have danced together for many years visiting each other one final time.

Ndede and Mom praying at the sundance tree together for the last time, following the August 2012 sundance described in this book.

Ndede, Shawon, and I on the roof of the Vatican after St. Kateri's canonization in October 2012.

Ndede and Mom in San Pietro Square, Vatican City, on the morning of St. Kateri's canonization.

Lisa and I at our traditional wedding ceremony in August 2014.

11

"HERE IT IS!" Ndede said.

He dusted off an old baseball cap he had found in a back room in his house and handed it to me to inspect its faded glory. The black cap had turned grey. Its garish neon-pink, -green, and -yellow design, all the rage in the 1990s, had not aged well either. Printed across the front in white was a medicine wheel and the words "20th Annual Li'l NHL Hockey Tournament."

"Try it on," Ndede said, laughing. I obliged, and we sat around his kitchen table grinning, perhaps waiting for the hat to say something to conclude the scene.

He had saved the hat from an all-Native hockey tournament twenty years earlier. Ndede had taken my friend Makwa, his older brother Mick, and myself to play on the Eagle Lake Selects, a rep team from Northwestern Ontario. We were badly outmatched that year, having moved up an age category to play older kids. But we had a ton of fun. For years afterward, Ndede would laugh and retell a story about Makwa being lifted from the oppressive grip of gravity by a hip check and crying out so loud the entire arena could hear him.

The old cap proved how much those memories meant to my father. He may not have shown much affection to us, but that didn't mean he was not feeling anything inside.

A few nights later, I began my speech at a dinner for the sponsors of the fortieth Annual Little Native Hockey League Tournament by pulling out the hat. I explained where I got it, put it on, and mugged for the crowd. They laughed and applauded. Later, my friend Deanna reminded me that I was a huge nerd.

My life had begun to change. I had gone from travelling here and there to cover stories for the news to darting across the country on speaking engagements. Meanwhile, my parents were gearing up for a different sort of race.

Ndede reached out to his good friend Dr. Brett Thompson, a man he had adopted as his son. Brett, an Anishinaabe from the American side of the border, had been headed nowhere fast before Ndede became his mentor. He confessed to Ndede that he had always dreamed of becoming a medical doctor. My dad was a firm believer in the importance of education and thought law was a higher calling than medicine. Still, he encouraged Brett and taught him about our traditional healing ways. The pipe. The sweat lodge. The language. All of it helped lay a foundation for Brett's future success by helping him heal from his earlier life challenges.

Brett became a medical doctor a few years later and set out to practise in Indigenous communities from Alaska to the Midwest. Now he was returning the favour by working to heal my father. He used his clinical experience as a palliative care physician to counsel Ndede and went out of his way to have oncologists at the world-renowned Mayo Clinic in Minnesota review Ndede's diagnosis and treatment plan. When they agreed with the plan proposed by the Canadian doctors, it gave my parents peace of mind and helped my father feel better about proceeding with the planned chemotherapy.

Brett also underlined the importance of nutrition and exercise in my dad's quest for wellness. He recommended books that all of us took turns reading. With so much advice, we tried to build an optimal cancer-fighting lifestyle for the old man. Finally, Brett told my mom to rest up, because she and Ndede were about to "run another marathon."

The marathon quickly grew serious. I came home from a public speaking trip one day to find my dad had suffered damage to his arm when a routine procedure had been botched. The complication was not severe, but he was in pain. We were left to realize that Ndede had a new life, and that much of it would consist of medical procedures and hospital visits.

I drove him to his next visit for chemotherapy. I did not want him to have to drive himself home. On our way into St. Boniface Hospital, I was struck by my father's familiarity with the place. He walked through the halls toward the elevators with the purposefulness of a man on a mission, a man who had carried out that mission many times before.

I studied his hands as he reached for the elevator button—the coarse fingernails that had seemed to thicken like his skin and helped shield him from the rough life he'd led, the bumpy knuckles that had developed when things got even rougher. He avoided meeting my gaze as we waited for the elevator. He was not happy to be here, and he took no joy in having his son along for the ride.

Upstairs, we checked in at the nurses' station and sat in a boring waiting room of the type found only in hospitals and medical clinics. When the nurse called out Ndede's name, we went into the treatment area, where two older men, also there for chemo, acknowledged our presence and a nurse arrived to administer the treatment.

"There is usually a younger guy here too," Ndede said. He must have been wondering what had happened to him.

We sat mostly in silence, making small talk now and then. I tried to lighten the mood with humour, but with an intravenous drip leading to a needle in his arm and sipping juice from a tiny hospital cup, Ndede was not really in the mood to laugh.

After enough time had passed for us to consider every possible negative outcome of this treatment, the nurse returned, disconnected Ndede from the IV line, and we left for home. I made something for him to eat, but it grew cold on the kitchen table. He walked to his bedroom and remained there in the dark for a long time.

I checked on him a little later. I watched him pretend to sleep. With eyes closed, he asked me if everything was okay. I told him it was, then left him and went to clean the house.

I WAS RIDING IN A PROP PLANE careening over the treetops of the boreal forest, headed for Pelican Falls First Nations High School, located between the town of Sioux Lookout and the nearby Lac Seul First Nation. It is a school for young people from northern fly-in communities in Ontario that do not have a high school of their own.

At Pelican Falls, I focused on a positive message. I spoke of the excitement of climbing that mountain in Mexico, how it reminded me that we have to expand our horizons beyond our neighbourhood, our rez, our hometown. We ought to see the world as a beautiful place full of mountains to climb, oceans to swim in, and wonderful people to meet. I closed by performing some round-dance songs on a hand drum, which I interspersed with rap lyrics I had composed. When I finished, the students stuck around to talk with me for a long time.

After that, I walked to get a view of the nearby lake and found a monument to Pelican Falls Residential School. Metal signs framed a walkway leading to a statue that commemorates the children who attended the school. The building itself had been torn down at the end of the residential school era.

I sat there silently for a long time under the shade of a tall pine tree, studying the water, and thought about my father's experience. I thought of his ordeal now. I offered tobacco and prayed for him, my sons, and my family.

It was difficult for me to ignore the parallels between Pelican the residential school and Pelican the high school. True, the old residential school buildings were gone. But what had been built in its place? A vocational school with a chapel at its centre; separate girls' and boys' dorms where the students lived. The young people had left their families and communities behind, and once at the school they were not permitted to leave the grounds.

There were some important differences. Today's students could study in their traditional languages, their culture was celebrated, and there was no corporal punishment. Perhaps most important, the students and their families had a choice about whether they attended the school. It might be illegal not to send your kids to high school, but at least there were no truancy officers tracking kids through the bush and hauling them away, kicking and screaming, as there were in the residential school era.

We had made progress. Yet we still had further to go.

12

"I AM GOING to adopt the archbishop."

The words hung in the air as Ndede and I sat beneath the towering pine tree that dominated his front yard. He studied my reaction with the trademark furrowed brow and piercing gaze I had come to know well over three decades.

I looked at the ground and urged him to explain more while I searched for a deeper meaning in the dead pine needles strewn about that had killed the grass. We were sitting at a small table, enjoying the early summer air, drinking tea.

"I am going to adopt the archbishop as my brother," Ndede repeated. "Phil, Bert, Fred, and I." He was referring to Phil Fontaine, Phil's brother Bert, and my uncle Fred. "What do you think?"

"Yeah …" I said, pausing to consider a diplomatic way to phrase what I was thinking. Part of me thought this was a waste of time. Another part worried that some might see it as a sellout move, another case of the Native bending over backward to appease the non-Native who does little in return. "Why do you want to do this?" was all I came up with.

"Jimmy has been like a brother to me," said Ndede. "I want to make it official." They had indeed grown very close.

Ndede described his vision for the adoption ceremony. He wanted to forge a lasting bond between our families and our communities, demonstrating how Indigenous culture offered a way forward in overcoming the pains of the past. If successful, it would repudiate the attempted cultural genocide in a much stronger way than words ever could.

The adoption ceremony is called *nabagoondewin* by the Anishinaabe. The Lakota call it *hunka*. Other First Nations people practise it as well. What unites these traditions is the insight that making our families bigger brings healing. For a grieving parent, adopting a new son or daughter will help them move forward by giving them an outlet for their love, as Ndede had done with Tommy Charging Eagle.

The adoption ceremony is also a peacemaking ceremony. It asks families, communities, or even nations to set aside their differences and commit to a rapprochement. It is hard to hate someone after you take them as a brother or sister.

I knew I would respect the decision my father had made to adopt the archbishop, considering the wisdom of the elders and all that. Besides, I figured, he was the one who would stand in the middle of the circle and be the public face of the adoption. So I was assuming I could keep my reservations about it to myself and take part by standing on the periphery.

"And I want you to conduct it."

Ndede's words snapped me out of my daydream.

"What?" I said, startled.

"I want you to run the adoption ceremony," Ndede said. "It is time we start not just teaching the young people but empowering you to lead the ceremonies. What do you think?"

So much for keeping myself on the periphery.

"It's a good idea, eh?" he summed up, taking my non-response as a vote of confidence.

THE PREPARATIONS BEGAN early at Thunderbird House, designed by First Nations architect Douglas Cardinal. The beautiful building takes the shape of our traditional roundhouses as inspiration. Cardinal added sweeping, modern lines in the form of a copper roof that evokes the contours of a thunderbird. It was a bright day, and sunshine flooded into the room through the skylights, reflecting off the polished hardwood floors.

Lisa and I rolled out a large buffalo robe in the centre of the circle and placed a buffalo skull on one end. Around this, we built an altar. Sacred medicines. Spiritual items. We added three framed photographs. One showed a group of children outside St. Mary's Residential School. Another a painting of a sundancer created by a Catholic priest. The final picture showed my father presenting the eagle feather to the Pope.

Recording and photography are banned from many Indigenous ceremonies because it can be a distraction for those praying. On this occasion, however, everyone agreed that we should waive this rule so that the occasion could be shared by the media and by the Truth and Reconciliation Commission of Canada, whose videographers were there.

I loaded the pipe with tobacco and prayed to each of the four directions, mother earth, and the sky. Then I stood and began with the traditional "*Ahow ndinawemaaganiidog ...*" I called out for everyone to be seated and welcomed them, explaining what we were here to do. I circled the buffalo robe in a clockwise fashion, recreating the path of the sun in the sky, from east to south to west.

"I have been practising the prayers to this ceremony, because if I get them wrong I might end up doing a wedding ceremony rather than an adoption," I joked.

I struck a match and lit a piece of sage. The smoke circled upward and my nostrils filled with the scent. I fanned myself, the smudge slowly climbing over me. Then we smudged the others sitting around the buffalo robe: Ndede, Uncle Fred, Grand Chief Derek Nepinak, Archbishop James Weisgerber, former federal cabinet minister and University of Winnipeg president Lloyd Axworthy, Phil, and his brother Bert. Lisa and I closed the loop on the eastern side of the buffalo robe.

Passing the smudge bowl to the crowd sitting in the outer circle, I could hear the soft sound of my leather moccasins tapping the ground. About half the audience was from the First Nations community, with a good number of them from our family and a sizeable contingent from the Fontaine clan as well. The other half were Catholics and members of Manitoba's church community. I explained the purpose of the smudge as a sacrament, which is perhaps not a difficult thing for a Catholic to understand.

When I lit the pipe, I thought of the men seated around me. Four residential school survivors. A grand chief. A former foreign affairs minister. The archbishop. I thought of my partner beside me. Of my children. I thought of the Creator.

I raised the pipe to the sky and rotated it clockwise, then brought it down to rest against my left shoulder. The stem pointed to the east, where the rising sun begins the day. "*Ahow kaa'anishinaa Nimishomis* ..." I invoked the spirits, our earth mother, and the Creator. We sang a pipe song.

Many people ask what the pipe is for, and some ask what we smoke in it. We fill it with tobacco, only tobacco. The pipe is a model of reconciliation. The bowl is feminine. It is of the earth, and it receives the stem. The stem is masculine. It is placed into the bowl, but also grows from the earth. Each has integrity on its own. When we place the bowl and stem together, the two elements form a new unified entity, which is stronger than each on its own. This is how we might think of reconciliation—two disparate elements coming together to create something more powerful.

Each adopted brother had an opportunity to speak. The archbishop went first. He said that if the government's apology was a wedding, we were now in the marriage, alluding to the hard work of making the relationship work. Then he presented his four new brothers with gifts.

My father spoke next, telling of his time in the residential school, the pain that followed, and the journey toward healing that he had walked for so long. He praised the archbishop for joining him on this same path.

My uncle Fred followed, as funny and eloquent as ever, switching from teasing the archbishop to praising him. He reminded everyone of the dark past that had brought us here on this day. He said while the goal of the residential school had been to turn him into a God-fearing Christian, he had instead become "a born-again pagan," which made me smile. Fred invited Lisa to sing a prayer song. As though her beauty, drive, and intelligence were not enough, she is also an amazing singer, and she captivated the audience with her soulful traditional song.

Phil was the next to speak. He talked about balancing Catholicism and Anishinaabe spirituality and of his visit to the Vatican with the archbishop. Phil even apologized to the Catholics in attendance for the anger with which he had sometimes spoken about them and other Christians while confronting his residential school demons. It was an act of contrition from someone who had suffered greatly, but that is Phil's way—he takes a conciliatory approach based on the remarkable strength and tenacity at the core of his being.

Phil's brother Bert passed on his opportunity to speak, displaying the quiet humility of many Anishinaabeg.

The four Anishinaabe brothers presented their new Catholic brother with four eagle feathers, representing each of them. Then Grand Chief Nepinak and I stood and gathered up a beautiful star quilt, raising it for everyone to see. The star in the centre was in red, yellow, blue, and green, the colours of the four directions for the Anishinaabe. In the centre, four pipes were set against the backdrop of a smaller star. The blanket was rich in the symbolic language of our people, but its message was clear: unity. The grand chief and I wrapped the archbishop in the quilt, the customary way of presenting someone with such a gift.

I picked up the hand drum and sang a song I had composed for the occasion, and the happy, celebratory melody rose above the drumbeats.

With Ndede, Fred, Phil, and Bert flanking the archbishop, the five new brothers danced around the outer circle, followed by Grand Chief Nepinak and Dr. Axworthy. Each of them shuffled along in the manner of the traditional powwow two-step.

Hearing the honour beats of the song, the archbishop raised the eagle feathers with his left hand as the beats were sounded, his head bobbing slightly in time. He wore the bright star quilt over his black robe and Roman collar. This Catholic holy man stood in the centre of a traditional Anishinaabe building adorned with the accoutrements of both cultures, participating in one of our ceremonies, dancing to one of our songs. There are few times in your life when you can say you have seen the impossible become possible. I witnessed such a thing at that moment. My father, the architect of that day, stood just to the side with a smile on his face, happy to stand near the spotlight rather than occupy it himself.

After a feast, we closed the ceremony with the Anishinaabe travelling song that we use to close all our gatherings in Lake of the Woods country. I explained the lyrics "*Ningosha anishaa wenjii-bimoseyan*"—"I am the reason you walk."

In Kwekwekipiness's roundhouse long ago, Ndede had explained that there are four layers of meaning to these words. They are from the perspective of the Creator, as though God himself were singing to you. The first meaning of "I am the reason you walk" is "I have created you and therefore you walk." The second meaning is "I am your motivation." The third meaning is "I am that spark inside you called love, which animates you and allows you to live by the Anishinaabe values of *kiizhewaatiziwin*." The fourth and final meaning is "I am the destination at the end of your life that you are walking toward."

On that day, the Creator spoke to us all, Indigenous and non-Indigenous alike, and reminded us of the reasons we walk.

13

LIFTING THE CANVAS FLAP, I followed my friend Eddy into the tipi and stood crouching so the slanted walls could accommodate my height. The air was thick with the smell of the wood fire. Orange light flickered and bounced around the space. Every so often, the crackle and pop of the fire would punch through the sounds of chatter and laughter.

The faces in the tipi belonged to strangers, yet they were somehow familiar to me—the same spectrum of skin tones, styles of haircuts, and types of casual clothing of the people I had grown up around. When we had shaken hands with everyone in the lodge, we sat and turned our attention to the man whose talk we had interrupted.

Rodney Elie looked the way you might expect an Anishinaabe spiritual leader to look. Studying the fire as he spoke, his long black hair falling down his back, he gripped a drumstick in his right hand and gestured with it as he spoke. In his left hand he held a drum, steadying it on his knee.

Then he cleared his throat and began to sing. The others seized the traditional melody, following his lead. They sang the song four times through. And then it was done.

My friends and I had travelled to this place, called Agawa Rock, for the same reason our ancestors had come there over many millennia: to fast, and to seek a vision. Agawa is on the eastern shore of Gichi Gaming, the great lake known as Lake Superior today. A sheer cliff rising out of the water marks the place where the ancient ones painted their visions. Some of the images show figures drumming. Others depict a group of canoes on a journey with the *odoodema'*, or clans, of each of the families in the canoes. One painting, however, is truly iconic and has been reproduced the world over. It shows Mishi Pizhiw.

Mishi Pizhiw is a supernatural creature that rose from the depths of the proto-Anishinaabe subconscious to populate our legends, traditions, and dreams with a presence that is alternately fascinating and terrifying. He (or she) may be a giant underwater panther or a massive predator, like a sabre-toothed tiger. At other times, Mishi Pizhiw has the head of a lynx and the body of a snake.

At Agawa, Mishi Pizhiw is painted as though looking directly at or through you. I have always felt called to this place, and to that image.

ON THIS NIGHT we laughed and sang until the sun set. When the stars began to spin slowly in the night sky, I had a good feeling about these people and this place. I had answered the call in my spirit, the call of Mishi Pizhiw.

Ndede's illness still loomed in the back of my mind, a persistent feeling I could not shake, even while I laughed and joked with friends. I had a smile on my face, but I kept looking over my shoulder for what might lurk in the depths around us. I prayed for my father a lot that night, placing tobacco in the fire over and over again as an offering. Finally, I said goodnight and walked back to my tent. The night sky was so clear, you could see the Milky Way in the distance behind the stars. *Nagekinaa*, I thought. The Anishinaabe word for the Milky Way means "everlasting road," the path the soul walks upon as it journeys to heaven.

A green light shot across the sky. A meteor. I thought of the legend of the wolverine, how he had crash-landed on earth as a shooting star. I smiled at this good omen. Then I prayed. "Show me what I can do to help Ndede," I said aloud.

A zip of the tent door later and I was fast asleep.

My uncle Leonard Crow Dog was telling me about a type of traditional medicine. I studied his face and the dark-brown skin with the reddish undertone that tells you this person's family has been in North America for a very long time. His black hair was pulled into a braid, and his mouth moved with the hint of an underbite that elders seem to develop as they enter old age.

Leonard was a medicine man's medicine man, the spiritual leader of the American Indian Movement (AIM) during its 1970s heyday. AIM had been the radical voice of the continent's original inhabitants as they cast off their colonial hangover, shouting, "We are still here!" Through a series of occupations at places like Alcatraz, Wounded Knee, and Washington, D.C., AIM proved a catalyst for social change, reinvigorating Indigenous politics and ushering in an era when its grassroots asserted themselves.

AIM was also responsible for its share of violence, perhaps none more inexplicable and disturbing than the murder of one of its own, Anna Mae Aquash, by other members of the movement. My Lakota relatives agreed that AIM may have made a lot of mistakes, "but it is what our people needed at the time," they would add. The movement wasn't perfect, but it was our wake-up call.

AIM helped clear space for the resurgence of Indigenous culture. Prior to its rise, sundances were held in secret, the result of having been outlawed for decades both in the United States and Canada. During this time, scouts would stand guard on horseback several miles from the sundance. If they spotted a missionary or police officer en route, they would speed back to the sundance camp with the news, and the dancers would pull out their Bibles and act as though they were engaged in Bible study.

Leonard was at the forefront of this cultural renaissance. He is also a strong advocate for an inclusive interpretation of Indigenous culture. When he says "*mitakuye oyasin*," which means "all my relations" in Lakota, he means that all people, all generations, and all beings are related. Leonard and my father became brothers after decades of sundancing together, forging a bond with blood, sweat, and tears.

Now Leonard was sharing a teaching with me. I looked to the ground as he spoke and studied the floor we were sitting on. It was grey mud caked in the heat of the sun.

Leonard's hand reached forward, holding a tiny peyote button. You could see where the roots had reached into the earth. Then he closed and withdrew his hand with the medicine in it.

A moment later, he showed his hand again. It was another medicine, a piece of a dog's jawbone with some meat still attached to it, spattered with blood. It must have been a small dog, maybe a puppy. The broken mandible fit neatly into Leonard's hand. I studied it for a moment before Leonard pulled his hand away from my view.

I woke from my dream. I was still in my tent. I was still at Agawa Rock. It was still nighttime. I thought about my vision. Three elements looped over and over again in my mind. The images cycled repeatedly. Dirt floor, peyote, dog meat ... dirt floor, peyote, dog meat ... dirt floor, peyote, dog meat.

WHEN IT WAS TIME to start the fast, I climbed the tallest rock I could see.

The summit of the rock was the flat pinkish colour familiar to those who have spent time on the Canadian Shield. On the western edge of the rock face, I found a small ledge overlooking Lake Superior. I set up my things and built my nest, a ring of cedar about eight feet wide. It was Thursday. This would be my home until Sunday.

That first afternoon, I prayed a lot for my family. As I prayed, I became more and more aware of my natural surroundings. I could sense bugs crawling on the edges of my peripheral vision, and I heard birds flying toward the trees.

I offered tobacco as I prayed for each person. I remembered the many times as a boy living on the reserve when my mom and Ndede sent me outside before a thunderstorm to put tobacco beneath a tree. They would tell me to ask the thunderbirds to take care of us. I cherished these memories of summer thunderstorms: the warm, wet smell in the air before the storm broke; the reddish hue of the sky that became more prominent during those moments; the perfect stillness that would descend for a few seconds before the first drops of water that would signal the beginning of the rain and I ran inside the house before the downpour was unleashed.

Now, from my perch, I watched the sun kiss the horizon and quickly set out of sight. The sky stayed light for a long time after the sun was gone. One by one, stars began to appear while the fading light from our nearest star became dimmer and dimmer.

As the sky grew dark, I thought of many nights spent stargazing with my parents. From the roof of our house in Onigaming, we would watch meteor showers. Ndede would point out constellations to me and share stories of wisdom that had been shared with him, always careful to acknowledge the name of the elder who had instructed him.

The next morning, I was awakened by approaching footsteps. I shook my head and wiped the sleep from my eyes. It was Rodney and two helpers arriving to check on me. He encouraged me to stay awake all night. "If you want to rest," he said, "try to do it during the day." After shooting the breeze a bit, they wished me well and left.

After their departure, I prayed and sang for what felt like an eternity. When I looked at the sky, I realized it was probably no more than ten o'clock in the morning.

I decided to visualize in my prayers what a day in the life of my loved ones was like. I would walk a mile in their moccasins.

I began with Dominik. Waking up in his mom's house, early in the morning. Watching the streets pass by the car window before being dropped off at daycare. Climbing the stairs with a low level of anxiety. Ringing the buzzer. Entering the room full of caregivers, the children who were already there turning to see who was at the door.

I walked through the rest of his day—the bus ride from the daycare to school, the school day, recesses, lunch break, a second bus ride back to daycare, the time there, being picked up, then his evening activities.

I opened my eyes and blinked a few times with a renewed appreciation for how hard it is to be a little kid. I offered some tobacco.

Then I visualized Bezh's day. I thought of his unique person- ality, more mischievous than his older brother's. The changing surroundings he encountered. The faces of the adults he interacted with. The children of all ages and backgrounds he met and played with. I pictured him lying in bed, watching his older brother sleep that night, knowing Bezh usually stayed up later than Dom.

I opened my eyes again. It was like a punch in the gut, the realization of how many other adults were helping to raise my children. Daycare workers, bus drivers, teachers, recess volunteers, and on and on. My sons spent time with these people, away from home, influenced by people who were instilling in them the values of mainstream culture.

Next, I imagined Lisa's day. Waking up alone in her house in Dauphin with only Guapo, her chihuahua, as company. Eating a quick snack and then heading to the clinic for work. I imagined what it would be like to assess patients, listen to them describe their symptoms, study their behaviour, and try to read between the lines to uncover other problems that may lurk beneath the surface. I pictured going through the exercise again and again for the forty or so patients Lisa might see on a busy day, followed by her extra-curriculars—teaching yoga, volunteering, mentoring. If I had fallen in love with her beauty, wisdom, and intellect, now I appreciated her work ethic.

I prayed for my mom and the life she was leading. Greeting the dark of early morning, smudging, and then feeding the dogs. Preparing meals for Ndede and putting them in the fridge to be reheated later. Riding the bus to work, which my sister and I had pestered her about, telling her to use their car to avoid the hour-plus commute on public transit. She had refused, arguing that Ndede needed his freedom. It didn't matter that he could no longer always drive himself where he needed to go. My mother's nature was extremely humble, even if it was at her own expense.

I visualized her days of meetings with First Nations leaders and government bureaucrats, doing all the research, policy-making, and proposal writing involved. After nine or ten hours of this,

Ndede would arrive to take us to dinner at Dessert Sinsations. There would be more work at home, writing proposals and marking papers for the university courses she teaches. And, of course, the demands of Ndede's illness interrupting the routine.

Finally, some time after midnight, I imagined her crawling under the covers in a darkened room, whispering prayers before drifting off to sleep, only to do it all again a few hours later. Which made me realize that I did not tell my mother I loved her nearly often enough. *Kiizhawenimin Nimaamaa.*

I pictured a day in Rome for my sister Shawon. Learning Italian, conducting research in ancient libraries, studying the works of the great Renaissance masters, communicating with her fiancé by video chat, butting heads with egotistical academics who sneered at her because she is a North American, an Indigenous person, a graduate student, a woman, or all of the above.

I prayed for my other sisters and all their kids, inhabiting their lives for a time as I thought of each of them. I opened my eyes to see a growing pile of tobacco on the rock in front of me. The sun had travelled a considerable distance across the sky. While praying with the pipe that morning had not taken much time at all, this exercise of carefully praying for my relatives' daily challenges had chewed through a large chunk of the day. It was now early evening and the light was beginning to change. The magic hour.

I thought of Ndede. It was time to walk a mile in his moccasins.

I envisaged waking each morning with the pain in my gut, the gnawing pain that could not be sated with food or subdued with pills. The growing ordeal that marked even the most monotonous daily routines. The car ride to the hospital. The squawk of an intercom. The wheelchairs.

I reach for the elevator button with thick, rugged fingers. The trip to the chemo ward. The familiar sharpness of the needle being inserted into my flesh. The waiting while the treatment is administered. The feeling of hunger and the need to eat, and not being allowed to. I want to eat, but I can't. I look at the other old men in the room and nod my head; they know what I'm going through.

I imagine the chemotherapy tingling. Maybe it is a combination of the effects of a narcotic and a low-level electrical current. It is dull at first. A soft rumble. I look over and see another patient mouthing words. I have taken my hearing aids out.

"What's that?" I ask, placing them back in my ears.

"You are making the sound of crickets," the man replies. He heard the alert the hearing aids sound when they are not in my ears.

I laugh and nod, closing my eyes and trying to ignore the feeling growing within me. Finally, I wander downstairs, where Shawon helps me find my way to the car. The sensation grows intense. The familiar sunlit side streets are lined with leafy green elm trees growing strong in the summer. The chemo is overtaking me. We pull into the driveway and I struggle to lift myself up out of the passenger seat. I hurry past the dog and stumble into the dark bedroom I left hours before. I feel as though I can barely make it, as though something is about to consume me, the same feeling you get as you rush to the bathroom just before you throw up. But there is no release, no vomiting, no catharsis. The feeling does not subside. It does not relent. It persists and it grows. The chemotherapy is working. It is killing the cancer cells. It is killing me as well.

Sleep will not come and give me reprieve. I try to read, but I cannot focus. I try to eat but cannot keep the food down. Instead,

I lie in darkness, alone with my thoughts. I know tomorrow will be worse.

I hear the door creak open.

"Hey, Ndede," Shawon whispers softly. "How are you?"

I tell her I am fine.

"Can I get you anything?"

"No."

"Did you eat?"

"No."

"Do you want to rest?"

"I want to go for a walk," I imagine saying. "I'll be ready in a few minutes."

She slides the door closed. I imagine sitting up, dizzy. I reach for my wool socks and dress slowly.

Soon we are on the highway heading east from the city toward the floodway, the massive channel Ndede helped dig almost fifty years ago.

We pull off the highway and drive down a dirt road, the tires kicking black mud up behind us. We stop on a hill overlooking the diverted river, which seems to stretch on forever.

This is where Shawon will let me off. I feel sick. A deep aching sickness that resonates in my bones.

"Are you going to be okay here, Ndede?" she asks.

"I'll be fine."

"You sure?"

"Everything's okay."

Everything is not okay. My body is betraying me. My medicine is hurting me. My family is reaching out to me, and all I want is to escape back to the land. I want to tell Shawon I love her, but something holds me back. Instead, that something pushes me out the door. I stand up with a hockey stick in my hand, a Canadian cane. The dogs bound out of the back seat of the car and I start walking. Then I imagine walking for three hours across the prairie landscape as the sun sets in the western sky.

I OPENED MY EYES. I was back in Agawa. I was back in my own body. It was nighttime.

Preparing for the night ahead of me, I moved with a slow pace, my thoughts calm and resolute. I saw my family for who they were. I was blessed to have them. All of them.

I loaded my pipe and smoked it. I prayed for my father. I prayed for my mother. I prayed for my sister. I prayed for my partner. I prayed for my sons. I prayed for my relatives. A night passed. Then another day passed.

The sun began to arc its way westward on the eve of my final night of fasting. I lit my pipe and prayed. Then I set it down, picked up my hand drum, and began to sing. I completed four repetitions of a song. I was pretty dry, but I finished. I sang another. Then another. And another. All while the sun sped toward the horizon.

Gichi Gaming was perfectly still, its surface had the smoothness of glass, the water mirroring the sky. When the wind picked up slightly, the glass began to undulate. The setting sun burned a furious orange, casting a red glow all around. The waves on the water caught brilliant reflections of the sky above, and the flashes of light on the crests formed a shining path toward the sun.

And my vision came to me. I did not hallucinate. I did not see angels or spirits rising up from the water. What I saw were things falling into place.

I saw the metaphor in front of me. The path of light stretching across the lake, reaching for the sun in the sky above. The sun was like the Creator, the goodness that exists in the universe. The waves in this inland ocean were like us, each rising into existence for a short time, then disappearing back into the expanse when our time is up. As we rise up, our lives can take different courses. We can turn away from the goodness in the sky above and reflect only darkness, or we can turn ourselves toward goodness and shine brilliantly, reflecting the light around us. Often, we alternate between the light and the dark, as I had earlier in my life.

We have a choice in life—we can choose how we are going to behave. We can determine whether we reflect the good around us or lose ourselves in the darkness.

Zhoomingwetaw. The Anishinaabemowin word entered my head as if spoken by someone nearby. It means "smile at him" or "smile at her."

I looked at the path of light in the water and considered the word. Then I repeated it to myself. *Zhoomingwetaw.*

Throughout my life, the Creator has smiled down on me. It began with my being born to such wonderful, loving parents. It continued with the gifts of good health, a good intellect, and good fortune. I was shown the strength of Indigenous cultures. I was given the chance to see the broader world, and to participate in it. I was gifted with two beautiful sons who helped me change my life immeasurably for the better. Now, a beautiful, talented woman was willing to put up with me. I remembered the challenges my relatives faced in their lives, and how they greeted all without complaint.

A tear traced a path down my cheek. All these gifts, and how did I respond? With a straight face. With anger. With dissatisfaction. I was not honouring the wealth of my good fortune. Until now.

Zhoomingwetaw. I spoke the word silently again. The Creator has always smiled upon me. I should do the same. I should be grateful. I should be happy. Yet even now, as I was seeing the beauty of life all around me, I was beating myself up. I laughed as I wiped the tear from my cheek.

I should turn myself toward the light, reflect the goodness that is all around me. I should walk that path. I thought of the Anishinaabemowin words "*waaseyaa miikanaa.*" "The path of light."

My heart swelled with gratitude and humility. I wept for the first time in what felt like a very, very long time. I smoked my pipe again and offered a prayer of thanksgiving.

Then I went to sleep and woke the next morning ready to head down the hill.

14

IT IS DIFFICULT, if not impossible, to communicate the ecstasy of a vision to someone who has not experienced it themselves. I discovered this when I returned to my normal life and tried to explain to Lisa and my parents what I had seen. They were supportive, but I could tell from their reactions that their lives were not about to be changed by what I had felt on that rock in Northeastern Ontario.

After a week or so, Ndede invited me to share my vision with him in more detail. The sun shone brightly through his living room windows that day as we prepared to smoke the pipe together. After lighting the pipe, I began to pray. When I finished my prayer, I looked across the room at my father. He was smiling, his eyes closed, listening. His face looked different without his glasses on.

I offered him the pipe. When he took it, our eyes met and the smile broadened. He sat back on the couch, made his invocation, and offered the pipe to the four directions, the earth, and the sky. Then he looked at me with kindness radiating in every direction. "Tell me what you saw," he said. "This is the right way to share your vision. With the pipe."

I told him what I had seen. I spoke about the first night in the tipi and dreaming of Crow Dog, the sand, the peyote, and the dog meat. I said I had prayed for Ndede and wanted him to be cured. Then I described the vision. I described the path of light I had seen stretching across the water toward the sun, the waves flickering in and out of it, and the goodness shining down from up above. "*Waaseyaa miikanaa*," I concluded.

"It's a good thing you did out there," Ndede responded. He was beaming with pride.

Things were changing. It was not often my father encouraged or congratulated me in such a way.

I thanked Ndede, and we put the pipe away. After I made him something to eat, he decided to lie down for a few hours before heading out for one of his long walks on the floodway.

OVER THE NEXT FEW WEEKS, our family settled into a number of routines. Some were geared toward helping my father, and we all became familiar with the diet recommended for him. Others were about improving the quality of life for both my parents. Shawon; her fiancé, Jesse; Diane; my mom; and I all pitched in. We cleaned the house thoroughly, repaired little things here and there, and Shawon and Jesse bought our parents a dishwasher.

I spent most days at my parents' home, carrying out various tasks, before picking up my sons from school or daycare and spending the evenings with them.

The change in my father's appearance was gradual but unmistakable. He used to wear baseball hats now and then, but now he wore one all the time, even indoors. He complained about the amount of hair that fell from his head each time he showered. He was self-conscious about the way he looked. I told him his hair loss was not noticeable, but soon it was.

The chemotherapy sapped his energy, slowing his gait. Through the first few rounds of treatment, he said it was not that bad. He persisted in his daily routines of teaching, errands, and exercise. But after a while it became clear that the treatment was hitting him hard. It seemed to be worse the second or third day after treatment. He did not complain. He just spent more time lying down each day, and slept less each night. Still, he continued his walks in the evenings, though some days, even if his heart told him to get up and walk, his body could not oblige.

"*Saabkeshi*," he said to me, sitting in his kitchen one evening. "That's the Anishinaabe word for cancer. It has to do with the shape of the tumour."

There, in the glowing yellow light, darkness outside the windows, I understood what he meant. *Saabkeshi*. Spider. It had been my first word, in any language. A growth with tendrils extending outward might resemble a spider. This term also tells an Ojibwe speaker that the thing is alive. It is animated. It is growing. It fits the fatalism that runs through Anishinaabe life.

Ndede continued his spiritual journey. He sought out medicine men to help him, and he attended mass at Kateri Tekakwitha Aboriginal Catholic Parish in Winnipeg's West End, an Indigenous congregation under the care of Archbishop Weisgerber.

My father may have been resigned to the fact that the spider was growing, but he would not give up without a fight. In his youth, the fights had been brawls and political spats. Now he waged a campaign using medical technology and prayer.

One day, pushing a lawn mower out of the garage while doing yard work for my parents, I noticed something on the asphalt driveway demanding my attention. Green shoots sprouted through a crack in the surface, and ants crawled back and forth across pine needles. I knelt to study them closely. Smiling, I realized I was happy. Perhaps it was the break from the pace I had maintained as a reporter over the past few years, or maybe it was the satisfaction of serving other people. Or it could just have been the simplicity of the routine I was settling into. Still, I was happy.

I seem condemned to make my most meaningful insights at the most mundane moments. Another vision. This time of a lawn mower.

IN MAY, I trekked through the traffic that separated Boston's Logan International Airport from Cambridge. My sister was about to receive her master's degree from Harvard. Shawon was actually working on her PhD, but because of Ndede's illness she decided to apply for a master's. That way, he could see her receive a piece of parchment from the best university on earth.

We met at a reception for graduate students who were attending the convocation. Inside a fancy white-walled ballroom beneath crystal chandeliers, Shawon and I picked at spring rolls and tiny sandwiches, cracking jokes about people around us. Just like old times.

After the reception, we took a selfie on the front steps of the building, Harvard banners draped behind us. Studying this picture today, it's clear I was totally overjoyed and proud of my sister. We were also quite sweaty. Then we went to meet our parents, who had arrived on a separate flight.

On the morning of the convocation, my parents and I were up early. We made our way to one of the staging areas while Shawon got her accreditations sorted out. She wore an academic gown with an Indigenous stole provided by the Harvard University Native American Program. Amid a heavy police presence, we wished her well and congratulated her again. She waved at us from the other side of a cast-iron fence, then moved on with her cohort, still wearing a big smile. I walked my parents to the entrance to their seating area, then I continued to my place in a viewing area further away.

As I watched the convocation ceremony, my little sister's enormous achievement really hit home. There she was, in a crowd of future world leaders, the best and brightest from around the globe. She had fought for a very long time to achieve this. I remembered the little girl I used to watch playing with her cousins on the reserve, and I recalled her tenacity, which was apparent from a young age. She would argue with our father even before she could walk. Everything she had accomplished over her journey to this moment was an undeniable testament to her intelligence, courage, and talent. I could feel a lump in my throat.

It was also a testament to the good job my parents had done in raising her, including all the work my mom had done to support and encourage her through her toughest times.

That night, we attended a dinner honouring Indigenous graduates from Harvard, held by the Native American Program. It was quite a sight to see twenty graduates from communities like mine being celebrated at such a pinnacle of academia. There were Lakota, Lummi, Mohawks, even Hawaiians and Maoris in attendance. There was, of course, our Anishinaabekwe as well. So many big, wide smiles. So many of our people celebrating. So many stories of overcoming odds to achieve success in medical, legal, and academic fields.

As I looked around at Shawon, Ndede, and others that night, it was apparent that things were getting better. A generation ago, education had been the tool of oppression used to hold us down. Now it was the tool of empowerment, and we were using it to lift ourselves up.

ONE DAY, on our way to school, Dom settled into a bad mood. He refused to leave my car and go to class. In the past, I might have forced him to go, but this time I decided to try something different. We walked Bezh to his class, then Dom and I gathered my camera and recording equipment and drove to his grandparents' house.

After visiting with Ndede for a while, we recorded some Anishinaabe teachings, preserving them in digital form so that Dom and Bezh and maybe their descendants would be able to hear the lessons directly from their *daankoobiitaagan*—their ancestor. Having Dom learn in a different kind of environment, one more culturally safe and less formal than the classroom, didn't hurt either.

I showed Dom the Record button, and demonstrated how to focus the camera. I checked the white balance and asked Dom what he thought would be a good background. When he chose a huge painting by Haudenosaunee artist R.G. Miller, we were ready. I gave Dom a pouch of tobacco and said, "*Miizh kidedenan.*" Without saying a word, he handed the tobacco to Ndede.

For the next few hours, Ndede held court on the subject of Anishinaabe names while Dom recorded every word and gesture. My father explained the etymology of the word *wiinzowin*, which means "name" in the Anishinaabe language. He recalled how he had been given the right to practise the name-giving ceremony, and explained the ceremony in great detail, including preparations to be made and the ceremonial clothing he was instructed to wear. Then he went on a more lengthy exploration of specific Anishinaabe names.

Throughout Ndede's talk, Dominik monitored the audio and video feeds, now and then making an adjustment to the focus. It was important for him to make this recording as high in quality as possible.

Someday, Dom will remember this moment. Perhaps he will remember the teachings. Or maybe he will just remember spending time with his grandpa. Either way, it will be a good memory.

We spent Father's Day at the Manitoba Marathon, where I ran my first full race. Lisa ran a half-marathon, and Dominik did the 2.6-mile Super Run with Shawon. It was a good day for a race. The only downside was that I had trained for only a few weeks, and once I hit Mile 20 my pace slowed considerably. Crossing the finish line, I grimaced. As Lisa and Ndede came up to congratulate me, I waved them off and hobbled away.

"He looks pretty mad," Lisa said to my dad.

"Well, he comes by it honestly," replied Ndede, referring to his own grim demeanour. They both laughed.

We spent the rest of the day eating, relaxing, and enjoying each other's company,

MY FATHER'S OWN MARATHON continued through rounds of chemotherapy. His physical stature had declined and his hair fell out entirely. I felt sorry for him when he removed his cap, revealing a smooth brown dome.

Yet through this time, his mood brightened. The permanent scowl he had joked about with Lisa disappeared, and an easy smile took its place. In the Ojibwe classes we held for kids, in the university courses he taught, and in the time he spent with us, he raised everyone's spirits.

Ndede continued his evening walks on the floodway. The river level had receded and the prairie grass had grown tall, more than waist high. He went out there as often as he could, a lone figure making his way across the land just as his ancestors had for generations before him. When he returned, he would laugh and tell me how the dogs he took with him would run ahead, leaving him alone. Now and then, one of the dogs, named Folsom, would come running back to check on him. Reassured that my father was still alive, Folsom would bound away again through the tall grass toward the water. A dog's intuition is remarkable.

Soon, we had another reason to celebrate. Shawon married Jesse, another Harvard PhD candidate, who had grown up in Florida and California. They had become engaged a year earlier, prompting Ndede to say, "I didn't know people still did that."

Shawon and Jesse had originally planned to marry in California in 2013, but due to my father's illness they decided to move the wedding up to the summer of 2012 and change the location to Winnipeg. It was another example of my sister making changes for Ndede's well-being. I admire her for that. She and Jesse scrambled to compress a year's worth of planning into a few short weeks, and in July things came together beautifully.

A day before the wedding, the two families gathered at Birds Hill Provincial Park, just north of Winnipeg. The picnic site was bordered on one side by forest and by open prairie on the other. Jesse's mother and her family arrived from California, and his father and family travelled north from Florida. My mom's sister, brother-in-law, niece, and nephew made the journey from Toronto. Ndede's brother Fred and the rest of our local crew rounded out the crowd.

As the sun sank low in the sky and the light grew long, Shawon and Jesse stood to thank their loved ones. Shawon took special care to highlight Ndede and praise him. Jesse in turn honoured his paternal grandmother, Wanda. Each was the oldest and most revered member of their respective clans.

The next day we took over Fort Gibraltar, the restored relic from the fur trade era that Shawon and Jesse had chosen as the venue for their wedding. Inside the great hall lay a beautifully restored room with wooden floors, antique chandeliers, and a giant stone fireplace.

With Uncle Fred officiating, and under the watchful eye of Ndede, we built an altar inside the hall, first setting a buffalo robe on the floor and placing a traditional drum, hanging from four staffs, onto it. We added a buffalo skull of Shawon's next to the drum, along with the eagle staff, cedar trees, sand, and ceremonial fabric.

When the sage was lit and the grand entry song was sung, Shawon made her entrance in a beautiful Vera Wang dress, her father by her side. She looked stunning. As the drum sounded and the traditional melody travelled through the air, they walked around the outside of the altar before entering the circle side by side. My sister walked down the aisle with her dad just the way she wanted it. A huge, sweet grin covered Ndede's face from cheek to cheek, and Shawon radiated beauty. They looked amazing together.

Jesse, dressed in a sharp navy-blue suit and adorned with a fresh lei, joined them in the circle, as did his best man, Riley, and Shawon's man of honour, David.

In Ojibwe, Uncle Fred delivered one of the best invocations I have ever heard. He described the union we were witnessing as an embodiment of the sacred precepts of love, kindness, sharing, respect, and humility. *Kiizhewaatiziwin* is the Anishinaabe word that captures these ideals.

Shawon and Jesse expressed their love for one another, then exchanged rings, each with a glimmer in their eyes. Jesse wiped away tears. Shawon brushed her cheek reflexively, though there were no tears there to wipe. She is definitely the descendant of a long line of stoic Anishinaabeg.

That night, we gathered in the south Osborne Street area of Winnipeg for the reception at a trendy bistro, Shawon's favourite restaurant in the city. Naked light bulbs hung from wires over neat table settings that contrasted with dark wooden floors. Lisa and I sat with my parents and Uncle Jimmy, the archbishop. Dominik and Bezh sat at the kids' table with their cousins from Toronto and Winnipeg.

After dinner in the main dining room, we offered a round of toasts. When it was my turn, I reminded everyone that before the recent adoption of the archbishop, Ndede had arranged for Phil Fontaine to adopt Jesse into his clan of Makwa, the bear. The message was simple, noting the patrilineal nature of our clan system. "He wants you to have kids!" I said. The crowd laughed and cheered for Shawon and Jesse. They will, of course, follow their own prerogative and decide for themselves if they ever want to start a family. Still, I never pass up a chance to tease them.

The newlyweds had their first dance together, launching the evening into party mode. The dance floor filled and kids ran around laughing at each other. When my mom tried to urge Ndede to dance with her, he refused. He must have been embarrassed. I hesitated for a second, then walked over and asked her to dance with me. She accepted, and halfway through the song Bezh came onto the dance floor, asking for a piggyback. With him on my shoulders, the three of us danced the night away.

When my father grew tired and he and my mother decided to leave, I walked them to the Buick and strapped Dom and Bezh into their booster seats. As they drove off into the warm summer night, the humid air seemed to amplify the vibrant colours being thrown off by the nearby street lights and awnings.

I watched the grey vehicle disappear into the distance, then walked back to the bistro. From the street I could hear the music playing inside.

15

WE WALKED down the dirt road just as we had so many years before. Grass grew between the two ruts pounded by vehicle traffic. Beyond the oak trees and tipis, I could see the outdoor kitchen. We stopped at a ceremonial altar in front of a beautiful canvas tipi and sat in beat-up folding chairs, the kind you see in the gyms of country schools.

A year had passed. The familiar scent was in the air, one I never smell anywhere else, a mixture of cedar, coals from burnt ironwood, and a tree sap indigenous to Mexico. It was good to be back at Crow Dog's Paradise, my home away from home.

Paradise is a plot of land on the Rosebud Reservation in southwestern South Dakota, home of the Sicangu Lakota people and the location of the sundance grounds where I made my original pledge as a teenager. I finished my first four-year sundance commitment there. It was the place I returned to after straying as a young man, and the place where I finished my second four-year commitment. I had pulled buffalo skulls there many times. I had been given a Lakota name there, and my son Dominik's Anishinaabe name came in a vision set there. This was also where my son Bezhigomiigwaan's name came from. I had been raised up as a traditional chief and finished my third four-year commitment there. *This place*, I thought, when I arrived, *has been the site of so many watershed moments in my life.*

We had come to Crow Dog's Paradise a few days earlier and made camp at a beautiful spot in the shade of tall oak trees. We spent the first few days setting up tents, digging outhouse pits, hanging a huge fifty-foot tarp from the trees overhead, and building the kitchen, with a barbecue, stoves, storage area, and dishwashing station. Now and then, we paused to greet an old friend or a relative walking by, and we would visit with them awhile. I would offer them a drink or something to eat, inviting them to sit down and enjoy a break from the sweltering August heat. On most days, the temperature approached forty degrees Celsius. We trimmed grass and rebuilt our sweat lodge. There was plenty of wood to cut and rocks to collect. Finally, my sons and I made a large firepit encircled by a sand turtle, the spiritual centre of our camp. Each night, for the better part of the next two weeks, we would gather around this fire, sharing teachings from the sacred way of life we were all committed to. We made and maintained the fire with the same care and attention we would offer a loved one.

"Keep the home fires burning," Chief Leonard Crow Dog would repeat, time and time again. And so we did. We kept it burning from the day we arrived until the day we left.

At Leonard's camp, Ndede and I sat across from the chief, who leaned back in a sturdy leather chair. My mom and Shawon, along with Lisa and our sons, sat to our left. Leonard's wife, Joann, joined him on his left. We exchanged pleasantries, and I offered gifts to Leonard and Joann. They nodded and thanked us.

The conversation soon shifted to my father's health. When Ndede explained his condition and the various treatment regimens he had been following for the past number of months, the mood became serious. He angled his face downward and looked over the frame of his glasses so that his eyes met Leonard's. It was his getting-down-to-business look.

As Leonard listened to my father, he nodded and looked off into the distance. Beads of sweat coated his face, and the deep creases in his dark-brown skin showed his age, yet he had few grey hairs. Both of his hands rested atop a walking stick, reminding me of Ken Dryden leaning on his hockey stick back in the goalkeeper's glory days. Leonard nodded more briskly as my father finished speaking.

"Mom … Mom," Leonard said, calling for his wife. It is a Lakota tradition to address family members according to their role, as in a father calling his wife "Mom" in front of the kids. "Get that medicine," he said to her. He said that he, Joann, and their helpers would prepare the root and call us back to their camp when it was ready. He said he would pray for my father's healing.

"Thank you," Ndede replied. "Thank you."

Each of us took turns shaking hands with Leonard, Joann, and the other relatives before making our way past the altar and back down the dusty trail toward our home fire. Others were setting up their camps. Soon, Crow Dog's Paradise would become a village with thousands of inhabitants. They all came to participate in the sundance, just days away.

We had a sweat that night. The medicine water was poured onto red-hot rocks, where it hissed and sizzled, enveloping us in a hot cloud of steam. We prayed and sang traditional songs. We opened the door three times. Then we had a feast of strawberries, blueberries, and Gatorade. After leaving the lodge, we visited around the fire until, one by one, we retired to our tents and went to sleep.

The next day was blazing hot. By mid-morning, the sun was high in the sky, scorching the earth, and the steady buzzing sound of thousands of cicadas throbbed in the air. Despite the heat, there was work to be done. Wood to be cut, piercing sticks to be sharpened, food to be made. Staying busy meant sweating all day long. My sons set up a concession stand where they sold candy, pop, and pickles to other children.

"How much is a pickle?" one child asked Dominik.

"Twenty dollars," Dominik replied with a straight face.

Later that day, while I sat in the shade with a cup of ice water, the PA system crackled and came to life. "*Hau*," a booming voice began in a Lakota accent. "Chief Peter from Canada. Chief Peter from Canada. Come over to the kitchen." The PA picked up another conversation for a moment before a loud click cut to radio silence. The buzz of the cicadas picked up again. The medicine was ready.

Five of us, including Ndede and my mother, made the pilgrimage back down the trail, through the pines, and toward Leonard's tipi. We found the members of Leonard's camp sitting in the nearby outdoor kitchen. We sat at one of the picnic tables in the large shaded area where three squares a day would be prepared and served to more than a hundred singers, security guards, and invited guests during the sundance.

I looked at the bare floor made of grey earth. I was anxious to hear what the medicine man had to say. After a few minutes, Leonard hobbled into the kitchen with his walking stick. He greeted us and sat down before calling one of his helpers. The helper reached up to a shelf in the kitchen and pulled down a piece of red cloth about eighteen inches wide, wrapped end over end. He handed it to Leonard.

Leonard carefully unwrapped the cloth to reveal the medicine inside and showed it to Ndede. He explained how to prepare and consume it. Ndede motioned for me to listen to Leonard's instructions. Perhaps he couldn't hear him clearly without his hearing aids. I leaned in and listened intently, staring at the floor to catch each detail.

I realized I was gazing at the same grey dirt floor I had seen in my vision at Agawa Rock three months earlier. When I looked up to study Leonard's face, he was looking at me while explaining the medicine and displaying it for us to see in his hand. Déjà vu. I snapped out of my memory as Leonard rewrapped the medicine and handed the bundle to Ndede, who gave it to my mom. We thanked Leonard, stood up, and walked back to our camp. I had seen part of my vision.

That night, we prepared the medicine according to the instructions and gave it to my father. He went to bed. He was awake all night.

The next day was Tree Day, the day we retrieve a large cotton-wood from the forest and plant it in the centre of the sundance circle. It takes the combined strength of hundreds of people to move such a thing. It is amazing how strong a little sapling can grow in the natural world. It is also amazing what you can do as a community.

Once our work was done, the tree stood in the arbour like a giant arm reaching for the sky, clenching a multicoloured bundle of cloth, prayer ties that each dancer had wrapped around the branches. The leaves shivered in the breeze, sounding like a thousand rattles. Ropes hung down and were gathered neatly near the tree's base. It was busy, it was chaotic, and it was beautiful.

The tree radiated life. It had come back to us for another year. The tree of life was reborn.

In the twilight that evening, with the campfire glowing, my father spoke about his condition. He said he was happy to be back for the ceremony we would begin in the morning and confessed that he was unsure if he should be hoping for a miracle or if any treatment might help him at all.

"Well, if anyone had a cure for cancer," I said, "they would be a billionaire." I paused and contemplated the flames in front of me before continuing. "Maybe the ceremony will make you feel stronger, though, and that will help you to beat this cancer."

Ndede nodded.

Not long after that I slipped into a dreamless sleep.

"SUNDANCERS! SUNDANCERS!" the PA system crackled when it sprang to life. "Sweat lodges are ready!"

The air in my tent was cold. It was dark outside. It was probably about four in the morning, but if you're keeping track of time at a sundance, you are missing the point.

I stared at the tent ceiling for a few moments, trying to decide if the emcee had really called us.

"Start lining up for the sweat lodges," the PA system bellowed in response.

I shook Lisa. She sighed. I kissed my sons, who were both still fast asleep, unzipped the tent door, and stepped out into the darkness.

It was time.

After a sweat, I lined up to enter the sundance arbour. There were now more than a hundred sundancers in their regalia, all of them ready. More were arriving every minute. I made my way down the line of chiefs, wishing each of them a good morning and shaking their hands. I could hear the inimitable laugh of my *hunka* brother, John Roy, snickering away at some joke he had made. This is the beautiful thing about Indigenous people. Even in our most solemn and sacred moments, we still like to laugh. We do not have a monopoly on humour—everyone likes to laugh—but I have yet to hear the Pope open a homily with a joke.

I asked the fire keepers to bring some coals and add cedar to them. As the medicine crackled and smoke circled in the air, I smudged my war bonnet before raising it to the sky, pointing it to the heavens. Lifting the bonnet and placing it on my head, I felt the feathers fall backward, some landing on my shoulders. A decade had passed since I had been given the headdress. I had come a long way.

Sundance leader Carter Camp stood in the centre of the circle, pushing a cane into the ground with each step. He began his oration. "Brothers and sisters, good morning ..."

It has been one of the great pleasures of my life to hear this man speak. He combined deep knowledge of the sundance way of life with an intimate understanding of the traditions of his own people, the Ponca. He had been a warrior in the American Indian Movement, participating in the 1973 occupation known as Wounded Knee II. Now, long after the dust had settled from those battles, he was still standing near the centre of spiritual power that had been fanned by the movement. He was shirtless, dressed in jeans, with an eagle whistle hanging from his neck.

He encouraged us to practise the ceremony in its purest form. "Use your eagle whistles," he would say. "Blow on them. When you do that, you are giving some of your moisture. That's the sacrifice you are here to make as sundancers."

Leonard walked into the circle, followed by his wife, Joann, and a few others. After greeting us, he spoke of visions he'd had that year and the challenges he had faced. He mentioned things happening in Indigenous communities that concerned him. Then he belted out a Lakota song. When he finished he called out, "*Hoka hey!*"

A giant sundance leader named Merle repeated, "*Hoka!*"

The sound of hundreds of eagle whistles rose from the crowd, each tuned to a slightly different pitch. The effect was of an eerie dissonance, though somehow not jarring to the ear. The hairs on the back of my neck stood up. *The time is now, the feeling is back, we are heading into the ceremonial place again*, I thought.

On the south side of the arbour, someone slammed a stick into a big drum. A thunderous sound emanated from the hide wrapped around the wooden ring, the singers started a drum roll and began to sing. We were off. Leonard, Joann, and the other leaders led us out, followed by the chiefs and the sundancers.

All along our path to the sundance arbour, people smiled, waved, and nodded as we passed. Many were young children and a few were elders, some in wheelchairs. My heart swells with pride every time I see the lengths to which people go to return to the sundance. One more time. That was the attitude that drew my father back that year, even while chemotherapy battered his physical being. No matter the toll he had to pay, the cancer would not conquer his spirit.

I turned back to inspect the line of sundancers trailing us, and there he was, dressed in a ribbon shirt, baseball cap, slacks, and moccasins. Ndede ambled toward me, smiling and nodding at the other dancers as he passed them. I offered him the spot in front of me, but he shook his head and took his place behind me. I saw hope glimmer in his eyes. He had made it back. Once a sundancer, always a sundancer.

After an hour of dancing in the circle, I looked to my right to study him again. He wore a huge smile on his face, and his shoulders swayed from side to side as he lifted his feet. It was not quite the two-step he had done when he was younger, but he still kept the rhythm.

A young cedar woman made her way down the line of chiefs, smudging each of them. As she came to my father, she scattered more cedar onto the coals in the can she carried. Smoke rose up, and Ndede bent from the waist. Holding his medallion and eagle whistle to his chest so they would not be burned, he inhaled deeply. As the medicine worked its way through his body, a look of bliss spread across his face. Then he stood upright again, opened his eyes, and fell back into the rhythm of the song.

Soon after, the sky turned white at a spot above the trees, paving the way for the sun's return. Its brilliant rays peeked over the treetops and bathed us in their warm glow. As the pure, bright light spread above the pines, Ndede said, "This is my favourite part of the sundance, seeing the sun rise overtop of the trees." He had told me the same thing each morning we had danced together here, going back some fifteen years. When the sun came into full view, the dancers let out a large cheer, with war whoops, ululations, and eagle whistles.

I looked around the circle. The ceremony was in full swing. Leonard stood with Joann, each swaying in harmony with the other, keeping pace with the beat. The leaders danced together, occasionally breaking off to straighten a line of dancers or rearrange some other element of the formation. That is how it went for most of the first day.

At about 4:30 the next morning, the sequence repeated itself, the dancers fasting all the while.

The hunger itself does not bother you much. It's the thirst that is a challenge. The lack of water drives your mind to distraction, in some cases even further. When I was a teenager, I found the thirst insufferable. The days without water seemed endless. Now that I was older, I could manage it better, but several times a day I would tell Lisa or Shawon the real vision I was secretly questing for was a large plastic cup filled with ice and cherry cola.

On the second day, the piercing ceremonies begin.

My niece Melissa, Darryl's daughter, decided to go first. After she and the others who would pierce that day were marked with ochre, the leaders called out, "*Hoka!*" and the round began. Melissa was ready. At a buffalo robe, she placed two ebony pegs in her mouth, each the size of a man's pinky finger. Merle studied the horseshoes painted on her arms before using a piece of sage to wipe them off.

"She's my niece," I told Junior, the cut man, and he nodded to me. Junior is an excellent cut man. He cuts deeply and with control for some, and very thinly and delicately for others. He is a real medicine man, raised in the sundance circle and gifted with a ceremonial altar at a young age. He is also eye candy for just about every woman at the sundance.

As my niece stared into the distance, Junior peeled back the sterile packaging enclosing a surgical scalpel. He raised the blade to the sky. Gripping the side of Melissa's biceps, he slid the scalpel through the layers of her skin and out again about half an inch away. Then carefully, sliding the blade upward, but not outward, he created an opening in her flesh large enough for Merle to slide the ebony peg through. Junior and Merle switched sides and repeated the process on Melissa's other arm. As the blade passed through her skin again, she pursed her lips and blew through them, as if letting off steam.

When Junior and Merle finished, Melissa shook their hands and thanked them. Then she turned to hug her daughter Zoe, a beautiful young girl with blond hair who almost shares a birthday with Dominik. They were born less than forty-eight hours apart. Junior placed the cap back on the scalpel and handed it to me. I shook his and Merle's hands and thanked them.

We circled the arbour again, and two of us led Melissa to a lineup on the west side, gripping her by the sage bracelets wrapped around her wrists. The sun shone brightly, heating everything in sight. The sound of thousands of cicadas pulsed continuously from every direction. The PA system blasted the voices of the singers and the beat of their drum as they sang a piercing song. The unmistakable smell of cedar and coals cut through the air. We were in that sacred place.

Crow Dog's Paradise is, of course, a sacred place in a very literal sense. But during the height of the ceremony everything comes together in a certain way, stimulating your senses, exhausting your normal mode of being, and drawing on a deep spiritual reservoir you may not even know you own. That is when something magical happens. Paradise becomes a different sort of place, not like the places we usually inhabit, but somewhere rarely visited. It is not necessarily a physical transformation, more like a change in perception. This is perhaps why Leonard and others refer to the sundance as the "centre of the centre of the universe." The ecstatic heights were coloured by song, smudge, spirit, and sun. That was the place we were in now. That sacred place.

When Melissa came to the head of the line, I took her rope harness from her and fastened it to a much longer rope leading to a fork in the cottonwood tree. On the other side of the tree, the rope led down to Chief Marvin Swallow, who sat upon Bocephus, a legendary horse. Bocephus had helped thousands of dancers pierce over the years. He never trampled on anyone, despite running around the crowded sundance arbour hundreds of times. He could dance to the beat of the drum, prancing in time to the

music and circling in spot when he passed a gate, just as human
sundancers did. On this day, he was painted beautifully with
handprints and other designs, with a circle around one eye.

I looped the harness around each of the pegs in Melissa's arms
and nodded to the man keeping watch on the rope. Two of us held
Melissa by her arms and braced ourselves in case she was dragged
forward. She leaned back slightly with an eagle whistle in her
mouth, eyes fixed on the tree.

The man watching the rope raised an eagle-feather fan high in
the air. On the other side of the tree, Marvin wrapped the rope
around his saddle horn and snapped Bocephus's reins. The horse
took off with a jolt.

The pegs broke through Melissa's skin and went flying forward
with her harness. The man guarding the rope caught them in
mid-air and handed them back to us. Melissa turned to kiss her
daughter. Then she circled the arbour once more before heading to
the tree of life.

At the tree, I removed the cap from the scalpel and studied
Melissa's cuts. They were deep. I cut away the little pieces of flesh
that remained and placed them into a small piece of broadcloth
she held in her hands. I congratulated her as she turned to hug first
her sister and then Ndede and other relatives who supported her.
Some fanned her with eagle feathers. Others wiped tears from her
eyes. All spoke kind words to her, lifting her and praising her spirit.

Melissa has lived through her share of challenges. Never having
had the chance to know her father, Darryl, she became the head of
her own household at a very young age, the de facto parent raising
her younger brothers and sisters. On days like this, you could see
how that challenging road had forged within her an exceptional
strength. She went through the entire piercing ceremony with the
same grim, stoic expression we all inherited from Ndede.

When she finished speaking to her supporters, we returned to our places in line. Melissa walked to the tree to leave her flesh offerings. Her lips moved silently, speaking words known only to her and the Creator. Moments like this would be repeated throughout the day before we retired for the evening.

This is what the sundance ceremony is all about. We sacrifice a piece of ourselves to back up our prayers with action, showing that we want good things for our friends and relatives more than we want comfort for ourselves. It is a beautiful thing. If you came to the circle to see for yourself, you would understand the power of this ceremony.

I WAS TRAVELLING through the skies when the voice of a Native American Church singer cut through my sleep and I woke from my dream. The singer's voice traced a haunting tune that reached out from the PA system and across Crow Dog's Paradise. He had probably left a peyote meeting in one of the tipis to sing for us, which meant it was a few hours before dawn, time to wake up for the third day of the sundance.

On this morning, my new brother-in-law, Jesse, chose to pierce his chest from the tree. As we do with many of our non-Indigenous relatives, Ndede had teased Jesse that he would have to shave his chest before piercing. I had also shared with him a teaching that dancers were supposed to pierce from the tree for their first four years, unless a vision told them otherwise. That he listened to this instruction revealed to me something about him: he was a soldier. I had learned this the year before, on the second day of his first sundance.

It had been pouring rain and was brutally cold that day, and we sat shivering during one of the breaks. The first day had been exceptionally hot. The heat had wiped out other dancers from our family, and all of them had stayed at the camp, leaving just myself, my adopted brother Gyles, and Jesse in the circle. Jesse had covered himself in a plastic garbage bag with a hole through it for his head. He had a defeated look on his face, but he'd refused to quit. I thought, *This is a good man, worthy of my sister.*

A year later, we found ourselves supporting Jesse, whose pierced chest was now connected to the tree by a long sisal rope. Soon the rope was taut and he began to dance, eyes fixed on the tobacco ties and branches in the sky before him. Shawon fanned him with an eagle wing. He prayed. Others in our family danced behind him. He walked to the tree, a friend coiling the rope beside him so that he would not get tangled. Jesse did this over and over again.

One of these times, with the rope taut, someone passed his mother, Gina, an eagle wing and told her to tap the rope with it. The idea is to support the dancer in a spiritual way, by touching the rope and lending him some of your power, but also to help him in a practical way, by expanding the piercing a bit and making it easier for them to break. Gina is a petite, polite medical doctor from the San Francisco Bay Area, so everyone was shocked when she grabbed the eagle wing and slammed it into Jesse's rope as hard as she could, over and over again. The rest of the family smiled and exchanged glances with one another, not wanting to laugh at her. Still, we would talk about it for years to come.

Finally, after praying to the tree four times, Jesse ran backward, pulling his shoulders back as he reached the end of the rope and breaking his skin. The pegs and rope went flying toward the tree. He hugged Shawon and they shared some words with one another at the tree. After he thanked our family members who had come to support him, we went back in line and concluded the round.

DURING THE SUNDANCE, my father had been speaking to members of the Native American Church, seeking help on his healing journey. The NAC combines traditional Indigenous spirituality—the tipi, the peyote, the fire—with some of the iconography and teachings from Christianity. The result is both unique and beautiful. It is at once both contemporary, a product of the post–Indian Wars era, and also a part of a very ancient tradition that stretches back thousands of years to those peyote gardens near Real de Catorce, Mexico. Many relatives and friends at the sundance are members of the NAC, and they are among the kindest, most respectful, family-oriented people you could meet. It is not our path. Still, something about it spoke to Ndede. Perhaps it was the beauty of the music and its melodies, or the way it fused the Indigenous and Christian traditions he had wrestled with all his life. He often mused about getting more involved in their ceremonies. Today would be that day.

Late in the afternoon, as the light shifted from the intensely bright sunshine of midday to the halcyon tones of late afternoon, Chief Dwayne Shields, a leader in the NAC, took the microphone and called my father and our family to the centre of the circle. Wearing a sundance skirt and no shirt, with a ceremonial robe draped over his shoulders, Dwayne was the very picture of a traditional man. The sharp features in his face harkened back to classic images of his Dakota ancestors. He spoke seriously, with the conviction of someone who has no need to impress onlookers, yet his voice and steady manner communicated a certain compassion and kindness. He laced his speech with expressions such as "respectfully," "at this time," and "forgive me," showing us his humility even as he took centre stage and led us in prayer.

Our family followed Ndede into the circle, each of us spinning in a clockwise direction as we passed through the western gate.

Dwayne directed Ndede to the western side of the tree and a little to the north. We sat behind the old man. Four generations of our family were seated on the grass, supporting the one we loved so much, the one who now suffered so greatly.

Dwayne's helpers prepared their sacred items at a spot to the west of the tree. Onto a bed of sage they brought a water drum, a rattle, and a staff beaded with the DayGlo colours of the NAC.

Dwayne held an eagle fan in his hand and called for cedar. When he asked Ndede to come forward, my father rose slowly and walked to him. Chief Shields placed cedar on the coals in a coffee can and shook the can until smoke began to pour out. He fanned the smudge toward my father and said a blessing, alternating between Lakota and English. He asked Tunkasila— the Creator—to help Ndede find health. He appealed to the Holy Father to heal my family's earthly patriarch. There were no divisions between the words of different faiths. Each expressed the same truth.

I sat on the ground looking up at my father—looking up at him for the first time in a long time. The sun drew lower in the sky and shadows crept across half his body. He extended his arms like a child ready to be lifted by his parent, his chin turned up ever so slightly. The breeze rose and blew cedar smoke across his body. For a moment, he was a man on fire, a silhouette in a billowing cloud of smoke as Dwayne fanned him down. Chief Shields prayed for him in a gentle, humble way, and the arbour fell silent save for the pulsating buzz of cicadas.

Dwayne walked to his helpers and knelt on the ground facing Ndede. When his helper struck the water drum and fell into the quick rhythm of the NAC, Dwayne closed his eyes, lowered his head slightly, and matched the drum's pace with his rattle. He began to chant. *"Ya wa noy, we ya no, hi niy yo wa ..."*

He repeated these vocables a few times, then began to sing. What emerged from his mouth was like light cast through a prism, creating a rainbow of colour. It was the most beautiful bittersweet melody I had ever heard. The entire experience of heartbreak, loss, and redemption that each of us had walked in our lives was summed up in the tones of his song, which he unlocked with the medicine.

Chief Shields's helpers joined in the song. Some matched his tone directly, others fell into harmony. Emotion washed over Ndede and our family. Other NAC members stood up in the shade of the arbour. Recognizing the song, they walked into the circle and sat behind Dwayne and his helpers. First there were five. Then ten. Then twenty. Then fifty. They all sang as one, a joyous wall of sound. Chief Shields concluded the song. The drummer tipped the drum quickly. The water sloshed around inside and the tone of the instrument shifted down sharply. Dwayne began another song and his people followed his lead.

Tones of happiness, gratitude, and prayer ascended from the dozens of peyote singers gathered in the circle to support my father. Cedar smoke continued to blow through the air and the sun burned our skin. My cheeks tightened. A lump appeared in my throat. I closed my eyes and prayed for Ndede.

The beauty of the dying day overcame me, this outpouring of support for a man many of the singers barely knew. Still, they wanted him to live, and were doing what they could to lift him up and make him well. They sang four songs for him. When they concluded and the drum was sounded for the last time, our family exchanged looks. What could we say? Our Native American Church brothers and sisters walk in beauty.

Chief Shields concluded the ceremony with a few remarks and shook hands with Ndede. My father took the microphone to thank him both in Anishinaabemowin and English. When Ndede was finished, Dwayne stepped forward and gave him a peyote button. It was small and plump, covered with a thin layer of translucent skin beneath which the rich forest green of the cellulose was visible. My father held it in his open palm.

I stared at the peyote button in his outstretched hand while my mind raced back to the hand holding a piece of peyote from my dream on Agawa Rock. I focused on the button, furrowing my brow, as if concentrating on it would make the meaning of this moment more apparent. We left the circle to sit down for a few minutes before the next prayer round began.

I held out hope that there would be a miraculous cure for my father, that he might live to see another year after this, his seventy-sixth. Perhaps all of this prayer would accomplish the impossible. Perhaps he would be the outlier, part of that small percentage of people who become victors over pancreatic cancer. He had already beaten the odds by living this long. He was a fighter. And he was fighting it with everything he had.

But maybe we don't get the miracles we ask for.

In the next prayer round, I danced next to a chief named Alberto from Colombia. With our feet moving, we spoke a few words together. I told him where we were from, and he told me he had just started a sundance near Bogotá. He also told me his own father had been stricken with cancer.

"We did some ceremonies like you just did for your father," he said in a Spanish accent. "We prayed for him, we honoured him, and we asked for healing." After pausing, he continued. "He passed away a little while later. But it was good that we did the ceremony. It gave him a chance to put things in order. It put him at ease, and it helped him on his journey."

I looked ahead and kept dancing.

When the day was over, we went to our sweats. I visited my sons before putting them to bed, then spoke to my parents briefly. I told my mother I loved her, "*Kiizhawaynimin Nimaamaa*," as I hugged and kissed her. Then I walked to my father, seated beside the campfire. "*Kiizhawaynimin Ndede.*" I leaned down to hug him. He was smaller than before. Something tugged at the corners of my mouth. I thought of those times we had not expressed our love for one another. The times we had not hugged each other or told one another how we felt. What a waste. I kissed him on the head, patted him softly on the back, and went to bed.

THE FOURTH DAY OF THE SUNDANCE began like the others, with sweats, prayer, and piercing rounds. Then came the ceremonies that set this day apart. The naming ceremonies. The water ceremony. And the clowns.

Late in the day, after almost everyone had pierced and we were relaxing in the shade, the drummers began to beat a loud drum roll. I turned to see a group of *heyookas* emerging from the sweat lodge area carrying a large pot turned black by the fire. The *heyookas* are the thunder dreamers, the clowns of the sundance. They dance in funny ways and have an extraordinary spiritual power.

Not wanting to reveal much about their ceremony due to its sacred nature, I can say that one *heyooka* made a beeline for Ndede and presented him with a very unique kind of medicine, one that might be described in other settings as dog meat. At first, my father objected, saying, "I may want healing, but I'm not desperate. I'm not going to eat dog meat."

"It's not dog meat," I said. "It's medicine."

When Ndede took the flesh, I knew it was the final omen from Agawa Rock.

Ndede turned to me with a serious look on his face.

"Eat it," I said.

He did not budge. He held it in his hand.

As the *heyookas* left, my father and I followed them. He still held the medicine in his hands. We walked to the sweat lodge area, where we saw the *heyookas* eating the remainder of the contents of the pot. Ndede walked up and showed one of them the meat in his hands.

"*Minopwaagad*," a large *heyooka* replied. It was odd to hear someone saying, "It tastes good" in Anishinaabemowin while in Lakota territory. This trickster was from Canada.

After speaking in Ojibwe for a while, Ndede headed back to the shade. I walked over to Junebug, Leonard's son. Bug is a long-time friend and a mentor when it comes to the sundance. I told him of the dream I'd had on Agawa Rock, that I had seen his father, the grey dirt floor, the peyote, and the dog meat. I said I had now seen all four omens over the past four days. He nodded his head and shook my hand.

"Dreams come true," I said to him.

He shook his head. "No, visions come true," he corrected me. He stared intently into my eyes, making sure I understood the message.

Walking back to the circle, I saw a line of chiefs being marked by one of the leaders. It was our time to pierce.

There is a Lakota adage that the chief should be the poorest member in his community. He should be poor because he gives everything away to help his people. We chiefs honour this belief by putting ourselves last at the ceremony, allowing all the others to finish their prayers ahead of us. Only after the other sundancers have gone do we do our sacrifices.

I walked to the leader, turned, and offered him my back. "Skulls," I said softly. I could feel his thumb make four quick strokes with the ochre paint. The round began shortly after that.

Though I was thirsty and hot, I felt a slight cold sweat. Nerves. *Best not to dwell on these feelings*, I reminded myself. I learned long ago at the sundance that if something frightens you, it is best to walk straight toward it and get it over with.

Entering the circle, I lifted my knees higher and bobbed my head and shoulders to the rhythm. Time to dance hard. Time to get to that sacred place.

When it was time, I walked to the buffalo robe. I put my ebony pegs in my mouth, wetted them with my saliva, and stepped forward. "Make it count," I said to Junior.

Ndede told me, when I was a boy, that he did not see any point in trying to make an easy thing out of piercing. It is supposed to be hard, so you might as well get cut deep. That was how he saw it.

I turned away from Junior. I felt the warm buffalo fur beneath my feet once again. Someone rubbed my back and grabbed a handful of flesh. Then came that familiar feeling. Stinging and burning, followed by openness as the scalpel passed through my flesh. I could feel the blade finding the other side of my back from beneath the surface. I could feel Merle push the peg into the opening, twisting it along the way. Then I could feel the peg embedded in my back, blood trickling down toward my waist.

I prayed for my father, I prayed for my sons, I prayed for my mother, I prayed for Lisa. I felt the scalpel go in the other side; I felt it find its way through the skin and emerge again. I felt the peg being pushed through and spun. I felt the blood dripping down. I sensed the air in the cuts; I could taste it. The metallic taste of blood you get when you have a bleeding nose. The elders say that when you are cut, you are fresh and open to everything around you, vulnerable to the spirit world.

Walking to the row of eagle staffs, I pulled my family's staff from the ground and put the bonnet on my head. The feathers, ribbons, and ermine skins rubbed the cuts and the pegs in my back. I walked to the western gate and waited my turn. Words escaped me, but in my heart and in my mind were the ones I came to pray for.

When it was my turn, I stepped into the lane that circles the arbour. They asked how many skulls I wanted to pull. "All of them," I said. They told me there were twelve. I nodded. They finished tying the buffalo skulls to each other with sisal, and I knelt beside each one, speaking to them. Then I walked to the front of the train of skulls and stood facing away from them. An experienced sundancer hooked my harness to the skulls and looped it around the pegs in my back.

"*Hoka!*" he called.

I raised my hand to the tree, then lowered it and walked slowly forward, testing the length of the rope. It tightened. The skulls resisted. Driving the eagle staff into the ground, I leaned forward. My skin stretched. The pegs were pulled back by the skulls. The skin did not break. Instead, the skulls began to move. They were heavy. I dug my feet into the ground and used the staff to keep moving. It is better to keep going than to stop once the skulls start moving, even if it hurts. Besides, it is supposed to hurt.

One step. Two steps. Ten steps. Fifty steps. A hundred. Soon, we were at the northern gate of the arbour. I stopped and faced the tree, as I had been instructed to do on the first time around the circle.

After praying for Ndede, my sons, and family, I stepped forward, leaned in, and began to pull the skulls once more. The rope tightened, my skin stretched, and the skulls moved. The sun shone brilliantly down on the earth ahead of me. I passed over some ruts in the earth. A few steps later, I felt the skulls dig into the ruts and pull me backward. I fought to keep moving. Supporters urged me on. I made it to the eastern gate. I stood and prayed to the tree.

Starting again, I passed the southeast side of the arbour. With each step I took, I could hear the drum grow louder. I reached the singers, the female backup singers standing behind them. At the southern gate I stopped to pray to the tree again.

Here we go, I thought. *Home stretch.* Leaning forward again, I began pulling the skulls back toward the western gate, where I had started my circuit. Here, on the southwest side, were more ruts. Again the skulls became difficult to pull.

At the west gate, they checked the harness and tightened the loops around my pegs. Sweat dripped from under the war bonnet and trickled down my face. It was hot. I took deep breaths of air. I could use this rest. The next time around would be made without any interruption.

After a few seconds, and without warning the others, I took off, doing my best to run. The skulls were too heavy for me to actually run, but I managed to surprise some supporters, including one who kept the train of buffalo skulls in a curved line behind me. Without him, the skulls cut through the circle and crashed into two buffalo headdresses on the northwest side of the arbour. The headdresses and their stands fell to the ground. The buffalo dancers to whom they belonged stared at me in disbelief. I would offer them gifts to make amends.

"Somebody watch the skulls!" I yelled behind me.

Junebug came over and told me to calm down. "Focus on your prayers, brother," he said. He was right. I should not be angry. I was not in that sacred place.

When the skulls, ropes, and ceremonial items were untangled, the dragging began again. Around the circle, passing the ruts on the northeast side, the supporters on the southeast, the drum on the south, the people on the southwest, and we were at the west side again. Two times around.

I inhaled deeply and bent over, leaning on the eagle staff. It's amazing how much sweat your body can produce, even when it is dehydrated. Ndede came forward with an eagle wing. He fanned my face. He lifted the bonnet's feathers and fanned my back. He fanned my neck. He nodded and smiled at me.

Pray hard.

Time to pull the skulls again. This time, supporters rose and let out war whoops and ululations. Chills ran down my spine. Jesse and the others shouted encouragement. Their words were distant. My legs were burning. The pain in my back had faded. The nerve endings were dying, or maybe I was going to that sacred place.

Exhaustion.

Heavy breathing.

Push forward.

My father stood in front of me at the east gate and asked me to stop. I shook my head and told him to move. He obliged and we went on, feet digging into the ground, staff propelling me forward, leaning almost horizontal to wrest the skulls onward. Approaching the south gate, I could see the elders in their chairs, shouting encouragement. On the southwest side I slowed, exhausted. The skulls grew heavier. I told myself to keep walking. With about twenty feet left to go, it was time to pick up the pace. At the west gate, I heaved a loud sigh.

Ndede, Lisa, Jesse, Shawon, and others fanned me while I struggled to catch my breath, standing bent at the waist. When they asked if I wanted to continue, I nodded. A moment later, I stood up. As I leaned forward, the rope tightened. I took a step. Now we were in that sacred place again. Our vision focused through a narrow tunnel, seeing only the path that lay ahead.

Shouting. War whoops. Shrill cries. People all around. The drum. Heavy legs. Skin stretched. Pain. The sun shining on trampled grass. The ruts. Forward. Keep moving forward.

The relatives were there. Even those who weren't. You were there with me too in that moment.

There was no more *you*, there was no more *me*. There was no more *Indian*, there was no more *white*. There was no more *woman*, there was no more *man*. There was nothing left. All that remained was unified.

We were in that sacred place, travelling around the circle, making our way around the northeast, southeast, and southwest sides of the arbour.

This must be what the Lakota mean when they say, "*Mitakuye oyasin*"—"We are all related." In that sacred place, we are all together, and we are all the same.

No thoughts. No words. No ego.

Only emotion, prayer, and love.

The tunnel showed ten more feet. *Ten more feet, and that will be four times around. Dig your feet into the ground. Finish what you started.*

We made it.

Now there was really nothing.

Gasping for air, I looked to the sky, searching. Hands on my hips. Sweat running down my face and back. Did I have the strength to break the skin on my back? I felt sorry for myself. Amazing how quickly the ego returns. These thoughts rushed to fill the vacuum in my mind.

Shawon stepped forward. My little sister fanned me for a moment, then began to speak.

"What?" At first I could not understand.

"Broddy," she said, looking deep into my eyes, "Ndede goes to chemotherapy. Then he comes home and goes for a walk. Three hours a night at the floodway. Imagine what he feels like when he's out there. Imagine what he feels like right now. Imagine how badly he wants to live. He hasn't given up. He is fighting."

As she spoke, the other dancers were seating children, including Dom and Bezh, on the skulls behind me.

"This is nothing," she said. "What you're feeling right now is nothing compared to what Ndede is going though. Show him we are walking this path with him. Do it for him."

Tears welled up inside me. I looked at my younger sister, then closed my eyes and prayed for our father.

Open your eyes. Take a step. Then another. Now sprint.

The rope tightens immediately. It stays taut. *Drive your shoulders forward. Push your feet into the ground. All of your strength …* and then snap! My skin broke. The pegs flew out. A cheer rose up. I ran around the circle and then to the tree.

Our ceremony was complete.

Every year, we return to the sundance with very specific prayers. That year, we asked for Ndede to be well again. That was the reason our relatives pierced. That was the reason my mother ran the camp. That was the reason I dragged skulls. We offered our sacrifices and asked that my father be healed. But the sundance is not a transaction. Your prayers and your sacrifices will be answered, though perhaps not in the way you expect. None of us can ever know what the Creator has in store. Yet maybe, if we return to that circle and that sacred place, we might begin to understand what this existence looks like through the Creator's eyes.

16

I SPENT A FEW WEEKS after the sundance readjusting to non-Indigenous life, helping my parents and caring for my children. Then it was time to head out for more speaking engagements and music gigs.

My travels took me over emerald waters to Cape Breton. Landing in Sydney, I was greeted by Chief Leroy Denny of the Eskasoni First Nation, the largest First Nations community in Nova Scotia. The chief introduced me to his brothers Dion and Wally. Wally was an RCMP officer, and as they spoke I was struck by their grasp of the Mi'kmaq language. Our languages are related, but the speed at which they strung together long sentences in their native tongue left my head spinning, and I doubted I could ever catch on.

I soon learned that this knowledge of Mi'kmaq was not confined to their family or their generation, which was even more impressive. I heard the language spoken everywhere in Eskasoni, by young and old alike. Even toddlers knew their language.

When I asked the chief how they had managed to hang on to the language so well, he said, "I think it's because we're isolated compared to the other communities." I found this hard to believe. They were bordered by neighbouring towns and were just forty minutes from the city of Sydney. Then he added, "We've also tried really hard to teach the young. We have an immersion school."

That was it. In Eskasoni, they had managed to cultivate an attitude that celebrated their language, using Facebook pages and YouTube videos, all in Mi'kmaq. One family had overdubbed the animated film *Chicken Run* in Mi'kmaq, produced DVDs of this version, and sold copies at twenty dollars each. It proved a popular Christmas gift and they had to make multiple runs of the discs.

Mi'kmaq was the first language used at their public events, something I discovered when I co-emceed a night of entertainment in the community with a teenage girl who had just been named Miss Eskasoni. She conducted all her hosting duties in Mi'kmaq and had the audience in stitches. This made me feel something of a third wheel that night, but I gladly played the role in order to study a First Nation relatively close to an urban centre that boasted a high level of language retention.

The community also had a deep Catholic faith. Sitting at Wally's house one day over a plate of mussels and salmon, we talked about the upcoming canonization of Kateri Tekakwitha. It would be the first time the Vatican declared an Indigenous North American a saint.

"I'm going to go. Are you?" I asked.

"Oh, yes," Wally said. "We are taking a big delegation. There might be fifty people from Eskasoni headed there."

I had long wondered about the role of the Church in Indigenous communities, given the history of colonization and the residential schools. Missionaries were the tip of the spear when it came to accessing our lands and disrupting our traditions. Yet it became clear to me that the Church had helped Wally become who he was: a Mountie, a family man, and a practitioner of Mi'kmaq culture. That was undoubtedly a good thing.

My partner in crime for a good chunk of my time in Eskasoni was Wally's brother Dion, who took me for a drive one afternoon to a trailer on the west side of the reserve. "This is where I work," he said as we pulled into the approach. "This is the Eskasoni Crisis Centre. We run a suicide hotline here."

When a rash of suicides erupted in the community several years earlier, Eskasoni had scrambled to respond, resulting in the establishment of this centre. The need for this kind of rapid response is too common in many of our communities. The First Nations youth suicide rate is five to six times the national average, and the rate for Inuit youth is even higher—about eleven times the national average. Suicide is a leading cause of death for young Indigenous people, and no one is able to explain it completely. Part of the cause has to do with learned behaviours and dysfunction, most notably from the residential school experience. I saw that play out in my own family. Generations were raised by strangers, and in some cases abusers. When those generations came home and started families, they treated us, their children, as they had been treated in those institutions. I know Ndede pushed Darryl away when the young man confessed to contemplating suicide not from a lack of love but because my dad did not know how to express the love he felt in his heart. My father was raised by people who didn't love him, and he was punished when he showed any vulnerability. And so the pathology is transmitted to a new generation. That void, that hole in our spirits that should be filled by love, is instead filled for too many young people by partying, violence, and other forms of destructive self-medication. Part of the problem is also a result of the ongoing inequitable treatment of our peoples. Mental health issues in particular are exacerbated by the lack of access to health care in many First Nations, Métis, and Inuit communities.

The problem is made worse by the loss of culture and language. Research conducted by two prominent academics, Doctors Chris Lalonde and Michael Chandler, showed that culture, language, and self-determination acted as hedges against suicide among First Nations communities in British Columbia. Simply put, where communities speak their ancestral tongues, practise their traditional culture, and determine their own destinies, they do not have suicide. We should be shouting this from rooftops.

Yet I know from my own experience that culture alone is not a silver bullet. Close relatives and good friends have taken their own lives even though they were exposed to Indigenous culture. In Eskasoni, they had their language, but still they needed to deal with suicide.

Another part of the problem is the lack of jobs. Job creation is no silver bullet either, but going to work each day provides structure, discipline, and a little more meaning to life. It offers an answer to those who ask themselves, "What am I doing here?" Well, you are cleaning floors, you are working in an office, you are filleting fish, or fulfilling some other worthwhile role. It may not be the most profound answer, but it is a start. You are contributing to your family, your community, and the world to some extent.

And then there's the question of limited horizons. It is difficult to understand how my fellow community members in Onigaming can feel like harming themselves when they are surrounded by stunning scenery a mere twenty-minute boat ride away in any direction. How could there be hopelessness in God's country? Unfortunately, some of our people focus only on the houses, the roads, and the highways that make up their community. They have forgotten how to live on the land. We can blame the Indian Act's restrictive policies for cultivating this tunnel vision, but it seems unlikely that legislative change alone will solve the problem.

Turning the tide of the suicide epidemic will mean fixing everything, not just one individual thing. It will involve bringing meaning and identity to our people through language, culture, work, and a connection to the land. It will also require equal access to education, employment, and mental health services. We also need to have justice for land and resources.

Walking into the crisis centre trailer with Dion that day, I saw the same type of office furnishings and desktop computers I had seen in countless reserve offices over the years. Dion introduced me to a young staff member, who took us to the back of the office and showed us the servers while Dion explained the novel approach they had taken.

The Eskasoni Crisis Centre had been started as a helpline for community members to call whenever they felt like harming themselves. The problem, of course, is that not everyone about to hurt themselves calls for help. So Dion and the crisis centre staff turned to social media. Whenever they saw a post that suggested the writer was considering self-harm, they would jump in a car and drive to see that person, talk to him or her, and refer them to an additional support service if they needed it. With the centre staffed twenty-four hours a day, this made a real change. At the time I visited, Eskasoni had not lost a young person to suicide in a couple of years. Sadly, this has since changed, but the community is still fighting for its young people.

IN LATE SEPTEMBER, I was back in Southern Ontario to deliver a lecture in Peterborough. Things started well enough, with some five hundred students and teachers from the area packed into a downtown theatre. An elder opened with a prayer, followed by remarks from the chiefs of two nearby First Nations and a powwow demonstration with dancers and singers. The crowd watched, displayed a super-positive attitude, and cheered with enthusiasm.

Then it was my turn. I stepped into the spotlight, introduced myself, and told a few jokes. About twenty minutes into my talk, I raised the subject of residential schools by acknowledging it was important for all of us to understand the issue and the impact that history has had on us. "None of us in this room is personally responsible for residential schools," I said. That's when I saw the tall, lean frame of the elder who had led us in prayer stand up, walk briskly up the aisle, swing open the door, and leave for the lobby. I went on as though nothing had happened. "Still, we need to learn this history, and work to make things right today."

The sight of the elder storming off threw me for a moment. After about half an hour, I wrapped up my talk and left the stage.

The elder was waiting for me in the wings to confront me. We were in the low light of backstage, but I could see he had his fists clenched and his feet positioned in a fighting stance. He started tearing a strip off me, stepping forward and leaning his face to within inches of mine.

When someone approaches me like this, I am no longer a public figure or the good Anishinaabe who respects his elders. The man may have been a quarter century older than me, but without thinking I squared my shoulders to face him, set my own feet in place, and leaned in too so he could sense I was not about to give an inch.

"Who the fuck are you to be telling these kids they are not responsible for residential schools?" he began.

"Were any of them alive when residential schools were created?" I said.

Instead of answering, he said, "Who the fuck are you? What the fuck do you know about it, huh?

"I was raised by a residential school survivor," I said. "My relatives went to residential schools. I know how bad it was."

"Yeah, but what do you know?" he spat at me. He brought his fist up to my face and pointed at it, showing me a curved scar that cut a path on the back of his hand. "Do you see this?" he said. "Do you see this? What do you know about getting beaten by a teacher when you're a kid? Have you ever been hit or abused in school?"

I thought back to the times I had been choked by a teacher and other authority figures and stared grim-faced back at him.

The elder kept pointing at the scar and berating me for suggesting that reconciliation was about more than atoning for the sins of the father.

We argued for maybe ten minutes, cranking up the heat the whole while. Finally, we were surrounded by organizers and dignitaries who could read our body language.

In the end, I was not successful at changing the man's attitude. I was unconvinced that my comments merited rage, but I had to admit that his anger was contagious. When I told him I wanted to pick up the conversation after we both had time to reflect, he walked away while I was in mid-sentence.

I turned toward the others, feeling a rush of adrenaline. Their comments, a mishmash of consolations and encouragement, were unintelligible at that moment. As nice as their words were, they didn't really help, and for the rest of the day I felt the hangover of guilt and shame that follows a conflict.

This encounter was a powerful reminder of how painful the residential school experience remains for many people. No amount of logic, no amount of persuasion, no amount of being "right" will ever be adequate for some people. Like the government apology, it will never be enough for everyone, considering all the pain that was wrought on our people.

I learned a few things that day. I learned to tread lightly when discussing residential schools, and to be damn sure you are prepared to help people if you dig up something from their pasts.

Some people have been able to find healing. Others have not. It is not my place to offer forgiveness on their behalf. I can only share my feelings about the path that I have walked.

17

THROUGHOUT THAT AUTUMN, we built memories with Ndede.

On Labour Day weekend, as the changing leaves ushered in the twilight of summer, we headed to Onigaming to rebuild our sweat lodge. In Ndede's Buick and Lisa's SUV, we drove along the winding, tree-lined gravel road leading to the "Old Reserve," a settlement on the Aulneau Peninsula we know as Shabashkaang.

With willow saplings in view of the road, we pulled to a stop. The two dogs, Folsom and Caravaggio, co-signed the decision, barking and panting. When the doors opened, they bolted, and a few minutes later they came back soaked and dripping with water. The gift of the Labrador.

I took out a pouch of tobacco and passed it to my sons and to Lisa. Each took a pinch without asking and offered it as a gift to the living beings we were about to take from the forest. Mom and Ndede made their own offerings, saying a short prayer in Anishinaabemowin before placing some tobacco on the ground near the willow trees.

With an axe in hand, I cut down the saplings. I showed the boys the type of trees we were after, and told them to feel the bark and remember the shape and colour of the leaves. They soon figured out the difference between the willows and other young trees around us.

In the soft light of the overcast day, I witnessed a scene I had seen play out many times before, watching different generations together on the land practising our way of life. Ndede lifted his cap to wipe sweat off his brow, revealing the short fluffy hair of a man recovering from chemo. My mom picked flowers and medicinal plants. The two boys reminded us we were all being pushed forward into new roles that had previously been occupied by those who came before. It felt good to be in the woods that day.

Our friends Doug Sinclair and Kathy Jack arrived with their grandsons, who were Dom's and Bezh's ages. With all hands on deck, we set to work building the new lodge.

As I split the jack pine, my sons asked to help. Bezh had a miniature axe he had bought earlier that year, and I told them to go ahead. Before he could take a wild swing, I positioned Bezh closer to the log, practised the movement of the swing with him, then stepped back and let him go to work. He chopped at the log four or five times before he looked up at me.

"Are you tired, Bezhie?" I asked, knowing the answer. He nodded. I repeated the exercise with Dominik. He took a few more swings than his younger brother, but then he slowed and I asked him to take a break.

"No sense getting tired," I said. "That's when you get hurt."

The boys sat on nearby logs and watched me split the rest of the wood. This is the way I was raised—supervised by my parents but also trusted by them to do serious work. Rez life and country living offer that kind of freedom, a freedom that helps you build a work ethic.

Bezhie, Dominik, and I built a crib of logs for the rocks. We placed the rocks—the grandfathers—in a pattern that represented the shell of a turtle. Studying the stone turtle, I recalled Ndede giving me the same teachings. I would look at him with reverence as he instructed me in the symbolism our people invest in every aspect of our ceremonies. My mom and dad sat on the deck of the house nearby, watching the traditions they had shared with me being passed on to their grandchildren.

Finally, we covered the crib and rocks with split wood and lit a match.

One of the other teachings my father passed on to me was that the sweat lodge ceremony is not just about the sweat itself but also about the preparation, including the visiting that happens before-hand and the feast and conversations that take place afterward. They are part of the ceremony as well. He told me not to just drive up to a sweat and jump in, then afterward take off.

I saw this play out that day. Doug was tending the fire with a pitchfork in hand, and Mom was walking back and forth from the shack to the house, carrying medicine water and other things for the ceremony. Meanwhile, Lisa was playing with Bezh, swinging him around by his feet while I helped Dom make kindling. My friend Makwa and his mom, Baatiins, were sitting with Kathy, helping her break the tips off cedar boughs so we could use this medicine in our ceremony.

Surveying all of this was Ndede. Gripping each armrest of his campaign chair, he watched us with a grin on his face. Occasionally, he would turn to Doug and say something in Ojibwe. Doug would snap back with a dirty joke. The women would laugh and join in. Lisa and Bezh giggled as they played, and Dominik, true to his nature, worked up a sweat. It was a wonderful moment of late-summer Anishinaabe life. Then the sun began to set.

As twilight descended, the snaps and pops of the fire slowed and the logs turned to coals. We entered the lodge.

My father spoke to us, then offered tobacco and cedar to the fire. He walked back into the shack holding a towel around his waist. Kicking off his shoes, he lowered himself to the ground so he could crawl into the sweat. We are supposed to humble ourselves as we enter the lodge, crawling on our hands and knees. His legs were skinny. He had lost a lot of weight the past year.

When we were all inside the sweat, Doug brought in the first seven rocks, glowing red from the heat of the fire. The sacred items were passed in, and then my father spoke, saying, "*Kiba'an ishkwaandem!*"

Doug obliged and closed the door, patting the tarps down at the base to make sure no light came in.

For a moment, there was silence. The sweltering heat radiated from the rocks. I heard a rustle, the sound of a spark, and the lodge was illuminated by the flicker of a match. Ndede lit his pipe and the ceremony began.

He made eloquent invocations in Anishinaabemowin before switching to English to explain his words. He led us in songs, scooping medicine water from a copper pail and pouring it onto the grandfathers and grandmothers. The water exploded on contact with the rocks, hissing furiously. I prayed.

By the time the fourth round came a few hours later, the grandfathers had made it very hot. I rocked back and forth in place, feeling the need to stretch my legs, though I knew I could not; there were hot rocks a foot or so in front of me. I could tell the others in the lodge were getting as antsy as I was. Through all of this, the two old-school Anishinaabekweg, Kathy and Baatiins, remained stoic. When it was their turn to pray, I could hear from their voices that they were sitting up straight and completely still. They prayed slowly and free of anxiety. When the door was opened at the end of the fourth round and light came in, I could see both of them, sitting on one hip with legs to the side, just as they had been at the start of the ceremony. The strength of Anishinaabe women.

Doug passed drinking water and berries into the lodge. Ndede offered some to the grandfathers and grandmothers, and soon the sweet smell of burning berries filled the air. When he passed the bowl to me, I grabbed a small handful and passed it on to the left. The berries tasted sweet and felt cold, welcome sensations after the sweat.

Finally, Ndede turned onto his knees and crawled out of the lodge. No one else moved for a time. We sat reflecting on the power of the ceremony we had just gone through.

When Kathy said in Anishinaabemowin she appreciated the chance to hear my dad pray, the chance to soak up his mastery of the Ojibwe language, we nodded silently. Baatiins offered a testimony to the power of the teachings he had shared with us, and we sat together sharing another moment of reflection, listening to the grandfathers and grandmothers hiss softly in the darkness. It would be the last time any of us would sweat with my father.

After the sweat, we went inside for a feast of wild rice, chicken, pies, bannock, and other food. We sat and ate, talking well into the night. The conversation was full of stories, jokes, puns, and teasing. Big laughs rang out and filled the living room. An old incandescent bulb cast everything in a warm glow. The stark night outside the windows seemed to push us all closer to one another.

"*Nitaa anishinaabemo.*" Kathy spoke of me to her husband, Doug, telling him I could speak Ojibwe. While I still felt I had a long way to go in learning the language, it was true that I had greatly improved my ability to speak my mother tongue. Over the summer, my father and I had begun to work on a database of Anishinaabe verbs. Actions are where our language really comes to life. At one point, Anishinaabemowin was listed in *Guinness World Records* for having the most verb forms of any language.

Initially, we thought our work could be published as a book. However, after some thought, I decided that an app would reach a broader audience, especially younger people, who are key to the future of our tongue.

Compiling the database, we would choose a verb and then run through its various forms, documenting how the prefixes and suffixes would change, depending on who was doing the action and who was being acted upon. "*Ni-waabam-aa*," for example, means "I see him/her," but "*Gi-waabam-ig*" means "He/she sees you." In both cases, the root verb *waabam* stays constant. Since the Ojibwe language is very regular in this sense—meaning it does not have too many exceptions to the rules—it really lends itself to automation and hence computer programming.

Ndede and I would often become sidetracked in discussions of the origins of a word, or in recounting some story associated with that word, and these conversations were some of the most amusing times we spent working together.

Through the summer and early fall, I spent many nights with Ndede, sitting at his kitchen table reviewing the database. Leaning forward in his chair, he would furrow his brow as he scanned an Anishinaabe word and the English sentence provided as a translation. He would repeat it to himself a few times and then either nod his approval or offer a correction. Now and then, we would take a break when my mom or Lisa walked through the room. More often than not, these breaks meant a chance to eat some pie.

My ability to speak Anishinaabemowin improved dramatically. Growing up, I had been self-conscious about speaking the language around my father, knowing I would be instantly corrected if I said the wrong thing. That fear was gone. Now, when I arrived at his house, our pleasantries would be in Ojibwe.

"*Shigo?*"

"*Gaawiin Gego, giin dash?*"

"*Nimino'ayaa.*"

And on from there.

By late September, I had a working prototype of the app, designed with the help of a developer I contracted online. I had done well with my public speaking gigs that year, so I paid the developer out of my own pocket. Ndede encouraged me to find funding, but I shrugged the idea off. It was important to me, and I could afford it, so I should pay for it myself.

When I handed him a tablet with a beta version of the app running on it, he studied it for a few minutes. "If … you … argue …" he said, swiping his fingers across the screen. "Translate," he said, touching the screen. "*Giishpin giikaawidaman,*" he read through his bifocals.

A smile broke across his face.

He swiped some more and read a few other translations. "This is awesome," he said, turning to me. "This is going to help the language reach young people."

He turned his chair so he could put his feet up on a nearby bench and settled in for a more in-depth review that lasted for hours. I found this amazing, because I could not recall ever seeing him sit at a computer in the past. Yet here he was, taking a belated step into cyberspace.

These were good memories of a father and son working together on a project we both loved. Some parents and kids work on a car together, or map out their family tree. Ndede and I developed a piece of software for an Indigenous language. That was our thing.

There is a dimension to this project that was bigger than just the two of us. My father succeeded in compiling a thorough database of many Ojibwe verbs, the first time they had ever been documented together in one place in all their various conjugated forms. It was an important contribution to our language's future. Part of Ndede's achievement on the nights we spent working on the project was to give us a very beautiful gift. He was leaving a legacy.

The work extended into the classroom, where we continued our after-school Anishinaabe language program. We brought in more science lessons, including ones that dealt with biology, astronomy, chemistry, and engineering concepts, all taught in the Anishinaabe language. Ndede contributed enormously with translations and by attending classes and sharing in the teachings.

There were a few rough patches, caused by the sad truth that some Indigenous people would rather tear one another down than lift each other up.

Some elders criticized me for teaching Anishinaabemowin. Their beef was that I was not 100 percent fluent in the language. My response was that, with a language in decline, we did not have the luxury of waiting for perfect language teachers to come along. Instead, each of us should do our best to spread the knowledge we had.

One of these elders challenged me in front of the class. I had named animals to be used in a classroom game, and when I reached the bald eagle I used its Anishinaabe word, saying "*migizi.*"

The elder, his arms crossed, spoke up to correct me. "No, that's wrong," he said. "It's *giniw.*"

I might have let it slide, but I knew he was mistaken. After all, my last name is Kinew, the same as *giniw*, so I was certain it meant golden eagle. "*Giniw* is golden eagle," I shot back. "*Migizi* is bald eagle."

"No," he said, "*giniw* is bald eagle."

I replied, "*Migizi*."

"*Giniw!*"

The rest of the class grew silent. We went back and forth in this uninspired argument until I turned to Ndede, the elder with seniority in the room, and asked his opinion.

My father was so furious he looked like he wanted to explode. Instead, he simply said, "It's *migizi*."

"Right," I said. "*Miigis* is the white shell, and the bald eagle has the white head. So there's a connection. *Miigis, migizi*."

I began listing other animals but could feel the elder's eyes burning a hole through me.

That night, while I drove Ndede home, we talked for a time before he mentioned the incident. "Listen, don't worry about those people," he said. "Don't worry about the 'culture police.' They didn't teach the kids the language. You did that. This is the only time these kids have ever heard their language. And you gave it to them."

His words meant a lot to me. Ndede had always been hard on us growing up, not in an abusive way but in the way of a demanding parent. This was one of only a few times that he offered me legitimate, unconditional praise.

We moved on, continuing to enjoy the time we had meant to spend together since I was a boy.

IN MID-OCTOBER, Ndede called for another ceremony involving a non-Anishinaabe person. This was a pipe ceremony honouring Dr. Lloyd Axworthy, the former minister of foreign affairs. Both my father and I worked with Lloyd when he served as president of the University of Winnipeg. During his ten years at the helm of the school, Lloyd dramatically remade it, growing its physical footprint and transforming it into a force for urban renewal in Winnipeg's downtown. A big part of this involved supporting Indigenous people, both on the academic and the student sides. Lloyd, of course, had been present at my father's adoption of the archbishop.

In recognition of his role, Ndede gave Lloyd a pipe, a high honour in the Anishinaabe community. I received my pipe as a result of a vision I had when I was a young boy, and have carried and feasted the pipe ever since. For others, the pipe comes as a result of sundancing. Here, it came in recognition of service in the community.

On the day of the ceremony, Ndede conducted things from a distance. He invited former national chief Phil Fontaine, Grand Chief Derek Nepinak, regional chief Bill Traverse, and other First Nations leaders to attend. It was both a personal gesture and a desire to have witnesses in the Anishinaabe community affirm the legitimacy of the presentation. Uncle Fred, who ran the ceremony, asked me to be the *oshkaabewis*, or spiritual helper.

We gathered in Convocation Hall, a large circular room on the university campus. In the late-autumn evening, the room was bathed in light from the setting sun. The chiefs wore their headdresses. Ndede, Lloyd, Fred, and I sat in a circle on a buffalo robe around an altar. About two hundred members of the Indigenous and business communities sat in plastic chairs. There was a buzz in the air.

The opening steps were familiar to me—the thunderbird pipe song, the invocation, the lighting of the pipe, the orations by each participant, and explanations of their roles. We were in that ceremonial place again.

When the pipe was presented to Lloyd, he appeared nervous, yet I knew he relished the experience. After the pipe was given to him, it was taken back, offered a second time, then taken back again. It was offered a third time, and taken back once more. Finally, on the fourth gesture of offering the pipe to Lloyd, he was allowed to accept it. It is the way we offer our pipes when sharing them with visitors to the sundance. It was a holy moment. When Lloyd accepted the pipe, I let out a loud war cry to celebrate. He laughed nervously. The chiefs did not flinch.

In the giveaway that followed, gifts were distributed to everyone in attendance. A giveaway song came next, and everyone was asked to dance with their gifts. I had fun pointing out to everyone in attendance that even our Mennonite brothers and sisters had joined in the dance. The crowd laughed, and some business leaders from that community would tease me later. All in all, it was a good, if politically incorrect, moment.

On our way to a restaurant afterward, Ndede told me his intent behind the ceremony, an indication of what he wanted me to do in the future. "Share our ceremonies with these business people," he said. "Let them see the beauty of our ways. Help them understand who we are."

Not everyone in attendance that night would have understood the symbolism and depth in the ceremony they witnessed. But I know that everyone who participated absorbed the sights, sounds, and smells of traditional Anishinaabe culture.

I imagine they left feeling pretty good, too.

18

STREET LAMPS SHONE on the cobblestone streets as we walked toward the basilica. A giant obelisk towered in front of us. We walked past it, getting closer to the massive marble structure looming ahead of us. We had made it to Rome.

My father wore a brown-and-blue-checked shirt, a brown blazer, and brown slacks. He wore his slacks a little higher now that his waist was thinning. His hair had grown back, and he had an air of calmness and happiness about him as he walked, chewing on *wiike*, a traditional medicine. My mother and Shawon walked next to him, conversing with each other. Shawon was dressed in black, with a bright pink-striped scarf. My mom wore a black dress with a thin brown hipster belt and an orange coat, her favourite colour.

The sound of our footsteps was swallowed by noise from a steady stream of pilgrims. Many looked as you might expect in a typical Catholic congregation here, with elderly nuns and priests among them. Others, however, made it apparent that we were headed to something more than a typical Catholic ceremony. They had brown skin and wore beadwork and cowboy hats. This was not your average mass in Rome.

We had all come for the canonization of St. Kateri Tekakwitha, soon to be made the first Indigenous North American saint of the Roman Catholic Church.

We entered St. John Lateran's Archbasilica. I am told that if St. Peter's Basilica is the father of all churches, then this basilica is the mother. We scanned the room for familiar faces. A cardinal came to shake hands with Ndede. They had met during the 2009 visit with the Pope. "You've lost weight," the cardinal said in a Québécois accent. "I should follow you?" he added, attempting a joke. My father laughed and the two men continued their small talk.

More Indigenous people entered the room, wearing Pendleton jackets and traditional regalia. I greeted some people from home, including Carolyn Bruyere. She had been taken to a residential school as a young girl. After we joked a bit in Anishinaabe, I asked why she wanted to come here.

She answered, "*Gaa pi gagwejimigoowaan gaa gichi-wii-piizhaayaan. 'Eya, ninga ezhaad. Ninga gichi-jiikendam ji-piizhaayaan anishinaa mii ganabaj awe nitam' ndinaa ngoozis, 'Awe nitam ganabaj Anishinaabe gaa-wii-Canonize-awiiyin' ndinaa.*" When her son had asked about the trip, she told me, she had replied that she was going because she would be overjoyed to witness the first Anishinaabe person to be canonized.

A smile broke across my face when I heard her appropriate the word *canonize*, conjugating it as an Anishinaabe verb would be.

I would later appreciate that scene: a residential school survivor and the offspring of another conversing in Anishinaabemowin in the heart of the same religion responsible for running most of the residential schools in Canada.

The mass that night featured a video retelling of Kateri's life, including the smallpox she suffered in childhood that left her permanently scarred, her conversion to Catholicism, and her refusal to renounce her faith under pressure. The film then described her life after death: the way in which miracles attributed to her warranted her beatification in 1980 and, now, her canonization, including details about the final miracle involving a young boy named Jake Finkbonner from Washington State.

In 2006, the boy was diagnosed with necrotizing fasciitis, commonly referred to as flesh-eating disease. He was hospitalized and the church community rallied behind him.

Jake was in the crowd, and I watched him while this portion of the video was played. His scars were visible, just like Kateri's. His mother was wiping tears from her eyes.

I turned back to the film. The broad community of Indigenous Catholics, searching for a way to elevate Kateri, became involved. Prayer groups calling themselves Kateri Circles gathered across the continent to appeal to the Blessed Tekakwitha to intercede. They held hands, they prayed, and they read from the Bible. They sang traditional songs with hand drums and rattles. Their prayers were answered when young Jake survived. The video ended and I saw members of the audience wiping their eyes and blowing their noses. I could feel their emotion fill the room.

I felt compassion and inspiration, but I did not make the leap of faith others had. I must have a cold heart.

The cynic, or perhaps the realist, in me has a tough time believing in miracles. If you follow enough people with terminal diagnoses, eventually one of them will undergo a seemingly miraculous recovery. Statistics tell us they are the outliers at the far end of the bell curve. This doesn't require divine intervention. Still, if this boy could be an outlier, why not Ndede? He had already outlived his prognosis. He was already part of that long tail on the bell curve that plotted survival time for people with cancer like his.

On one side of the crowd, I saw a Native priest and two helpers wearing vestments adorned with traditional beadwork. On the other side, three nuns stood in their own version of traditional regalia, wearing stark black and white. Above it all hung an image of Jesus, crucified and bleeding from a cut on his ribs.

We were in a holy place. Some things reminded me of the sundance: the reverence, the suffering, the goodness. Yet it was also very different. The elevation of the holy men above the rest of the participants was evident, and the riches held by the Church were on display. And the stories of sacrifice were read from a book rather than re-enacted in ceremony.

There was something good in this way, but it was not my way. I like to feel the blade of the knife and stand on the same level as the one leading the ceremony. I prefer to hold a giveaway rather than pass a collection plate.

Perhaps the Church is a glimpse into the future if our ways get set down on paper. Some of our traditional languages are becoming like Latin, known only to the holy men and women and used only in a ceremonial context. But if we go that route, we will lose some of the beauty of our ways—the freedom, the vitality, the visceral power.

This way was good. But our way is good too, in a different way. I am not sure the Church agrees.

In the film about Kateri, a priest explained the concept of "acculturation," the religious doctrine that allows for a Catholic to smudge or for a statue of a saint to be dressed in peyote vestments. In this view, the Indigenous culture is merely a host for Catholicism. The priest called our culture a "prism" through which the "truth" of the gospel is revealed. This was not the interpretation of the canonization's significance I would hear from my father and others the next day. To them, it was about the freedom to continue practising their traditional spiritualities while it simultaneously lifted the veil of racism in the Church that had cast a shadow over their attempts to also practise the Christian tradition.

The movie faded to black. The crowd rose to its feet and gave a standing ovation. The Finkbonners hugged one another. And the mass began.

A lilting melody wove its way through the massive halls of the archbasilica as a priest led a beautiful hymn in French and a procession of bishops, priests, and cardinals, including the top members of the Catholic Church in Canada, made their way to the front of the altar. There they were smudged by an Indigenous priest. The women who had smudged the hall earlier were not allowed to take part in this portion of the service. Prayers and speeches followed, and the mass was finished.

When the audience rose to its feet, I could see smiles on many faces. The Finkbonners were swarmed. Young and old alike approached Jake and his mother, asking them to pose for photos while Jake's father stood off to the side, smiling.

Ndede stepped forward and patted Jake on the shoulder. When Jake turned, Ndede said, "Can you hug me? I have cancer."

"Aww, I'm sorry," said Jake. My dad leaned to hug the boy. Something subtle yet unmistakable in the way he moved his hands during this embrace reminded me how much weight Ndede had lost.

"Keep in mind we'll be praying for you," Jake said as they ended the hug.

"I'll pray for you too," Ndede said, switching to the "bro shake" known across Indian Country.

They posed for a photo, and the crowd moved in to surround the boy.

Jesse, fresh off a plane, met us and we found a restaurant nearby to enjoy good food and company for the rest of the night.

The next day, we woke to an absolutely beautiful morning. The sky was clear and the air already warm. We cabbed it down to St. Peter's Square, and the closer we got to the Vatican, the more the traffic thickened. The square was still half empty when we arrived, but it was quickly changing as the steady stream of people walking toward us became a torrent. Shawon and Jesse walked ahead, past a long row of satellite trucks. I turned and pointed my camera at my mother and father.

Ndede and my mom smiled back at me. My father put his arm around my mother's shoulders and they waited with expressions of teenage lovebirds while I snapped a few photos. As I put the camera away, my father turned to my mother, leaned down, and kissed her.

My parents were never ones for public displays of affection, but this moment became frozen in time for me. There they were: the Anishinaabe man, dressed in a blazer and slacks, skinnier and a little slower than he once was, hugging his wife and planting a kiss on her lips; the blond-haired, blue-eyed woman with her eyes closed, receiving his love and kissing him back; the sun rising above the buildings behind them, bathing them in a shower of light and grace and spilling down onto the soft grey faces of the bricks beneath their feet.

They had been through a lot together. They had lost some of their closest loved ones and celebrated some of their greatest joys. One had hurt the other and been forgiven. They had raised many children together, plus nieces and nephews as well. None of this mattered at the moment. It was all in the past. No one knew what awaited them in the future, but that didn't matter either. What mattered was that they were here together now. In love.

Then they smiled, laughed, and walked past me.

In the few minutes it took us to walk to the security fence, the square filled and we were in the midst of a crush of people. I dropped my shoulders and placed my arm around my parents, trying to keep people from pushing them as they worked their way to the front.

The slow crawl became a standstill as police officers searched bags, patted people down, and checked for tickets. We all had tickets for assigned seats, but it became clear that the seating section was full and the officers were turning people away.

As I stood behind my parents with my arms folded in front of me, I could feel someone pushing against my back, trying desperately to squeeze by me. Not wanting to cede my spot, I made sure this person could not move me, but he kept trying to force his way by, even placing two hands on my triceps and attempting to push me out of the way. I held my position. This person scraped their sternum against my elbow trying to squeeze through the non-existent space between me and the person to my right.

"You're hurting my chest!" the usurper cried with exaggerated urgency.

"Well, quit forcing your chest into my elbow," I shot back. I turned to see that the pushy one was a non-Native priest about fifty years old leading a group of Filipino tourists.

"You're hurting my chest," he repeated. He grappled with my elbow, still trying to get around me.

"You know today is supposed to be a celebration?" I asked, with as much condescension as I could muster. He continued to push as I added, "Today is a good day. You should be happy."

The priest said something under his breath and changed direction, leading his flock to another entry point further down the fence.

The Creator must have been laughing at both of us in that moment, seeing the Catholic and the Anishinaabe, neither in his finest hour. I guess we all have a lot to learn about living the good life—*mino-pimaadiziying*.

After my parents found seats, I went off to look for a different spot from which to take photos.

The canonization ceremony began. Church bells sounded from St. Peter's Basilica, a multitude of tones emerging from the clanging metal, and the brass rang out, trumpeting a triumphant tune. The crowd murmured in anticipation.

Scanning the tens of thousands of people in St. Peter's Square, I could see a strong Indigenous presence scattered throughout the crowd of pilgrims from every continent. I saw the beaded caps of the Mi'kmaq, the jingle dresses of the Anishinaabe, and the deep-burgundy shirts and turquoise jewellery of the Diné and Hopi. Looking toward the basilica, I could see a man wearing a war bonnet. It was Chief Wilton Littlechild, commissioner of the Truth and Reconciliation Commission of Canada. To the east, I saw someone wearing a Mohawk headdress. There were flags showing the many nations of those about to be canonized, including the United States, the Philippines, and Canada. But there were also the flags of many Indigenous nations: the red-and-white cross of the Mi'kmaq, the purple-and-white wampum of the Haudenosaunee, and tribal flags from South Dakota, all symbolizing Native pride worldwide.

The sound of the organ began, and bishops walked to the pulpit two by two, followed by the Pope, who was guided to the altar by an entourage. He swung a thurible back and forth at the end of a long chain, smoke pouring out of it, smudging the pulpit. I thought of my son holding a cedar bucket and smudging everyone at the sundance. A choir began to sing.

The Pope read a long speech that included a call for a "renewal of faith in the First Nations." Any hope that he might have been celebrating traditional spirituality was dismissed when he noted that Kateri had stayed "faithful to the traditions of her people, although renouncing their religious convictions until her death." I sighed in disappointment; some, at the height of this spirituality, were still convinced theirs was the only way. The Holy Father finished his speech. Then came a moment of silence.

The organ began to play again and the Pope led a hymn. During the singing, I looked around at the immense church riches on display, the massive basilica and the square it inhabited, the immense marble columns, the statues of the saints, the gold on the fingers and around the necks of the thousands of holy men in the crowd. It is a very different way of looking at the world and the spirit than is our own. One focuses on the accumulation and preservation of things in a static condition; the other embraces flux, motion, and constant renewal.

At the end of the ceremony, a massive procession left the stage as the hundreds of priests, cardinals, and bishops exited. The day had grown warm, and the sun blazed down on the huge crowd as the Pope was driven off in the Popemobile, making the sign of the cross over and over. As he was whisked by, I was able to look at him up close, and he did not look well. He had the expression and unsteadiness of someone suffering from nausea. I said a prayer for this old man.

People began to turn to leave, a few groups of tourists breaking off to tour the Sistine Chapel or the basilica. As I was making my way through the crowd, I heard someone call "Wabanakwut!" Only people who have known me since childhood refer to me by my full name. *Who could this be?* I turned to see Harold Condin of the Charging Eagle family from Cheyenne River, South Dakota. I rushed to hug my *hunka* uncle. He was with a delegation of Lakota people from America. We laughed and marvelled at the odds of us running into one another on the other side of the world in a crowd of tens of thousands.

When Harold asked about my father, I told him Ndede was here but at the moment I had no idea where. We tried to arrange to meet later, but his tour group was moving on, so I snapped a photo of him just before he disappeared into the crowd.

About fifteen minutes later, when I met Shawon, Jesse, and my parents near a café on the east side of the Vatican, I was at least able to show Ndede the photo.

When Phil Fontaine met us a short time later, Ndede and I left with him for a reception at the Pontifical North American College. In the mingling crowd, Ndede found his *nabagoondewin* brother, Archbishop James Weisgerber. The archbishop wore his formal red vestments and a beautiful golden crucifix around his neck. Ndede wore a black velvet vest adorned with colourful Anishinaabe floral beadwork. They both sported similar modern glasses with black frames. How different they looked. How similar they were.

Their friendship had started here, in the Vatican, years back. It had taken them to a sundance, through an adoption ceremony, and now back to the Vatican again. Two Catholic ceremonies plus two Indigenous ones.

In some ways, the lives of my father and the archbishop could not have been more different. They had dramatically different experiences with the Church when they were young, and very different experiences growing up in Canada. The archbishop was raised among racist attitudes toward Indigenous people, and Ndede was on the receiving end of that thinking.

Yet they were also similar in important ways. They were both from small-town, rural Canada; they both came from humble families; and they both had answered a spiritual call to lead their flocks.

Through a lengthy, topsy-turvy journey, they had found and embraced each other as brothers. Reconciliation in action. Reconciliation is not something realized on a grand level, something that happens when a prime minister and a national chief shake hands. It takes place at a much more individual level. Reconciliation is realized when two people come together and understand that what they share unites them and that what is different about them needs to be respected. Reconciliation happens when the archbishop and the sundancer become brothers.

AS WE LEFT THE RECEPTION, Ndede complained his legs were sore from all the standing and walking. Still, he said it had been worth it. We rode home in silence, or at least as much silence as rush-hour traffic in Rome affords.

Late the next day, we made our way back to the Vatican, this time with Phil, his partner, Kathleen, Shawon, Jesse, and my mom. We waited in St. Peter's Square for our host to meet us. As we sat in the hot sun, Ndede walked to a public fountain and turned on the faucet over a small stone basin. He removed his glasses and splashed water on his face. Our guide walked up and introduced himself. Father Bettencourt was a priest, originally from Canada, who had spent much of his professional life working in the Vatican. He explained that he wanted to help celebrate the canonization of Kateri by giving us a personal tour of the Holy See, including some areas off limits to the public.

The priest led us through halls adorned with frescoes by Raphael, into the room where the State of the World address is given, and in through a back door to the Sistine Chapel. From there, we made our way through more corridors into a brightly lit private art gallery.

Bettencourt ushered us outside through some doors to a rooftop patio overlooking St. Peter's Square.

We were now perched high above the place where we had witnessed the canonization the day before. Long shadows reached across the square as the sun set behind us. The yellow, grey, and terracotta cityscape of Rome bathed in the warm sunlight far in the distance, a beautiful sprawl.

I turned to my father and asked what he thought.

"I'm impressed," he replied, turning his palms to the sky. "I think anyone would be impressed."

I looked to the west at the darkening statues of saints. The glow of the sunset formed halos around them. I looked at the dome on the basilica, then turned back to face the west.

My father was sitting on the parapet lining the patio. Behind him was a two-storey drop to the roof of an adjacent building, and below that a few storeys more to the ground. Ndede sat on the ledge with his feet crossed and his hands in his lap, wearing green slacks and a fine ribbon shirt. He had a deep smile on his face. Not a wide, beaming smile but the sort of calm and effortlessness expression that identified a man at peace with himself. He was staring off into the distance.

Shawon and I sat next to him for a moment while Jesse took a photo. We were living a watershed moment in our family's history. Serenity. Calmness. Togetherness. Then Ndede spoke to me in Anishinaabemowin for several minutes, explaining the significance of this trip to him.

"*E'ii Aapichii nimaamookaadenaan. Gichi-inendaan sago gemaa piizhaa'aan. Awe Shkiniikwe gegit igo apichii giimino' aatizi. Okiizhawenimaan manitoon. Okiizhawenimigoon gaye. Kimiinaa dash che'eyaad. Chi-naanaandawe'ii'ed. Naanaandawe'ii dash Kateri. Mii'e gaa-waabandamaan. Ngiiwaabamaa gaye owe gwiiwizens, gaa-gii-naanaandawe'ind. Daagii ishkwaa pimaadizi gwiiwizens. Mii dash awe Kateri ogiishaabowii'aan. Ngiiwaabamaa dash* *dibikong. Gwiiwizens ngiiwaabamaa"* —he nodded, before concluding— *"Mii'e, Mii'enendamaan.** That's what I think of this trip.

"Awe dash gaye," he picked up again after a beat, pointing at Phil. *"Buddy* [Phil's nickname]. *Minochige. Eya, aapichii minochige. Nimaamookaadenimaag sago, James Weisgerber, Aa gaye a'aa Baribeau. Aapichii onishishin. Maamookaadendaagoon. Gaawiin wiikaa gii-inawendaanzii gii-gwiizensiwiiyaan giinamaademoon gii-ayaayaan, wiikaa chi-naateshinaan awe noongom waabandamaan. Aapichi dash gii-gichi-ezichige Phil Fontaine. Gii-baakinang owe. Mii omaa wenjii-eyaawaad Niibowa-Anishinaabeg. Awe gaye Oshkinii' ikwe noongom Ogichitwaa Kateri gaa-inind. Mii gaye'e gaa-taagookishkootood Phil chi-waabamind awe Oshkinii'ikwe. Gegit Ogichitwaakwewid. Mii'e bezhig. Mewinzhaa e bi-onjise. Mii dash omaa noongom waabandamaang.†*

"Niminwendaan gaye niibowaa waabamagwaa Anishinaabeg pii-andowenimaawaad. Wiinawaa go ozhooniyemiiwaan, odabajii'-aawaan chi-pii-ezhaawaad omaa. Eya gaye nimaamaa'inenimaag ikwewag, mindimoweyag baateniwag pii das-ininiwag. Kaa anishinaa mindimowe, ikwe odonbii'aan abinoojiiyan chi'aanid ogikino'amawaan kiizhemino'aadizinid, mii dash omaa wenji-eyaawaad mindimoweg, ikwewag. Mii sago minik."‡

---

* "Well, I am very amazed. I am proud to have come. This young woman, she really lived a good life. She loved the Creator. And she was loved too. You gifted her and she was gifted. She was healed. Kateri heals too. This is what I have seen. I also saw a boy, he who was healed. This boy should have passed away. But Kateri worked through him. I saw him too last night. I saw that boy…. That's it. That's what I think."

† "And he as well, Buddy [Phil Fontaine] does good work. Yes, he really does good work. I am very amazed with them too, James Weisgerber and Pierre Baribeau [lawyer for the Catholic Church]. It's really great. Profound. I never thought when I was a boy in that sad state that I would ever be witnessing that which I am seeing now. And really, Phil Fontaine has done a great thing. He opened this up. For all of us Anishinaabeg to come here. That young woman too, now, Saint Kateri, so they say. This too. Phil managed to see that young woman. Of course, she is a saint. That's the one. A long time ago she came here. And now, here today, we see it."

‡ "I am glad too for all these Anishinaabeg I see who sought her out here. Their money, they used that to come all the way here. Yes, I think highly also of the adult women,

When he finished, he nodded and then sat in silence. We spent about a half hour together on the patio. Except when posing for a few more photos, Ndede maintained his position on the ledge. And his smile.

Watching him sit there, with that smile, I realized something. He was resting now, enjoying the moment, as if he had just completed the victory lap after an important battle in his life. He was looking back and enjoying the view. What an amazing achievement it had been.

There he was, sitting atop the home base of the religion that had sought to "kill the Indian" in him, and in hundreds of thousands of children like him. It had failed. The Vatican, the global Catholic Church, with billions of dollars at its disposal, its religious doctrine and ideology, couldn't destroy him or his culture. Four other Canadian churches had tried, as had the government of Canada, a nation then bent on erasing Indigenous identity.

All those forces had been levelled against my father when he was just a boy, and he survived. The combined weight of the churches and the Canadian state had been set on crushing children like him when they were just little—barely five, six, or seven years old—but they did not break. They survived. They may have lost some of their friends, and may have been damaged along the way, but they did not give up. They kept speaking their language. They kept practising their culture. They kept praying the way their parents had taught them to. And they waited.

Ndede had waited. He waited until the last of the residential schools was closed, a move spurred on by leaders such as himself and others of his generation. He waited until it was okay for him and

---

elderly women, and also the many men. I acknowledge the elderly woman, the adult woman who raises a child giving teachings of a good life of kindness, and that's why the older women and the adult women have come here. That's about it."

others to tell their stories, a moment brought about in large measure
by the leadership of his good friend Phil Fontaine. He waited while
the class action lawsuits piled up and the churches began to apologize. He waited until the government, pressured by the threat of
billions of dollars' worth of liability, finally came up with an offer
of compensation. He waited until the prime minister apologized,
his words shaped in part by Ndede's brother Fred Kelly. He waited
until the Pope told him he felt sorrow for what Ndede endured.

He waited until someone who looked like him and came from
a community like his was lifted to the greatest heights of the
religion that had caused him so many sorrows.

He waited for the country to change, for the churches to
change, and, finally, for the government to change.

He waited for the world to start seeing him and his people
differently.

This is part of what my father and all the residential school
survivors achieved. The full force of colonization had set out to
change them, yet these brave young boys and girls held on to who
they were and instead changed the colonial state and the colonial
religions. That is a remarkable journey.

The path began when he was taken from the home of his
parents in a poor but beautiful village on Lake of the Woods, and
it culminated at the very heights of global power, both literally and
figuratively. No wonder Ndede was smiling.

He had grappled with his pain, with his anger, and with his
grief. Now, we had seen him conquer those things with love, a
love he extended to his fellow human beings, including some who
had hurt him.

The worst things one human being can do to another had
been confronted by the very best that the human spirit has to offer.
On this day at least, the best part of us had won out.

In the midst of a stormy sea, Ndede had found a way to turn himself toward the sun and reflect that goodness back into the world around him. Now he was enjoying the victory on our behalf.

Miigwech Noos.

PART THREE

Giiwekwaadizid
The End of Life

19

WITH THE ARRIVAL OF WINTER, the trees shed their leaves and stood naked, their black shapes contrasting with the snow that blanketed the land. The air grew bitterly cold and the windswept prairie once again became an arctic tundra. The summer was long gone; this was the season of things coming to an end. The elders tell us that it is necessary to have a cold winter for the medicine to be strong the next year. It is difficult, however, to believe in the beginnings of new life all around you when you are standing in a blizzard.

It was late 2012, and as the snow fell my father's body was changing too. Even though he lost more weight, his stomach began to swell. When I brought him a Hugo Boss shirt I had picked up on a trip, he pointed at his protruding belly and said he did not want to wear it. I tried to assure him that a slim-cut shirt was fashionable and no one would judge him by his stomach, even while I wondered how he could be growing thicker at the waist and losing weight at the same time.

My mother called me the next night. "Your *ndede*'s stomach is filling up with fluid," she said, searching for the right words. She softened her tone. "It is really painful for him, but he doesn't want to make a big deal out of it. He is going to the hospital tomorrow to have it drained."

I thanked her for telling me and asked if I could do anything to help, knowing there really wasn't anything.

The procedure involved draining several litres of the fluid collecting inside his body as it turned on itself. Afterward, his belly was visibly smaller, and some of his joie de vivre returned.

Ndede and I completed the development of the Anishinaabemowin language app, and released it online. Visiting my father the night of the app's release, I handed him the iPad and he swiped through the verbs, reading them aloud to himself and peering through his bifocals at the translations that appeared.

He kept doing this until Dominik and Bezh came running around the corner from the living room, chasing one another. When they bumped into him and fell into a fit of laughter, Ndede grabbed Bezh by the waist and Dom around his shoulders. As he squeezed, both boys squirmed and giggled because he was tickling them. Soon, all three Kinews tossed their heads back in laughter, the smiles wide on their faces, their eyes squinting with joy.

This is a wonderful memory, etched as a moment of pure bliss in my mind.

A few days later, I returned to Ndede's house to video-record him speaking Ojibwe and sharing teachings again. He expanded on the name-giving ceremony and related teachings. Naming a new child or community member is one of the ceremonies Anishinaabe elders are called upon to conduct most often.

We sat in his living room for several hours that morning while he held court and spoke in elegant and eloquent Anishinaabemowin. I listened carefully, understanding most of what he said and noting any words I had difficulty with. Now and then, I would ask for clarification, and he would circle back before continuing with his lecture.

As I stared at the tiny monitor on the camera, I was struck by how different the little man in that viewfinder was from the man I had known just a short while before. He had trouble with his voice and tried to clear it constantly, but the frog in his throat refused to leave. His nose was running and did not stop, as much as he blew it. He was becoming even skinnier. His arms were lean, his face was thin, and he seemed to have more grey in his hair than before, although I may have just imagined that. Yet his mind was still sharp, and his spirit was perhaps more fully realized than ever before.

Our time studying the language and the culture of the Anishinaabe was drawing to a close. We had done some remarkable things together in this way, documenting our tongue and the teachings it revealed. More significantly to me, we had, in the process, become very close. Growing up, I had never felt close to my father. Now he was my best friend.

A few nights later, my father felt well enough to teach his university course, "Pathways to Indigenous Wisdom." It was the last class of the term, December 3. When I heard he was going to teach that week, I called my mom to check if he was up for it. "Yes," she told me. "Since he had his stomach drained, he's feeling so much better. He really wants to do it."

I was concerned but knew better than to say anything. Ndede was nothing if not proud, and while battling his illness it was important for him to feel he still controlled his destiny. We were cooking for him, escorting him to his medical appointments, and helping him dress. Teaching his course was one thing he could do, and perhaps had to do, on his own.

When I spoke to him after his lecture, he was disappointed. Only a few students had shown up. I logged on to Facebook later and saw a message from a friend who was one of his students. My friend was asking if my dad was well enough to teach. He and some other students had seen his condition and didn't think he would make it, so they skipped class.

It was too bad. They missed his swan song.

Ndede held court that night for a full three hours and stayed to visit and counsel those who lingered. He knew what lay ahead for him, and he wanted to invest everything he could into them. The message he left with them was inspiring.

In the lecture, Ndede reflected on his life, his political career, the progress he had forged, and the changes he had witnessed. He spoke about fighting for political recognition, fighting for civil rights for Anishinaabe people, fighting the apathy among our own people, and fighting for recognition in the courts and in the streets. He talked about the culture and his work on language revitalization, about his personal path to wellness, and about his quest to be a better husband and a better father. He described his drive to reconcile his spirit to his residential school experience and summarized the journey he had walked in his life.

"This is what I have done for my children and for my grandchildren," he told the students. "Now, what are you going to do? What will you leave for your children and your grandchildren?"

Class dismissed. This would be the last lecture given by one of the greatest orators I have ever known.

AROUND THIS TIME, I started noticing a hashtag circulating online. I first saw it used by a woman named Tanya Kappo, who was organizing a teach-in on the Louis Bull Cree Nation in Alberta.

The teach-in, named after a series of events that had started earlier that fall in Saskatchewan, was called "Idle No More."

I did not attend that Louis Bull event, but I watched my Twitter stream fill up with tweets about speeches delivered by Tanya, Janice Makokis, Pam Palmater, and Sylvia McAdam. The main thrust of the discussions was to criticize two provisions in that year's federal budget omnibus bill, titled Bill C-45. One of the provisions drastically reduced the number of federally protected waterways. The four Indigenous women, all lawyers, argued that this opened the door to the degradation of the environment generally and water specifically, which is the responsibility of women in many Indigenous cultures. Importantly, they argued that environmental degradation would not just affect First Nations people but all Canadians. The other provision that offended them was one that opened the door for reserve lands, now held communally, to be transformed into fee-simple property. This was reminiscent of the Dawes Act in the United States, which led to the loss of reservation lands through privatization while doing nothing to improve the long-term economic prosperity of the communities it affected.

Within a few days, #IdleNoMore had grown far beyond the event at Louis Bull. It focused attention on earlier events in Saskatchewan and the four women who founded those meetings: Nina Wilson, Sheelah McLean, Sylvia McAdam, and Jessica Gordon. Soon #IdleNoMore would become more than a protest about the federal budget. It would be the spark that landed on the tinderbox of grievances and challenges faced by First Nations, Métis, and Inuit people in Canada and the United States. In short, it was explosive.

A few days after the hashtag began to pick up steam, a group of chiefs walked the complaints that had been circulating online right into the seat of federal power. Okimaw Wallace Fox, Chief Isadore Day, and grand chiefs Patrick Madahbee and Derek Nepinak, carrying a wampum belt, a drum, and a pipe, scuffled with RCMP officers when they tried to enter the chamber of the House of Commons. The incident may not have led news coverage that day, but it appeared on the political shows and was widely circulated on social media.

The four Saskatchewan-based founders of Idle No More called for a national day of protest on December 10. With the social media buzz creating a feedback loop that amplified the actions at the teach-ins and by the chiefs on Parliament Hill, the stage was set for the movement to take off.

I accepted an invitation by the local organizing committee to emcee the Winnipeg event, expecting it to be another poorly attended rally like others I had experienced that fall. Starting with a few dozen students at the Aboriginal Students' Council lounge at the University of Winnipeg, we marched down Memorial Boulevard, picking up supporters, who rushed to join us and unfurled flags and banners along the way. Looking around, I felt a little uncertain about what we were doing. *Should I really be here in the streets carrying a picket sign?* Then I thought back to my childhood. I remembered holding a sign that asked, "Policeman, are you my friend?" after the shooting of J.J. Harper, and wearing a T-shirt that read "Elijah Power!" during the Meech Lake Accord days. And I had visited the Peace Village across from the Manitoba Legislature during the Oka Crisis. *Yeah*, I thought, *I belong here with my people.*

As we walked up to the intersection with Portage Avenue, Winnipeg's busiest street, a non-Native guy driving an ugly hatchback on the opposite side of the street from us scowled and flipped us the bird. He had no idea what Idle No More was. The only thing he knew was that we were brown and we were blocking a few lanes of traffic. For this, he hated us, which captured in a nutshell much of the criticism the movement would eventually face.

That day, about five hundred people joined us in the snow and the cold to protest Bill C-45. The crowd was rowdy, but things went well overall. We heard from many good speakers on a variety of topics. At the end, we all joined hands and formed a ring around the legislative building, round-dancing together to show our solidarity, the round dance being the friendship dance of the plains Indigenous nations.

I had thought this was the end of the event, but I was wrong. A few young people shouted for everyone to rush the doors, and soon more than a hundred ran inside the legislature to occupy the lobby. My friend Leonard and I visited with another friend, who advised us not to go inside, that we should keep the protest peaceful. Leonard and I looked at each other, and I said, "Should we go check it out?"

Without hesitating, Leonard said "Yup," and in we walked. We joined the mass of teenagers and other young people voicing their fears and frustrations, expressing their desire for unity to make things better for their people. I remembered the idealism I felt when I first got involved with the activist scene as a teen. And I remembered the eventual disillusionment when the personal flaws of some protest leaders got in the way of us reaching our goal. I had seen too many so-called revolutionaries make fewer demands for social change and more for food and gas money. There were also other warriors, men and women alike, who could be counted on to fight with one another rather than take on the challenges in our communities. The memory made me smile, and I stood for awhile studying the sight of a new crop of avid and determined protesters, Leonard and I left just as the police began showing up.

The next day, a newspaper ran a large photo of me on its front page, along with the headline "Idle No More Ends in Legislative Lockdown." I laughed when I saw it, but when I showed the newspaper to Ndede, he was not amused. I couldn't tell if he was upset or feeling the after-effects of his medication.

Scenes like the one at the Manitoba Legislature occurred all across the country. They were the beginning of Idle No More's march to the forefront of national attention. There would be Chief Theresa Spence's hunger strike in Ottawa and an audit revealing a lack of financial oversight on her reserve. There would also be beautiful moments of Indigenous cultural renaissance, such as flash mob round dances that took over shopping malls across the continent, from the West Edmonton Mall to the Mall of America. All of this would occur among bouts of internecine fighting, moments when the message would cut through the media landscape, and incidents when racists tried to hijack the agenda to advance their own trumped-up ideas.

MY FATHER AND I sat at his kitchen table discussing what was happening, but we had no idea what was to come. All we knew was that Ndede was very ill. His energy was fading and he looked increasingly gaunt, even as his belly grew larger again. We did not discuss it directly. There was no point. Besides, it is not the Anishinaabe way to commiserate about a physical ailment that cannot be changed. My father was too proud to ask for pity, and I respected him too much to offer it.

That night, we ate pie and laughed at the spectacle of the protests, joking that someone always called the cops whenever the "Indians" showed up.

The discussion turned serious when we debated the issues being addressed in the online discussions of Idle No More and analyzed the different courses of action pursued by the four chiefs and the contrasting position of the national chief. Both of us remarked on the two-steps-forward-one-step-back nature of Indigenous affairs in this country.

This was the type of talk I really enjoyed with Ndede, but it was clear things were changing. Politically, the national conversation about Indigenous issues had taken on a dramatic sense of urgency. Personally, there was a difference in Ndede's demeanour. While he was still intelligent and thoughtful, his linguistic faculties were tempered. He had always been blunt, but now he lost the luxury of being able to couch his thoughts in language whose meaning was disguised by its eloquence whenever he wanted it to be. What he said next caught me off guard with its candour.

"We will never be free as long as we are under their Constitution."

Then he cleared his throat and looked away.

Perhaps he meant we should separate from the rest of the country. That did not match, however, with the mission of reconciliation he had pursued earlier that year. Nor did it match with the type of politics he had practised since the 1960s—direct and confrontational, but one that never saw him leave the table.

Or maybe he was resigning himself to the notion that Indigenous people will never truly be "free" in Canada. But Ndede always demanded the best, whether it was on important things such as my sister's education or relatively trivial things like the thread count in his bedsheets. It seemed far-fetched to me that this man, who had grown up dirt poor and fighting for basic rights in Northwestern Ontario and had managed to achieve a comfortable lifestyle, would now accept being a second-class citizen.

Instead, I believe he was referring to a rather technical distinction—Section 91.24 of the Constitution, where powers are divided between the provincial and federal governments. "Indians and lands reserved for Indians" falls under the jurisdiction of the federal government, placing us, as Ndede said, "under their Constitution." Many Indigenous nations seek to become a constitutionally recognized order of government in their own right. Their powers do not derive from the Constitution; Indigenous sovereignty existed before contact. Rather, I believe Ndede's point was to fight to be taken out from under the nanny state of the federal government in the Constitution and have us stand on our own. This would create three orders of government in that document: federal, provincial, and Indigenous.

This was quite a technical point, but it was no surprise coming from a man who sat me down when I was just nine or ten years old and explained the injustice of the St. Catherine's Milling decision.*

Section 91.24 of the Constitution had very dramatic results in the real world. Consider my father's own experience with cancer treatment. In Manitoba, the provincial government has a program to pay for all drugs necessary for cancer patients. As an "Indian," however, my father's health coverage was paid by the federal government, making him ineligible for the provincial program. As a result, he was denied access to the first-choice cancer drug recommended to him in 2012. It likely would not have made a difference to his survival, but why must First Nations people still wonder whether they would live longer were it not for Section 91.24?

---

* This 1888 decision is a deeply problematic precedent in Aboriginal law. Essentially, an English court held that my ancestral title to the land was allowed at the Crown's pleasure and could be taken away at any time. That case was also settled without hearing from First Nations legal representatives, because it was illegal for a lawyer to represent First Nations at the time.

In the end, my father did have a choice in the matter. He could have appealed the decision about drug coverage or paid for the drugs out of his own pocket, something I offered to help him with. He chose not to do either. His oncologist told him that if he were to seek out the more aggressive option that he had been denied access to, he might live marginally longer, but he would suffer more. The doctor told Ndede to think about his quality of life, and about the things he still wanted to do.

Ndede took the message to heart. He accepted the shorter prognosis, making sure that he would live each of his remaining days on this earth to the fullest.

His comment about the Constitution was the last time I heard my father discuss politics. After this point, although Idle No More would grow louder, and First Nations issues were brought to the forefront of the national agenda, politics ceased to matter to him.

He had devoted much of his life to politics. Now, he left it behind.

20

WHEN SHAWON RETURNED FROM ITALY she hadn't seen Ndede since the canonization. Her first sight of him shocked her, but she adjusted to it quickly and spent many late nights visiting him.

Along with my sons, Ndede and I continued the Anishinaabemowin classes as the streets filled with snow. Everyone's minds turned toward the approaching holiday season, and one night in class we taught the young people Christmas carols in Anishinaabemowin. We were singing together as a group when Ndede walked into the room wearing a huge smile on his face. Walking toward John Mclean, a fluent speaker from Pinaymootang who helped us teach the language, he rested his hand on his stomach, which bulged through the sweater he was wearing. Fluid was refilling his stomach cavity, and I could see the pain beneath his smile as he reached to shake John's hand. They talked in Ojibwe while the young people around them soaked up the sounds of our tongue.

It was the holiday season, so we gave gifts to the children. Ndede's gift to us was his presence; he was fighting through pain just to be there. When the class finished, we walked out into the gentle winter night. The thick snowflakes seemed to cling to one another as they fell to the ground. This would be the last Ojibwe class Ndede would participate in.

As the snowbanks grew, I would wake up early with my boys and we would skate on the hockey rink across the street from our house before they went to school. April and I shared custody, but I took them to school most days. One morning, Bezh surprised me when he threw down his hockey stick, picked up my shovel, and skated around clearing the snow off the ice for his older brother.

Later that day, I found myself at my parents', eating with my mother and father in their kitchen. It was a scene that had played out countless times before, but this evening, in the warm incandescent light, Ndede suddenly turned serious.

"I know I am going to die," he said to us, "but I don't want you to be sad. I am basically dying from natural causes."

I could have drawn a technical distinction, but on some level he was right. He had lived a long life, and eventually—whether it was because some cells chose to replicate out of control or from some other process—his life would come to an end.

But for him to say this, he must have been suffering. After Darryl's death, Ndede had always said suicide was not an option, insisting he would always fight to stay alive. Now, he was accepting the inevitable. Accepting, but still prepared to hang on to the end.

"I know you will cry when I go," he went on, "but I don't want you to cry. And I know the sundance will be hard for you too. The first time you go into that arbour without me, I know that you will cry."

We studied each other in that moment.

"But don't cry too much."

Our eyes were locked in a steady embrace. Perhaps we were afraid to look away because neither of us knew if we would see each other again. Finally, I looked from him to my mother, who looked down at her empty plate. I felt so much pity for her.

"There will be a time for grief," Ndede went on, "but don't grieve for me too long. Don't be like those people who cry on and on and on. I don't want you to cry for me."

His stomach was growing. The fluid claimed more space from his viscera in their see-saw battle. The trips to have his stomach drained were now a weekly occurrence.

My sister Patricia and her son Derek came to visit. She was the baby who had been born when Ndede and her mother were in residential school and adopted by her relatives in Southern Ontario. She had made her life and raised her family there on the Saugeen First Nation on Georgian Bay.

We sat together in my parents' living room while Ndede asked to bring out the possessions he wished to bequeath to Pat and Derek. They were keepsakes, traditional items and photographs. We laughed at some of the pictures. One showed my dad in a big, curly coif straight out of the 1970s, a hairstyle that had not aged well.

Diane and her son Pishanakwut were there as well that evening, along with Dominik and Bezh. The house was full of people, full of energy, full of laughter.

Before Diane and Pishanakwut left, we crowded around Ndede for a photo. He sat on the couch with his arms folded and legs crossed, a grin on his face. His face was thin, and his features seemed smaller.

Later, while Pat and my mother sat together in the kitchen, I joined Derek and Ndede in the living room. Now in his thirties, Derek was eager to learn about Anishinaabe culture. He had grown up on a reserve where the prominent spiritual influence was the United Church rather than Anishinaabe tradition.

Derek asked Ndede in various ways for him to pass along some teachings of the true Anishinaabe way of life, but each time he tried, Ndede returned to the topic he wanted to speak about. It was a name he had given to a young person recently: Nanisoobiness. A poet might translate the name as "Holy Trinity Thunderbird." It speaks of three thunderbirds being encompassed into one being, a syncretic reflection of my father's spiritual journey grounded in Anishinaabe spirituality but making room again for the Catholicism that had made an imprint on him as a young boy. The Trinity and the thunderbirds were together in one name.

As Ndede explained this, Derek kept asking about other things, which frustrated my father, who at one point shook his head and looked away.

The disease metastasizing inside Ndede took away more than just his physical stature. It also affected his mental acuity, his sharp demeanour, and his verbal facility.

I watched my father shrink before my eyes. He seemed to be feeling the nauseating vibration that affects your mind when you take powerful narcotics. He searched with subtle exasperation for the right words and made points that did not land with the same impact his arguments would have made in the past. He was fighting through a haze, and my heart sank, because I knew what was happening. I had read the pamphlets.

They say never count a fighter out, and the old man was not done yet. He tore through this haze and delivered a line with all the characteristic bluntness he had mustered during his prime. "Do you have a problem with the Church?" he asked his grandson.

Derek paused, then said, "Yeah, I guess so."

"And why is that?"

"I guess I am not crazy about the Church because of what they did to you and to our people," Derek said.

My father sat with his arms crossed, staring ahead, his lips pursed. "You know," he said, "I am the one that was in residential school. I was there."

Ndede tilted his head back, then refocused on Derek before continuing.

"I do not have much time left in this world," he reminded us. "I can't be angry. I don't want to spend the rest of my time here being angry. I have to make things right. Not for those other people, but for me. I want to leave this world in a good way. So I am making things right with the Church."

And that was that.

A FEW DAYS LATER, I was in my office at the university when my phone rang. It was Shawon.

"What are you doing, Bruddy?" she asked. Before I could answer she said, "We need your help with Ndede. He just fainted coming out of the hospital."

"What?" I didn't know what else to say.

"He was coming out of the hospital, St. Boniface Hospital. He just fainted when he was leaving the building. They had to get a wheelchair for him."

"Is he okay?"

"He had his stomach drained again, and it was really hard on him."

"What do you mean he fainted?"

"He passed out. Leaving the hospital. And then again, trying to get into the car."

I asked if he was injured.

Instead of answering, she said, "Can you meet us at the house? They didn't send the wheelchair with us. We need your help getting him into the house. Mom and I can't lift him on our own."

I sped through traffic, cursing each stoplight that slowed my progress on the way to my parents' home in the suburbs. Rounding the bend near their house, I could see the grey Buick backed into the driveway. Shawon and our mother were waiting outside. I could see a silhouette in the passenger side of my dad's car.

"He's feeling very weak," my mother said as soon as I hopped out of my car. "They drained his stomach again, but this time it was different. They must have taken a lot more out. He's very weak. He passed out."

I opened the door to the Buick.

"Hi, Ndede," I began. "Everything is okay. I'm going to help you get into the house. Is that all right?"

He did not speak. He sat there, his eyes open, his gaze fixed straight ahead, head cocked downward. He was awake and he was conscious, but he did not speak. I imagine when you are feeling the worst pain of your life, you do not have much use for conversation.

I reached over and unbuckled his seat belt and said, "Okay, Ndede, let's try and get up together. I'll lift you up, okay?" I tried to lift him by his arms. All I did was pull his arms without moving much of his body.

"You're going to have to help him more," my mother pointed out.

I wrapped my arms around his torso and clasped my hands together in a Gable grip, the sort of fingers-over-the-back-of-the-other-hand grip favoured by wrestlers. I squatted down and tried to power him up out of the seat.

Ndede immediately let out a groan that almost eviscerated me. "I'm sorry, Ndede," I spat out. "I'm sorry, I'm sorry, I'm sorry. Shit."

Why the hell had I squeezed his torso, the part of his body causing him the most pain?

Sweating more from anxiety than exertion, I tried again, this time more methodically and with more thought. I swam my right arm under his left armpit, securing what a grappler would call an underhook, then slid my left arm under his right armpit to secure double underhooks, and clasped my hands together in a Gable grip. This time, the pressure was on our chests and his back rather than on his belly.

I made this a grappling exercise the way I would do with my friends at the gym. *Do not think about what you are doing*, I told myself. *Take one step after the other and keep moving. Ignore any emotion you may feel carrying your father.*

My mother and Shawon helped guide Ndede's feet out of the car and I pulled him forward, inch by inch, so that the pressure remained on his chest and away from his abdomen. "Okay, Ndede, let's try and get up," I said. "I've got you."

He moaned again. My legs straightened, and I was now holding my father in a tight bear hug, arms under his. He was facing the door. My back was toward it.

"All right, let's try to walk."

I began to inch backward toward the front steps.

Suddenly, my father became very heavy. I tightened my grip and lowered my hips so my centre of gravity was below his. I felt him go limp in my arms. *There is no significance to this*, I told myself again. *Focus on keeping your hands clasped behind his back; keep your hips lower than his. Keep him on his feet. Do not let him fall. That is the only thing that matters.*

"He fainted!" my mother and Shawon shouted.

I tried to reassure them. "I've got him."

"We've got to get him inside!"

Some part of me will forever be frozen in that moment. The black asphalt peeking through the white snow. The pine boughs of the giant tree. The cool, wet air. The birds singing. The overcast day. The feeling of Ndede's chest against me. The moisture in my palms gripping one another. The warmth of his face pressed against mine. My mother's presence. My sister's.

Then he came back to us. Slowly, he grew less heavy. His head moved slightly and I felt him lock eyes with my mother. Ndede had returned.

"Okay, Ndede," I said. "Everything is okay."

But nothing was okay.

I walked backward to the front steps and up them, one by one. We shuffled across the landing, through the open door, and into their home. Ndede fainted again as we made our way through the living room and kitchen. We waited for him to return and then made our way toward the back of the house.

"Bring him here," my mother said from the bedroom. She cleared their bed and lifted the blankets for him. We sat him down and he groaned again, his belly now compressed by his bending hips. His shoulders relaxed and he lay back and closed his eyes, furrowed his brow, and let out a sigh. My mother and Shawon straightened his covers and tucked him in. I walked to the living room and sat in silence for what felt like a very long time.

My father did not leave the house again. This man had travelled so much when I was growing up that it often seemed like he was never around. Now he had come home for good. The rolling stone had ceased to move. Travelling no longer mattered.

That night, I drove to a bank. I felt so terrible about my father's condition that I thought, *Maybe if I give him five thousand dollars he will feel better.* The idiocy of that sentiment immediately left me dumbfounded. My father was unable to speak, unable to walk, and confined to his home. What the hell was he going to do with five grand? Money ceases to matter so early on in our journey toward our final days, it is a wonder we spend so much of our lives worrying about it.

I drove out of the bank parking lot and went to a pharmacy. I bought every mobility device I could find—a wheelchair, a walker, accessories for the bathroom, and on and on. I spent the evening assembling devices, fastening safety bars into wall studs, and doing what I could to make the house more comfortable for Ndede.

We tried to persuade my father to let us help him with some of these things when he needed to get up, but he refused, waving us off as he tried his best to get out of bed on his own. We helped him anyway. I would secure the underhooks and lift him out of bed, and together we would walk to wherever he wanted to go. We had to pause so that he could rest along the way. The distances were small. Five feet, and then pause. He would be hit with a dizzy spell and need help steadying himself. Each time we returned to his bed, we would rush as he tried to propel himself forward in a race against gravity. We would make it just in time, laying him down. He furrowed his brow and sighed.

If suffering brings you closer to the Creator, my father was very close indeed.

We began a round-the-clock bedside vigil. Shawon, Diane, Pishanakwut, my niece Melissa, my mother, and I divided the day and night into shifts, usually four hours at a time. During those hours, we would stay awake, even if he was not. We were at his beck and call, helping him with whatever he needed.

I was amazed at the quiet strength of my family. We all wanted to believe that the Ndede we knew could return. Shawon tried out many recipes that were considered part of a cancer-fighting diet. She understood the reality of the situation but didn't want Ndede to feel as though we had given up on him. Ndede rejected much of this food. Sometimes he refused to eat. Sometimes he had no appetite. Sometimes he would spit the food back up. Shawon finally discovered that he liked to eat sautéed spinach in small amounts. He liked the taste and could keep it down. From then on, there was more spinach in my mom's fridge than in Popeye's.

I found reprieve from the vigil with my father by spending time with my sons and volunteering at community Christmas events.

At work, we rushed the creation of the Dr. Tobasonakwut Kinew Fund for the Promotion of Indigenous Culture, Language and History through the University of Winnipeg Foundation. Lloyd Axworthy and I made founding contributions of five thousand dollars each. I brought the press release to my parents' house, where I sat on the edge of Ndede's bed and explained what we had done. "Ndede, we set up this fund in your name," I said, "to continue all the work you've done with your students. We'll keep that work going in your honour."

The words were meaningless to him. I tried to simplify.

"Lloyd and I put some money here in your name."

Ndede responded, but only with sounds, not words. He would look at me and his eyes would wander away to different spots on the ceiling. None of this was getting through to him. I tried again in Ojibwe.

"*Ndede. Gigiimiinin zhooniyaa. Gigawiidookawaag minawaa Anishinaabensag*," I said. At this, he turned his gaze to me. My words seemed to cut through. I spoke to him a few minutes more. Eventually, his attention lapsed and his gaze wandered back across the ceiling. I wondered what he might be seeing in those moments.

I folded the paper and placed it on the dresser. The fund may have been a nice way to commemorate him, but it came too late for its namesake to appreciate it. I sighed to myself, my father and I alone in that dark room. Money didn't matter anymore, and recognition probably didn't matter either.

The next night, I brought my sons over to see their grandfather for what I knew would be the final time. I see-sawed back and forth about whether it would traumatize them to see him in this condition, but in the end I decided we had nothing to hide or be embarrassed about. In a few decades, they would be thankful they had been given one final chance to see their *dedenan*—their grandpa.

Before leaving home, I dressed the boys in matching knit Christmas sweaters. Dom's was orange, Bezh's was blue. I bundled them up in their winter clothes and helped them put on their boots. As we got ready, I sang some of the Anishinaabe songs we knew. Some were traditional, and others were nursery rhymes translated from English.

Driving through the dark wintry streets, I tried to explain their grandfather's condition.

"Dedenan is very sick," I said.

"Why is he sick?" Dom asked.

Exactly, Dom. Why is he sick? "I don't know," I answered. "He just is. He is very, very sick. He is going to be different than the last time you seen him."

"What do you mean?"

"Well ..." I paused, "... he is sick and he is in pain. He probably won't be able to say anything to you."

"Why not?"

"He is using all of his energy to fight his sickness. So he doesn't have much left for talking or walking."

"He's using all his energy to fight the cancer?" Dom asked.

"Yes," I replied, "and he'll probably stay in bed the whole time we are there. He may not look at you the way he did before, but he still sees you. He knows you are there. And he loves you very much."

We drove the rest of the way with me reminding them how to say certain things in Ojibwe. The boys obliged me.

At my parents' home, when we entered the bedroom I saw Ndede sitting up in bed. My mother sat beside him, feeding him with a spoon. They both smiled as soon as they saw the boys. The two brothers were tentative.

"Hey, guys!" Mom said.

Ndede smiled and sighed the way someone does when they see a sight for sore eyes.

"*Ojiim Kidedenan*," I told each boy, urging them to go kiss their grandpa.

They did, one after the other, hugging him carefully. The old man smiled. His eyes seemed to see something far away.

The boys found their way to the foot of the bed and stood next to each other, with their arms at their sides.

"Go ahead," I said gently.

"*Kinibaa na? Kinibaa na nimishomis?*" They sang softly, in unison, to the tune of "Frère Jacques." As they wound their way through the song, their voices carried the sounds of their ancestral tongue, their grandparents as silent witnesses. The melody was a school kid's tune, but the words and sounds were of their grandfather's language, the first sounds he heard at birth. Now, at the end, they were his lullaby. He did not speak much anymore, but when he did, Anishinaabemowin seemed to come most easily.

When the boys finished, we all applauded.

Next, they sang a traditional song about an old hunter who lost everything before being brought back from the brink by a little bird. They glanced at each other as they sang. The song's melody was given to the hunter by the bird hundreds of years ago and passed down through generations of Anishinaabeg, eventually finding its way to Ndede, who in turn had shared it with me. Now the song would live on in the memories and voices of two little Anishinaabe boys. Perhaps it would live on beyond any of us in the room. Or perhaps this would be the last time it was ever sung. Songs are fickle like that.

I watched the boys sharing songs for a few more minutes. The cartoon monsters on their matching sweaters eyed each other. They gave their *dedenan* a gift that night.

Our ancestors said that in life we need both the young and the old—the old because they pull us onward in life, the young because they push us forward. For a moment, I stood in the middle as the older and younger generations acted on me from both directions.

When the boys finished all their songs, we clapped again and complimented them on how well they had done.

"Okay, I guess we should go, then," I said, before repeating myself in Ojibwe. "*Ani-giiwedaa.*"

I looked to the boys for a second. Their eyes met mine. I nodded.

"*Kiizhawenimin Ndedenan,*" Dominik said—"I love you, grandpa"—walking forward to hug and kiss his grandfather again.

"*Kiizhawenimin Ndedenan,*" Bezh repeated, and followed his brother to kiss his grandfather's forehead.

With that, we turned and walked out of the room, leaving the two grandparents smiling. I pursed my lips as we walked to the door. Both boys were silent.

They left him walking forward, not looking back. This is how our ancestors tell us to leave. Their last words to him were not about closure or finality, but simply about love, in the deep familial sense, and then showing their love for him with a simple act.

The drive home was long and quiet. When we got home, I stared at the only Christmas present I'd had time to buy. It was a large canvas of an eagle I bought at a charity art auction and planned to give to my parents. I decided it couldn't wait.

The next evening, I entered the darkened room where Ndede lay. He was in a waking dream, his eyes open, his hands reaching in front of him, swiping and feeling for the things he could see in his vision.

"Ndede," I whispered. I told him I was giving him this. *"Gimiinin iwe."*

I turned the lights up slightly and raised the canvas over his head so it entered his field of view.

"Ohhhhhhhhhhh." It was a surprised, pleased tone that let me know the image reached him, wherever he was.

I put the painting away and sat with him, starting my overnight shift at his side.

On those nights, I would sit with a drum, keeping him company by tapping out a gentle rhythm and singing four push-ups, or one cycle, of a song. This would last about five minutes. I would stop and explain in Ojibwe who the song had been given to, or who had composed it. Then I would start another.

Sometimes, Ndede would nod his head to the rhythm. Sometimes, he would tap his foot under the blanket. Perhaps he was dancing, one foot already in the spirit world. More often, he would simply listen, arms outstretched, reaching out for the dreams and visions he saw before him. His hands would close on themselves as if he had grasped something. He would roll his fists, one around the other, in a "wheels on the bus" motion. He would extend his hands cautiously in different directions as though he couldn't see and he was feeling around for something. He was finding his way.

I worked through a dozen or so songs over the next hour. Then I went to sauté some spinach and tried to feed it to him. He chewed it, then spat it out. I tried more, and he spat that out as well. After several tries, he appeared to swallow it. I was overjoyed. After I put the food away, I walked back to his side and asked him if he was okay. He was licking his chops. I asked him what it was. I looked closer. The spinach came back to the tip of his tongue. He had not swallowed anything. I plucked the spinach out of his mouth and put it away.

I don't know if he ate anything after that. Food had ceased to matter.

Back in my chair, I picked up the drum and started singing more songs. This time I sang "Kopichigan," the melody his mother had sung to him so long ago. I hoped the song brought him back home. Back to mother. Back to earth.

Singing softly, I heard Ndede muttering, so I stopped to listen. I leaned in to place my ear closer to him and asked what he had said. I heard him mutter again, and listened more closely.

"I've got to get out of here," he said, this time clearly enough for me to understand.

"Okay, where do you want to go?" I said, a little panicked. "The living room?"

"I gotta get out of here," he repeated.

"Okay," I said. "Let's go."

I helped him up slowly and we made it to the hallway, my arms wrapped around him, and into the living room, but this was no better.

Ndede looked around, worried. "I gotta get out of here," he said again.

I was straining to understand what he meant. I asked him a few times what I could do, why he had to leave, where he wanted to go.

"He's gonna kill me," he said.

I stopped trying to answer him. He was living through a nightmare. Ironically, he knew exactly what was happening to him in the waking world.

We made it back to the bedroom, and I reassured him that everything was all right. He relaxed and fell asleep a few minutes later while I sang the lullaby that had been given to his mother when she was a little girl.

It went on like that. A little singing, a little talking, a little bit of cooking, but not much eating. A little bit of drinking water or tea.

Every so often, he would need to use the washroom, and when we got up he would faint in my arms. Sometimes it would happen twice, once on the walk there, once in the washroom. It happened so often, I should have grown accustomed to it. But I never did.

The next night, Jesse arrived. Straight off a plane from Istanbul and severely jet-lagged, he jumped right into the rotation at Ndede's side. I went to the mall and did all my Christmas shopping in a few short hours. We put up a Christmas tree and decorated it, but it was a subdued occasion.

Pishanakwut, Melissa, and Diane stayed by Ndede's side the next day. Nothing changed. He did not speak, he drank very little, and took only a little bit of medicine.

When Uncle Jimmy arrived to visit, the archbishop sat with us in that darkened room.

We spoke softly, reminiscing about the year that was. The adoption. The canonization. The meals together. The laughs.

Permeating our conversation was the wheeze from Ndede's chest. This seemed to be the only noise he made now. His eyes were closed. Occasionally, he reached out in front of him, searching for what he saw in his mind's eye. His hands looked plastic. Ndede had passed the point of no return. He did not even notice us anymore.

James did what he could to cheer us up, given the situation. When he announced that he was leaving, I said, "I think we would all like it if you could say a prayer for our dad."

"Of course," he replied, and he knelt beside Ndede, clasping my father's hands in his own. He bowed his head and we bowed ours. Then he lead us in a prayer to our Lord Jesus Christ. He blessed my father and appealed to the Creator to be gentle and merciful. He crossed himself. "Amen," he concluded.

"Amen," we all repeated. "*Aho.*"

The archbishop shook my father's hands gently. "Pray for me too," he asked Ndede, his rural Saskatchewan accent not entirely hidden by the years in the black robe. The tone in his voice told me he did not expect my father to reciprocate. Yet as the archbishop stood to leave, Ndede reached out to grasp his hand again, furrowing his brow as if summoning all his energy to focus on the task at hand.

Then, suddenly, he broke his silence.

"*Aho kaa'anishinaa Nimishomis, Kizhawaynimin,*" he began, invoking the Creator, telling God that he loved him. He continued. He asked the Creator to bless this *mikitekone*, this black robe. He told the Creator this black robe was his brother and thanked the Creator for all of the gifts we encounter in this world, for loving all children. He concluded his Anishinaabemowin prayer with "*Mii'e*"—"That's it." After he finished, Ndede lay his head back slightly into his pillow and relaxed. He had let go of a heavy burden. It was a burden he had shouldered for a very long time.

When James left, we remained quiet for a long time. We had witnessed our miracle.

All year, I had been praying for a miracle that would save my father from his illness. Instead, we were given a different sort of miracle. My father had lived long enough to see an apology. Now he had lived long enough to show us forgiveness as well.

THAT NIGHT, I sat with my father again.

I shared with him the songs I had learned over my years of travelling in our homeland to ceremonies and to powwows. I sang him the songs he had taught me. I showed him songs that I had composed.

He was on his journey, dancing in place slightly, reaching up from his bed toward the heavens. He returned to his vision, like a sundancer heading back into the arbour after a break.

I helped him use the washroom once more. He had not been drinking anything for the last while. Perhaps water had ceased to matter too.

He lay back. He rested his eyes briefly, then opened them again and reached for the sky, resuming his quest.

He opened his mouth and said, "*Ninibaa*"—"I am going to sleep now." This was the last word I heard Ndede say.

I sat watching him, thinking, *What a journey I have traced his footsteps on, especially this past year.* Now, there was another journey for him to take. On this one, I would not be able to follow. Not now. Not yet.

Jesse's alarm clock sounded at 4 A.M. Time to change shifts.

I waited twenty minutes as Jesse fixed himself some tea and found something to read.

Something told me to stay a little longer.

Jesse and I sat together with Ndede for a few minutes. There was nowhere else to be and nothing else to do. A rattle shook with each breath he took. The sheets whispered when he shifted beneath the covers.

I stood to leave but stopped. I knelt down again beside my father and kissed him on the forehead. I whispered to him, "*Kiizhawenimin Ndede.*"

I went downstairs and curled up beside Lisa, who was sleeping on a futon.

We were woken up a few hours later when my mother shouted down the stairwell, "Lisa, Wabanakwut—come quick!"

We ran upstairs. On the way up, I held out hope that the other miracle I had asked for was still possible. For an instant, I pictured Ndede sitting up in bed, smiling, on his way to a full recovery.

We turned the corner.

He lay on his back.

He was still.

Shawon sat at his side holding his hand.

Mom's face bore a look of anguish.

Lisa jumped onto the bed beside him and leaned on his chest, her ear pressed against his sternum, searching for any sign of life. There was nothing left.

She sat up and shook her head slowly, pursing her lips.

"Noooooo," my mother wailed. That cry was likely the worst sound I have ever heard in my life. She cried out only once, however. She remembered his words. She composed herself.

Tears welled in Shawon's, Lisa's, and my mother's eyes. Jesse joined us in the room.

A few moments later, I called Diane, who arrived almost immediately. I phoned Uncle Fred and told him the news. He came over and we sat together with Ndede.

Over the previous month, as this moment came hurtling closer and my father had walked steadily toward it, we had watched him stripped down to his base level of humanity. To our common denominator. To face our universal destiny.

He did not look for a way out. He did not cheat. He walked toward it as he walked toward all things, with courage, strength, and grace.

We had witnessed what Søren Kierkegaard called a levelling process. The divisions we obsess over—money, politics, race—were stripped away first. They did not matter in the end. Then the travelling was taken away, followed by the independence of the individual, the ego. They did not matter either.

Then you got down to what really mattered.

Food.

But then you can't eat.

Water.

But then you can't drink.

Air.

But then you stop breathing.

Finally, all he had left was the final resource that all of us will exhaust—time.

But then his time was up.

And then he was gone.

What's left behind?

All that remains in the end is love.

The love he had for us.

The love we still have for him.

And true love never dies.

21

FOR THE REST OF THE DAY we took things slowly.

We spent the morning discussing funeral arrangements with my uncle Fred. I sat in Ndedeiban's* old chair in the kitchen, calling people he had known well. Friends, relatives, and young people he had mentored. Many cried. I consoled them. I did not shed any tears myself until that evening.

That afternoon, a few close friends came by to visit and bring gifts of food. Alan Greyeyes. Namowan. Leonard Sumner. These friends I will remember until I go for my own walk on the everlasting road.

Dr. Brett Thompson arrived as well, someone Ndede had mentored in the past and the man who had sought a second opinion from the Mayo Clinic months before. I could tell from Brett's expression that he was very upset. Yet he did not burden us with his pain; he simply did what he could.

---

* In Anishinaabemowin, we add the suffix -iban to signify that someone is deceased.

The front doorknob had fallen off. Brett took it upon himself to replace it, making our lives a little easier. Brett may have done great things for my father, helping him immensely to have a better quality of life as he approached the end, but to me he will always be the guy who fixed our door on that difficult day.

As a member of the Jiibay-Midewin, I have the responsibility of conducting some of the ceremonies to do with death. And so I helped prepare Ndede's body.

My mother, Shawon, and I decided that he should leave in his finest sundance regalia.

We fixed his hair. We cleaned his face. We wrapped his favourite blue-and-red sundance skirt around his legs. We put moccasins on his feet. We dressed him in a ribbon shirt. Then we placed sage bracelets on his wrists, sage anklets above his feet, and a sage crown on his head. Finally, we chose two beautiful eagle feathers and arranged them in the crown, as a young sundancer is taught to do.

He looked like a warrior going home.

I sang four songs for him on the hand drum, songs he liked to use for ceremonies.

First I sang the thunderbird pipe song.

Then I sang a bear song.

Then I sang a sundance song.

As the words *Wakan Tanka* left my mouth, I was overcome. My voice shook. My mouth trembled. Tears welled in my eyes.

I thought of the beautiful life we had shared together. The memories in the sundance circle. The name he had given my son. The healing ceremony for him. The long journey I had walked with him, from being a young boy sitting on the skulls behind him to being the one pulling the skulls with my own sons sitting on them.

We would not walk on this path together anymore. At least not in this life.

I finished the song, then fell to my knees and sobbed. My mother, sisters, and Lisa were around me. They were crying too. The grief washed over us.

I remembered that we could not cry forever, so we stopped and I composed myself.

I sang the fourth song, the final song, the travelling song. That song we sing before we leave one another to journey home.

"*Ningosha anishaa wenji-bimoseyan.*" I pushed the lyrics out from my gut, staring at Ndede's peaceful face, his eyes closed, his gaze cast upon the heavens, so beautiful in his traditional regalia.

In the little roundhouse in Wauzhushk Onigum, I had been taught the song when I was young. Kwekwekipinessiban explained the lyrics in Anishinaabemowin, and Ndedeiban translated the teaching to me. I had been told the four layers of meaning to the words "I am the reason you walk," delivered as though it is God speaking to you. Now the Creator was speaking to my father.

I am the reason you walk. I created you so that you might walk this earth.

I am the reason you walk. I gave you motivation so you would continue to walk even when the path became difficult, even seemingly impossible.

I am the reason you walk. I animated you with that driving force called love, which compelled you to help others who had forgotten they were brothers and sisters to take steps back toward one another.

And now, my son, as that journey comes to an end, I am the reason you walk, for I am calling you home. Walk home to me on that everlasting road.

With a loud, echoing drumbeat, I brought the song to an end.

"*Gigawaabamin minawaa*" were my final words—"I will see you again."

The men from the funeral home arrived shortly after and took Ndedeiban away.

WE SPENT CHRISTMAS EVE making arrangements for a funeral on the reserve and a memorial service in Winnipeg. We placed an obituary in a national paper. I picked up the boys late that night and we drove through the snow to my mother's house.

After Lisa and the boys had fallen asleep, I lay awake for a very long time. I did not feel restless or compelled to get up. I simply wanted time alone in the darkness with my thoughts.

I asked myself the questions that have haunted people long before me. I wondered why my father had to suffer as he did. I remembered the journey he had gone on, how he had become a living embodiment of courage, grace, and resilience. How his spirit had so deeply enveloped itself with love that the love remained even after every other earthly compulsion deserted him.

For all this, here was his reward. Not just to die and to be taken from us, but for him to suffer in excruciating pain and nausea for many, many moons. He had walked the Creator's path and done everything he was asked, and in return he withered and wasted away in front of us. First, his strength was sapped. Then, his mind deserted us. Finally, the fire within him slowly burned out.

"What sort of Creator would allow this?" I asked of the darkness. I heard no response. "How is this just?" I wondered. "What was the point of all that prayer and sacrifice?"

A few hours before dawn, I turned onto my side and pulled the blanket over my shoulder. I closed my eyes and went to sleep.

On Christmas Day, the boys slept until eight o'clock. Not bad, considering all the presents waiting for them. They forced a groggy

Shawon and Jesse out of bed, then laughed and shouted as they opened their gifts, lifting our spirits in a beautiful way. The boys deserved to feel good even if they were aware of what had happened.

On Boxing Day, Lisa and I went to the mall. Idle No More Winnipeg had called for a flash mob round dance, an urban take on the traditional friendship dance of the Plains.

The mall was crowded enough, but the halls were impassable as we approached the main square. Pushing through the mass of people, I saw familiar faces smiling and mouthing hellos. Christmas greetings were exchanged. Those who had heard the news offered condolences.

When the time came, I found my way to a group of singers I had travelled with on the powwow trail in my late teens and early twenties. The drums kicked in one after another, falling into the *boom-chicka-boom* rhythm of the round dance.

One singer kicked out a lead, and all of the other singers grabbed it, following the melody he had set, with an explosion of sound. Chills went up my spine. As I sang, I looked around at hundreds of people joining hands and sidestepping to their left in time with the beat.

I felt the power around me. The power of the drums. The power of the voices. The power of community.

The singers struck their drums in unison, dropping the beat down to the level of a soft tap as we moved to the second half of the first push-up.

Slowly, a wild chorus of war cries, whoops, and ululations rose from the crowd around us until the singers were drowned out by the sound of hundreds of voices raised together, showing their pride, their love, and their sense of community.

The nearby jewellery stores and coffee shops began lowering their shutters and closing their doors. They were witnessing the original cultures of these lands taking their rightful place in the public sphere, but they interpreted it as a threat of shoplifting. We have a long way to go before reconciliation becomes reality.

The first song ended. The war cries and ululations rose up again. The language of the sundance was being spoken in a shopping mall.

The second song began, an Idle No More anthem composed in the western prairies. "As long as the grasses grow, and the rivers flow," we sang in unison, harkening back to the language of the treaties that had been signed here some 140 years earlier. Our cultures had been targeted for destruction. The attempt had failed, but it left indelible marks on the practitioners of those cultures. Our people had been targeted and we had endured. Constant friction between Indigenous nationhood and the eroding forces of globalization continued unabated, yet we were in the midst of a resurgence.

This, to me, is the key achievement of Idle No More—the flash mob round dance. Our cultures were marching back into the public spaces and the national collective conscience. We are still here. We are still strong. We are never going away. Don't call it a comeback—we've been here for years.

THE NEXT NIGHT was Ndedeiban's memorial.

Outside the funeral home, I gave interviews to media outlets, talking about my father's legacy in education and politics.

People began arriving early—extended family, politicians, including the premier and cabinet ministers, members of the Catholic community led by Uncle Jimmy, plus university colleagues, students, First Nations elders, and two former national chiefs.

It was a packed house. My biggest regret of that day is that our uncle Phil Fontaine, having arrived a few minutes late, had to sit in an overflow seating area. Given the important role he played in my father's journey, his brokering of the apology, the trips to the Vatican, and his participation in the adoption, this was an oversight. We had no idea he was there until the service was completed. For that I am sorry. I had a lot else on my mind, having been asked to emcee the event by my family.

I took to the podium and began in Ojibwe. "*Aho Ndinawemaaganiidog, miigwech kipiizhaayeg*," I said, thanking them for coming.

I spoke about my father, describing how he had passed, comfortable and at home. I told them about the pancreatic and liver cancers and reminded them of the journey that he had taken, how he had set a strong example for all of us to fulfill his vision of reconciliation. His example taught us to see our fellow human beings as our brothers and sisters, each deserving of our love and compassion, and each of us deserving of respect from others.

I thanked many of the dignitaries and relatives by name, and began introducing the night's speakers.

My uncle Fred led us in an invocation and delivered an eloquent speech tracing his and my father's journey from Lake of the Woods through politics and on to the contemporary era of reconciliation and empowerment.

Diane spoke beautifully about how Ndede had been one of her closest friends and greatest mentors as she followed his path into politics.

James Weisgerber told how he had thought he was embarking on the Church's work with reconciliation but ended up gaining a brother.

Premier Greg Selinger spoke, saying that during this time of Idle No More, my father's example was especially relevant.

Eric Robinson, the deputy premier and minister of Aboriginal affairs, followed with a funny recollection of the times he and Ndede spent together, from partying days to respectability.

One of the highlights was having legendary Cree entertainer Winston Wuttunee eulogize my father with humour, song, and dramatic storytelling. He closed with a round-dance song. "When the sun sets"—his voice hung in the air over the round-dance beat—"over the world, / I'll be thinking of you. / I know you are far away. / No matter where you are, / I still love you just the same." It was a fitting song for the occasion.

I cracked a few jokes, telling everyone, "When I was a kid, I used to think that my name was Enigok, because that's all my father used to say to me." Many people in the crowd laughed. The Ojibwe speakers knew this meant Ndede had been telling me to "try harder." He had been a taskmaster.

Growing up with him had often been uncomfortable. Part of the discomfort came from residential schools, part of it came from the era in which he was raised, and another part was probably just him. Looking at my siblings now, there is not much sense arguing with the results. We are all lucky to have been given opportunity, and lucky to have had a good dad.

We stayed long after the memorial, visiting with friends and relatives, thanking everyone who came. Shortly before midnight, we packed up and went home.

That night, I had stood as the leader my family and my father expected me to be. I conducted the proceedings. I stood in the spotlight. I did the public speaking. I said the things that needed to be said. I carried on and spread the message he held on to until the very end.

Yet beneath it all, nihilism lurked. I cared for the pipes and skulls as always, but now I doubted their potency. I said "*aho*" and "amen" after each prayer, but I did not really believe my words. I appreciated each song, but only as a song, not as a sacred communication with the spirits.

I was standing deep in the winter snow and could not see the medicine growing around me. The next day, we drove to Onigaming for the wake. In typical Kinew fashion, we arrived late.

I PUSHED OPEN THE DOORS to the traditional roundhouse and circled the middle in counter-clockwise fashion, carrying my father's urn. After building an altar and setting up a drum in the centre, I greeted the assembled community members in Anishinaabemowin and we sang four songs on Ndedeiban's drum. Joined by my first cousin Sonny, my nephew Derek, my friends Trevor and Makwa, we sang traditional Anishinaabe songs.

Looking around the room, I could not help but wonder where everyone was.

When the songs finished, I trudged outside through the snow to light the sacred fire that would burn for four days. As Anishinaabeg, we are told to keep a sacred fire for four days while the spirit of the departed walks the everlasting road on his journey to heaven. Along the way, we are to burn tobacco and food, which he will take with him.

With the fire burning, I said a prayer to the Creator and offered some tobacco. I burned some food. Then I slept a few hours in the middle of the roundhouse

The next morning, I carved Ndedeiban Odoodemi'atig—my late father's totem pole—out of poplar. This wood is chosen because it decomposes quickly, allowing us to move beyond grief.

Uncle Fred conducted this ceremony. I silently judged everyone in the room and damned everyone who failed to show up. *Where were the others? Where were the people he had conducted ceremonies for and taught across Canada? Where were the people he had shared the culture with, from Minnesota and Wisconsin, during my*

*teenage years? Where were the First Nations politicians from across
Canada to whom he had devoted the prime of his life to helping?*

This was not a fitting tribute to the man. I turned my ire on the
speakers who were present. *Who were these people? Who cared what
they thought?* It was pretty negative. I also began to grow restless
at the length of the ceremony. *Why was it dragging on? Was it really
necessary to spend four hours on more eulogies?*

Finally, Uncle Fred concluded the instructions for the departed
on how they are to make their four-day journey. He picked up a
rattle and walked around the urn, stopping in each direction.

At the cemetery, we carefully lowered the urn into the grave
before placing the totem pole. In Anishinaabe custom, all the
children stood beside the grave. Then we each took a handful of
dirt and spread it lightly over the hole in the earth.

When everyone had had a chance to put dirt in the grave,
my nephews, cousins, friends, and I picked up shovels and filled
in the rest of the earth. As the grave was covered, the women and
children came forward to lay wreaths and flowers on the fresh
earth.

In front of Ndedeiban were the graves of his two sons Danny
and Darryl. Beside them was our cousin Pee-wee. Nenagiizhigokiban,
Tobasonakwut's mother, was nearby, and his nieces and nephews
lay beyond her, along with his brothers Tootons and John. Many
years had passed, but they were all here together again.

I looked back at Uncle Fred, the last man standing. "When
you leave here," he said to the group, "don't look back."

We walked to our vehicles and drove away down the hill to
share a feast.

That night, I set my alarm for every two hours. When it woke
me, I would dress, get in my car, and drive across the reserve to the
roundhouse to check the fire. In the darkness of night, I would

split a few logs to help build the fire up and add a few whole logs that would burn slowly.

I would sit for a time, staring at the fire and mulling over the questions that continued to run through my head. I was there out of duty, a duty I owed to my father and my culture. Selfish thoughts seem to be the best company at moments like these.

Before leaving, I would say a prayer and offer some tobacco and food to the fire. I would ask the Creator to find my father on the everlasting road and give him these offerings to help him. *Why was I praying? Was there an everlasting road? Was there even a Creator?* Still, I prayed. Then I climbed into my car, drove home, and set my alarm for two hours later, save for the times my mother offered to check the fire.

During the day, I played with the boys. Inside, we would play games. A few times, we went out to cut wood. Lisa was at work in Dauphin, seven hours away, on call and in the emergency room over the holidays.

Three nights later, she arrived; it was my birthday. I was spoiled with cakes from my mother, Shawon, and my second mom, Baatiins. That night, we celebrated the New Year with my sons, spraying each other with whipped cream to mark the end of the year that was. The boys and I had baths, then we all went to bed. A few hours later, the alarm on my phone rang and I rose to go and tend the fire.

It was one of those crisp, clear, and tranquil nights that come only in the depths of winter. Everything was so cold it seemed as though the air itself was about to crack and break.

The woodpile was dwindling, and each log was covered in a thin layer of ice crystals. That was fine, because this would be the last night of keeping the fire. Tomorrow, we would let it burn out. It was four in the morning. I felt as though the rot inside me had started to ferment.

The same old questions echoed within me. *Why did my father have to suffer as he did? Why would the Creator make him die in such a shitty way? Why, after he had done so much good at the end of his life, did the march toward death have to continue unabated?*

And what was with all of the prayers, ceremonies, and holy people? From the Vatican to our own ways, wasn't it all worthless? Hadn't it all failed to save him?

I stared into the fire, trying to burn a hole in it with my angry eyes. I cursed. I swore. I wrote off a lot of things. I questioned my faith, I questioned the Creator, I questioned our ways, I questioned all ways. I decided that we are all mortal, we were all alone, and that this coil was all that mattered, that spirituality and religion were—

I stopped and looked up.

About thirty feet above me, a single cloud flew by in the night sky, the firelight reflecting from it. The cloud was small and translucent. It passed over my head in silence and moved on.

That low-flying cloud.

That Tobasonakwut.

Something left me as the cloud floated away. I was still angry, I was still upset, I still missed my dad. I was not healed, but something that had broken apart in me began coming together again.

There was something happening in this world and in this universe that was bigger than me, bigger than my pain, bigger than any of us, even Ndedeiban.

As I saw his namesake float by that night in the sky, I remembered that he would still be with us. In our hearts and in our minds.

His message was still true. It still mattered. It did not cease to matter just because it didn't give him everlasting life. It mattered because it gave him a better life while he was here. And now, even after he's gone, we are better for having learned from his example.

Those lessons are ephemeral. But they are real. And maybe that is what faith is too.

Everything did not immediately get better in that moment. But having spent the four days keeping the fire, I knew that even though I was hurting, things were going to be all right.

How wise our ancestors were to leave us with this path to walk on, this way of life. These traditions may not always make sense or seem important, but somehow, when we walk the path as others did before ourselves, we get what we need.

I built up the fire again and went home to sleep for a long time, knowing I would not be looking back.

EPILOGUE

It's been so hard
Watching you from the other side
I never meant to hurt you
Never meant to make you cry
It will be a long time
Before I see you again
So until then
Take care

IN THE TIME since my father died, new titles have come my way. Correspondent. Executive. Honorary witness for the Truth and Reconciliation Commission of Canada. Husband, after marrying Lisa at a beautiful traditional sundance wedding ceremony. And, of course, I continue to bear the title that is most important to me: father.

After working with Al Jazeera's Washington, D.C., office, I would joke that I had become a Native kid from Northwestern Ontario working for a Qatari-owned television network in the United States of America. More than a joke, it also revealed the truth that we are all part of a pluralistic, multicultural, global society.

That's why reconciliation must be considered in a global context, an understanding reaffirmed by the travels I have made since my father walked onto the everlasting road. Istanbul during the Gezi Park riots, where tear gas and water cannons cut through joyous expressions of freedom in one of the more prominent secular states in the Muslim world. Kiev in the midst of a shadow war between Ukraine and Russia. Both sides of the American border—Arizona, Sonora, Texas, and Chihuahua—as the influx of refugees from Central America became a humanitarian crisis. Some of these travels were as a reporter, others in my role as university administrator, and still others to visit the fascinating places our globe has to offer.

Everywhere along the way, I have been struck by the differences and unique expressions that humanity navigates and negotiates around this world. The salmon feasts of the Okanagan, the futuristic vision of the Emirates masking a deep inequality, and the intersection of Western-style capitalism and Chinese culture.

Beyond these differences, we are united by those qualities bubbling up from beneath the surface. I have heard the universal human language of laughter both in a Sonoran slum and a petrostate shopping mall. I have witnessed the devastation wrought by the loss of a loved one in some of the most dangerous cities on earth and in the affluent suburbs of the so-called First World. I have recognized the love of food, the need for sleep, and the desire for companionship everywhere.

Today, a majority of us are likely of mixed race, living proof that regardless of whether political and economic reconciliation is realized, our biological compatibility will always force us to be invested in one another's fates. Along the way, often while staring out an airplane window at the setting sun or through a windshield down another lonely stretch of open road, I have wondered about Indigenous identity in the twenty-first century and beyond.

What does it mean to be Indigenous when you are no longer Indigenous to the place where you find yourself? What does the deep tie to my traditional homeland mean if I can visit only a few times a year? What role does a traditional Indigenous culture, or any local culture for that matter, have in a globalized, interconnected world?

The answers to these questions underline why we need to think of the path my father walked, and his vision of unity. It is a very Anishinaabe story and a very Canadian experience—to be born in the bush, taken away to residential school, and for the rest of your life push for justice and healing. Yet it is also a story that is told over and over around the world, whether by survivors of the Shoah, apartheid, or other genocides. One need not suffer an injustice as great as the attempted destruction of one's people or culture to heed the lesson embodied in Ndedeiban's life. One only has to have felt some small transgression and responded with fury or pain to be able to appreciate the beauty of what my father achieved.

The underlying message of my father's life, and especially his final year, is one that wise women and men have known for millennia: when we are wronged it is better to respond with love, courage, and grace than with anger, bitterness, and rage. We are made whole by living up to the best part of human nature—the part willing to forgive the aggressor, the part that never loses sight of the humanity of those on the other side of the relationship, and the part that embraces the person with whom we have every right to be angry and accepts him or her as a brother or sister.

It may have taken Ndedeiban the better part of seventy-six years to learn this lesson, but in the end he took the steps necessary to leave this world in a good way.

This is not to say we should always forgive immediately, or ignore demands for justice. The anger of previous generations of Indigenous people won some of the most basic freedoms that my generation now takes as a given, including the freedom of movement, the freedom to eat in any restaurant we choose, and the freedom to grow up with our own parents, and among our own people and culture.

Challenges remain. First Nations children begin life facing longer odds on the road to success than others, because they lack equal access to education, health care, and social services. We must correct these problems where they exist. Indigenous people must also take more responsibility for our own affairs, which is something most members of my generation strongly believe.

As a result of colonization, many Indigenous peoples have been prevented from contributing fully to our globalized society. Consequently, the Indigenous cultures practised by those peoples have not been able to share their strength, wisdom, and beauty with the rest of the world.

I envision Indigenous people rising above their challenges to become the leaders this world desperately needs. I see them helping to chart the way to a more sustainable society and a more meaningful way of life.

Many solutions to the challenges of our time—from income inequality to environmental degradation—can be found in Indigenous cultures. If we start to see the earth as our mother, we will likely chart a course to a more environmentally friendly way of life.

If we grow up hearing that the chief ought to be the poorest member of the community and that true leadership is about service and sacrifice, we might think harder about income inequality.

And if people on opposite sides of seemingly intractable showdowns over land and resources began to take one another as kin, perhaps we might find peace in situations that we currently consider lost causes.

While there are political and economic lessons to heed, we cannot forget that, at its core, reconciliation is a spiritual and emotional journey.

My heart still aches for the man who walked ahead of me on this path, the man I see now only in visions.

IN YEMEN, I visited a man named Mohammed who had been imprisoned at Guantánamo Bay detention camp for a decade. His crime had been that he was an Arab in Afghanistan after 9/11. His incarceration without charge so offended an American judge that his immediate release was ordered. Mohammed was a walking example of forgiveness. He held no grudge. He only wanted to sell honey and pray at his local masjid in his home city of Taiz. In a soft voice, he revealed to me that his greatest desire was to find a wife.

During our time together, he led me to his father's house. We walked through narrow alleys and climbed a steep set of concrete stairs before reaching a small apartment. There, in a room painted the awful blue that adorns a million rez houses, sat his father.

A picture of the old man in his prime, wearing a Yemeni army officer's uniform, hung above him. Now, he lay on cushions on the ground, confined to his bed after suffering a stroke. He moaned for his son. His skin had the pale, plastic quality of someone not long for this world.

"He looks good," I told Mohammed, attempting a smile.

This man, the falsely accused terrorist, slowly cut an apple. He slid next to his father and began to feed him the fruit, slice by slice. The old man sighed as his suffering body found nourishment. Mohammed whispered to him while he fed him the rest of the food.

Mohammed moved so that he was next to his father's legs. He rubbed the man's limbs, massaging them, the tree branches that could no longer carry the weight they were designed to support.

Tears welled in my eyes, and I felt a sudden need to swallow. It had been six months since Ndedeiban left us.

Mohammed interrupted my thoughts. "If a son helps his father when he is sick," he told me through an Arabic interpreter, "then *his* son will help him when he is old."

I asked him to repeat himself.

"If a son helps his father when he is sick, then his son will help him when he is old."

Ndede had stood by his father in that residential school cemetery all those years ago. In turn, his son and daughters had stood beside him as he walked to the spirit world. Standing for him there, waiting on that side, were his two eldest boys. Now, in this place near the Gulf of Aden, on the other side of the planet from Lake of the Woods, another child stood beside his parent.

We stand by those who came before us, hoping that those who come after us will honour us in the same way. We love, and we hope to be loved.

Whether we are young or old, whether our skin is light or dark, whether we are man or woman, we share a common humanity and are all headed for a common destiny. That should bind us together more strongly than divisions can push us apart. So long as anything other than love governs our relationship with others, we have work to do.

When the divisions win out, we need to work hard and bring that which has been broken apart back together again.

We ought to recognize that our greatest battle is not with one another but with our pain, our problems, and our flaws.

To be hurt, yet forgive. To do wrong, but forgive yourself. To depart from this world leaving only love.

This is the reason you walk.

KIMIIGWECHIWII'ININIM (ACKNOWLEDGMENTS)

In thanking the people who made this book possible, I first need to acknowledge that many more than I list here have played a pivotal role in my life. They say it takes a village to raise a child. Well, it takes an army to redeem a wretch like me. So to all my friends, extended family, and professional colleagues, I honour you and hold you in high regard.

I begin by raising up the four people most responsible for shaping me: my parents and my two sons. Mom and Ndedeiban, I feel as though I won the lottery in being born to you. You taught me lessons I have taken to heart, including the value of hard work and the importance of family. As for the kindness you showed me, I am still working on that. Dom and Bezh, you are my greatest motivators and the primary reasons I have been able to shift my life onto a more positive course. I owe you everything and will spend the rest of my life trying to repay the favour.

Nichiimens Shawon, we have spent more time with each other than almost anyone else. You are my closest friend and best source of advice. Lisa, I love you and am grateful to have you in my life. You were interested in helping me become a better person even before we were romantically involved, a sign of your giving nature. April, you have given me my two sons and you had my back before others believed in me. It may not have worked out between us, but I will always honour you.

To my sisters, Pat and Diane, I love you and thank you both for the time we've spent together on this journey. Here's to many more years together! And to *nichiimens* Nenaa'ikiizhigok, you are loved and valued by all of us. Our father is in the spirit world looking out for you. Live your life to its fullest and know that he smiles down on you.

To my nieces and nephews Dan, Jay, Jenny, Wendy, Missy, Mike, Jeff, Lisa, and Matthew, we've had a lot of fun so far. Let's keep it going, and I hope the Creator blesses all of your children. To my cousins Don, Brad, Mike, Byron, Rhonda, Ben, Dawn, Bev, Val, Neech, and Delores, a thousand *Miigweches! Gichi-miigwech* also to my best friend since birth, Makwa, my brother from another Gyles, Mick, Eagle, Baatiins, Makate Giniw, Richard Kelly, and everyone in Onigaming and Treaty #3. *Wopila* to our Charging Eagle relatives, including Harold and Geraldine, Cam, Cricket, Richard, Valerie, Wambli, and little Steve.

Tatagiins, Uncle Fred: the wisdom and support these few years has been an important source of strength. "Ehhhhhh!!!" To Aunt Nancy, I honour you and raise you up. To Buddy, Uncle Phil Fontaine, I am very grateful for the role you played in Ndedeiban's journey. *Miigwech aapichii.*

And of course I commemorate those we loved who left us behind: Danny, Darryl, Billy, Leah, Danielle, Sonny, Tab, Pee-wee, Michelle, Uncle John, Uncle Tootons, and David, the cousin I always tried to emulate growing up.

This book is the product of many new friends in the publishing industry, including Nicole Winstanley, Diane Turbide, Stephen Myers, Alex Schultz, John Lawrence Reynolds, and everyone at Penguin

Random House Canada. Also, Jackie Kaiser and Westwood Creative Artists. I would also be remiss if I didn't shout out everyone at CBC Books and *Canada Reads*, including Tara Mora, Erin Noel, Erin Balser, Ann Jansen, and Dayna Shiskos, among others. There are many other friends in the literary world who helped me out with advice and insight along the way, and so I say *miigwech* to you as well: Joseph Boyden, Richard Wagamese, Waubgeshig Rice, David Robertson, John K. Samson, Niigaan Sinclair, and John Ralston Saul.

To everyone who has helped me on my spiritual journey, I thank you as well. Kwekwekipinessiban, Auggieiban, Kweki'egiizhik, and Vernon Skead for helping to show me the Anishinaabe *miikanaa*. I thank Ndedeiban, Kwekwekipinessiban, and Allan White for naming me. Tommy Jayiban and Anna Gibbs for initiating me. *Wopila*, Uncle Leonard Crow Dog, Auntie Joann, Junebug and Victoria Crow Dog, Alden Daily, Pedro, Anwah, Junior, Merle, Richard and Lonnie Street, Al Bino Garcia and family, Thomas Lopez and family, Oscar and Elena Moreno, Pete Beebe, John Moreno and Adhi Guevara and family, Oscar Jr. and family, the late Carter Camp and family, Chuck Scribe and family, Shane Patterson and family, Dwayne Shields and family, and all of our sundance relatives. I thank the Whitehorse and Lake of the Woods singers for teaching me how to sing powwow. *Miigwech* and *Wopida* to those I like to sweat with, like Tom Decoteau Jr., Marcia Anderson-Decoteau, Doug Sinclair, and Kathy Jack; and to those I've fasted with, such as Eddy Robinson and Muskie Rice, as well as Rodney Eli and family, Kelly, and everyone at the fasting camp. And of course all members of the Pizhiw clan.

Shout out to everyone I came up with in the hip-hop community, especially P-nut, Kenny G, Kenny Ross, Kenny Wu,

Big Bear, Poetics, Daybi, Jaymak, Stomp, Helly, Drezus, Tomislav, Henny, and Boogey.

Shout out to everyone at the Canadian Fighting Centre, especially coaches Giuseppe, Jerin, Beach, Dirty, Tino, and Naka. You have taught me a lot of techniques, but more importantly you've given me an outlet in mixed martial arts, kickboxing, and jiu-jitsu, which helps keep me sane.

Special shout out to my good friends Leonard Sumner, Namowan, and Alan Greyeyes. You were there the day my old man passed away. I will always remember that.

I would like to apologize to everyone I have hurt along the way, physically or emotionally. I spent part of my life as an angry, self-centred young man. I was wrong and have worked hard to make myself a better member of our society. Still, I pray this apology is accepted.

I would also like to apologize for misogynistic rap lyrics I have written or performed in the past. At the time I thought it was funny or had shock value. With the epidemic of violence against women, and Indigenous women in particular, there is no excuse for this. We have to do better, all of us, and hip-hop musicians can play an important part by ending the use of terms, images, and themes that degrade or disrespect women. I am committed to doing that and encourage other rappers to do so as well.

Writing this book has been cathartic for me, but it has also been a journey of self-discovery, or in some cases rediscovery. There are lessons I relearned in spending hours staring at my laptop screen, writing on planes or in Assiniboine Park. I have really enjoyed the process and feel as though I have grown from it. What is more, my late father always wanted to write a book but never had the opportunity. In some small way, this book is my contribution toward fulfilling that dream. I hope that some of the immense wisdom and the powerful message he left with us can be shared with the wider world in this form. I say this to convey how much these pages mean to me. With that in mind, my final thank you is to you, the reader, whose support has made all of this possible.

Miigwech aapichii., Mii'e (That's it).